OFF

TRADITIONAL DATING TRUTHS

THE

FOR THE MODERN

SHELF

CHRISTIAN WOMAN

RUTH HARDING

Ark House Press
PO Box 1722, Port Orchard, WA 98366 USA
PO Box 1321, Mona Vale NSW 1660 Australia
PO Box 318 334, West Harbour, Auckland 0661 New Zealand
arkhousepress.com

© Ruth Harding 2020

Cataloguing in Publication Data:
Title: Off the Shelf
ISBN: 978-0-6489194-5-2 (pbk)
Subjects: Christian Living; Relationships;
Other Authors/Contributors: Harding, Ruth

Design by initiateagency.com

This book is dedicated to every Christian girl who has cried herself to sleep at night, wondering when God will bring her a husband. Stay the path, sister!

CONTENTS

INTRODUCTION

This book is for older Christian girls who are committed to the faith, feel 'normal', and want to get married – but find themselves in a dating drought. If the cry of you and your single girlfriends is 'Where are all the good Christian guys?' then this book is for you. If you aren't a Christian, or 'religious', you will probably find this to be reminiscent of a 1950's domestic science class, pre-feminism. It's written specifically for Bible-believing Christian girls who are living in the modern world but want to do things God's way – and you are most welcome to jump on board!

If you're a young woman who is keen to have success in dating… you are ahead of the curve. It's crucial that you put yourself out there and secure yourself a good man, before they all get snapped up! I've observed that the best places to meet a husband (or to at least have access to a large pool of single, like-minded guys) are in high-school, college, youth group and young adults group at church. Once you grow beyond those age groups, it can be tricky to meet many single men. So if you're between 16-25, this is your time! You'll still find lots of helpful tips in this book, though, so read on!

There are *some* good Christian books out there about how to cope with being single, how to pursue God while you're waiting, and how to transform yourself into a (potential) Godly wife – but as far as I know, there aren't *any* books out there for Christian girls about how to throw yourself into the dating scene and get guaranteed success. Because if I know you…and I think I do…you and the Lord are all good, but you just want someone to PUT A RING ON IT already.

You've come to the right place. There's nothing super-spiritual about this book. In fact, if you are used to the warm fuzzies you get from women's conferences, ladies retreats, and mainstream Christian books, you may find this a little confronting. But I'm not going to waste your time with platitudes like 'The Lord is in control' or 'He'll come along at the right time' or 'You are still beautiful' (although these statements may be true). You've heard them all before and they haven't helped you, yet!

This book contains 100% guaranteed, practical strategies and rules for sorting yourself out, getting dates, choosing a decent man, and getting married! You might find I circle around the same topics time and time again, and that is because changing your thinking can be really hard and may take a little while. It's confronting and scary to widen your perspective and consider that there may be a totally different way of approaching the dating game. It takes some time to process.

I've broken the book into six main sections or topics, and within each section there are a bunch of chapters looking at various facets of that topic, or building on the previous chapters. You'll find that the opening sections of the book drill down into your personal life; what you're feeling and how you're dealing with being single right now, along with any baggage you might be carrying into your dating life. There's a lot to cover on those topics, but it's important that you sort yourself out first, so you can present your best self to your new man! After that, we start getting into the nitty gritty of the dating scene itself.

Feel free to dip in wherever you like, and skip around the chapters as much as you want. You can treat it like a textbook or dating handbook, if you like. It's a big book containing tons of information, so I wouldn't recommend reading it in one sitting – you may need to work through it over a period of months, as you process each chapter and apply new things to your life.

I often reference some of my favourite authors and presenters, so do take the time to check out other resources written by experts in the field – psychologists, dating coaches, and of course the Bible!

In terms of demographic, I'm a white Australian woman in my late 30's and I'm speaking from a middle-of-the-road conservative, urban, Protestant Christian perspective. You might be living in an ultra-conservative community where you still have to get your dad's permission to even talk to a man, or you might be a nominal Christian who lives mainly in the secular world but still holds on to a few strands of faith. Either way, I hope this book can be of benefit to you. And I guarantee that no matter what country you live in, this book will have relevance to you.

Read it with an open mind, and question your disagreements. It's a great technique for expanding your thinking and also adjusting and solidifying your personal values.

So grab your journal and pen, highlight your favourite chapters, play with some mind-mapping or goal-setting as you go, and explore and ponder the sections you don't agree with. I'm so excited that you are working towards growth in the area of dating and relationships! May God bless you as you start this journey of change.

Come to me, all you who are weary and burdened, and I will give you rest. Take my yoke upon you and learn from me, for I am gentle and humble in heart, and you will find rest for your souls. For my yoke is easy and my burden is light. – Jesus (Matthew 11:28-30)

A NOTE ON THE AUTHOR

Here's the goss on Ruth Harding. I started out as a really sheltered, small-town Christian girl, and when I moved to the big city for college, I was totally clueless. I had no idea about relationships, dating, playing it cool or making the best of my appearance. As a result, I missed tons of chances with good guys because I just didn't know what I was doing. I did have a lot of dates in my late 20's, and a number of very short relationships, but I was choosing guys for the wrong reasons, I wasn't emotionally healthy, and didn't have the relationship skills to actually maintain a mature connection.

By the time I got to my early 30's, I couldn't believe I was still single. I was sure I'd be married by 25! So, after stagnating in my career, spending all my money on travel and clothes, burning out in church ministry, and dealing with yet another heart-break, I ended up seeing a counsellor. She helped me work through some of my family of origin baggage and personal hang-ups, and taught me how to approach relationships in a different way. Finally, I was emotionally ready to hit the dating scene.

But – to my horror – I realised that there were literally NO single Christian guys to be seen. (Except for *those* ones…you know what I mean.) But did I sit around on my couch every night, crying into a tub of ice-cream? Did I start hitting the nightclubs and throwing myself at every male propping up the bar? Did I give up altogether and join a convent? (I actually considered that one). Well – no, I didn't do any of those things. I sorted myself out, glammed myself up, moved churches a few times, gave guys a chance, and I GOT MARRIED at the age of 34. I now have two small sons, and I am a stay-at-home wife and mum just kicking back and baking cookies all day long. (Ok, that's not exactly true. But sometimes.)

If you're thinking, *Well, I'm older than 34 and still single, so I don't think Ruth can understand my situation* – that's fine. Put the book down and walk away! But may I suggest that our issues are the same. Perhaps you can take away a little something from my journey. And do you want to be proud and alone, or humble and married?

FYI although I'm not a registered psychologist or ordained minister, I do have degrees in teaching, ministry and counselling, so everything you're about to read is basically gleaned from the amazing books, professors, and experiences I've had in my own life. I'm not an expert, but I have been in your shoes and I am the real deal. So, now that you know I'm legit, and I've walked the path myself, I hope you'll treat this book like your 'dating Bible', so to speak, and put these strategies to good use. Because if you do, this could be your future:

- No longer being seated at the singles table at weddings.
- No one repeatedly asking you: 'So, any guys on the scene?' or worse: 'How's the crochet club going?'
- No one telling you: 'You should really think about freezing your eggs.'
- Being allowed to have sex.
- Not being treated like the church slave.
- Having your own place where you don't have to worry about your room-mate bringing her boyfriend over 24/7 to eat your food, decimate your bathroom and watch loud movies.
- Not having to rely on Netflix to fulfil your emotional needs.

- To stop being 'the strong one'.
- To have financial support so you can stay home and bake cookies (YES).

IT IS POSSIBLE. LET'S DO THIS!

SECTION #1
The Single Life

Let's face it. Being an older single totally sucks. You have to live with younger people who are noisy, irritating and can still wear cute shorts. You constantly have to put up with varying degrees of pity/concern/mockery from your family members at major events. You're too old for the church young adults group, but you can't join the young families group. It's tough!

Will you ever meet Mr Right? Will you ever know the feeling of not having to cart your own groceries into the house? Will you ever be a mother? These are big, scary questions and in this section we are going to dive right into the emotional component of being single. It's hard, and I get it.

CHAPTER 1

Why do I feel so exposed & exhausted?

This might sound weird – but do you ever feel that your nerve endings are kind of raw? That the edges of your body are always tense? That your mind feels like it's in a vice, and it's always racing? Do you feel jittery, untethered, or unable to 'ground' yourself? Are you always **rushing from one thing to the next**, stressing about meal-prepping and getting enough exercise, and just trying to keep up? Do you struggle to get to sleep, have panic attacks, or find yourself binge shopping or binge eating to get relief? Do you feel like you're on the outside of life, looking in?

Perhaps you even feel like you wish you could just leave this life and **go to heaven** where you can rest and stop worrying about the future. These feelings are surprisingly common among today's women. And I would suggest that these are symptoms of a common problem facing many women in the church today – stress and anxiety with no place to feel safe.

It's pretty obvious that a lot of us women push ourselves way too far. Although (in the western world, at least) we have more opportunities, more money, more technological support and in some cases less responsibilities than in previous generations, there is no doubt that we are also under **a crazy amount of stress**. This is bad enough when you have a wonderful husband at home who provides a shoulder to cry on, or who will at least pay some of your bills so you can sleep at night, but it's absolutely terrible when you go home to an empty apartment or share-house, where no one really knows what's going on for you – or even cares.

There's **a psychological construct called 'containment'** that we all need. It's basically the idea that when you are out of control, what you need is a safe space to ground yourself and to be able to regulate your emotions. (Or in layman's terms, you need a hug.) When you see little kids throwing tantrums, or teenagers pushing the boundaries, what is needed is a strong person to hold them (physically and/or metaphorically) and to communicate to them: 'I am here. I'm not moving. You can push against me and I won't fall down. You can express your emotion here and get it out of your system. You are safe here with me.' Is there a person in your life who is this strong, safe space for you? We all need one. And technically, this person should be your dad.

Now I know this might sound archaic, patriarchal or anti-feminist. But the links are obvious, and research consistently shows the importance of stable parenting in a child's life. Mums obviously have an incredibly vital role, but let's just talk about dads for now. For a daughter, **her dad initially represents all men**. She sees him as a type of hero, a noble leader and a willing provider. He is her protector and her guide. (If a woman doesn't have a dad who is able to fill this role, she will spend her whole life looking for someone to fill this void.)

Now when a single woman leaves the 'covering' of her dad, for example she moves out of home and becomes independent, she is exposed to the world. **She becomes 'uncovered'.** And this is when both her vulnerabilities and her powers become apparent to her. There is one simple reason for this: biology.

I'd have to write a thesis to explain how this all works, but let's just cover some basics. Don't hate me for saying this, but **the truth is that**

a woman without the covering of a good man is highly vulnerable. She is completely unprotected from the various advances of random men, everywhere, anywhere, and all the time. She is physically weaker than men, she is sexually desired and pursued by men, simply because she is a woman, and she is vulnerable to pregnancy and sexually transmitted infections. And yes, she is also more susceptible to the oppressive patriarchy, which does exist in some environments. She is exposed to the elements.

Back in the day, women of the middle and upper classes who came out from under the covering of their fathers for whatever reason would usually then move straight under the covering of a **chaperone** (if they weren't getting married). The chaperone was an older, wiser person who was a responsible type and was obligated to the woman's family to protect her from the dangers of the world (including her own foolishness).

These days, we have dismissed the idea of a formal chaperone as old-fashioned, thinking 'I can look after myself!' (Can you, though?) And because women are getting married later and later, I've noticed that a dad will kind of opt out of the fatherly role as a woman moves into her mid-20's. I mean, he's not going to tell his 30-year-old daughter that she can't go to the movies with her male work colleague. So she is essentially alone. But she is exposed, and she can feel it.

Why do you think single women in the workplace **form alliances** with the most powerful men in the office? (Or at least the most powerful men whose loyalties they can win.) It's so they have someone to stand up for them in the lunchroom banter, the staff meetings, and the competition for promotions. And have you ever noticed how the boss's daughter at work, or the pastor's daughter at church, seem to get special treatment all the time? It's not because they are great people – it's because of their dads' authority.

It's interesting that whenever you have an important male in your life, who is seen and known by the community, that you are given a little **more dignity, respect and care.** At least, this is what I experienced. And this used to really bug me. I thought, *Why can't I just be enough in my own right? Why can't I be treated properly simply because I'm a human being? Why does being single mean I'm on my own?* But no matter what changes in society, biology doesn't change.

You must realise that there are tons of advocacy groups out there designed to protect women and children. Why? Because a woman alone is uncovered and unsafe. Maybe you can relate.

The annoying truth of the matter is that being 'covered' by a respected man in the community does in fact bring you a much higher level of honour. This idea of 'covering' is entirely anti-feminist, but does in fact line up with the biological drives of both men and women. **A man wants a woman he can pursue, provide for and protect, and a woman wants a man to do those things for her.** Both men and women spend most of their lives trying to attain this!

Think of the story of Ruth and Boaz in the Bible, particularly Ruth chapter 3. Ruth was a widow who went back with her widowed mother-in-law Naomi, to a land that was not her own. And with Naomi's wise instruction, Ruth strategically positioned herself to catch the eye of a local man 'of standing' who was in line to be her 'kinsman-redeemer' (a man whose link to Ruth's late husband obligated him to take her in and care for her). Naomi knew that they needed a good man to marry into the family and become responsible for them, so she didn't mess around.

You probably know the story. When Boaz discovered that Ruth was lying at his feet, essentially offering herself to him in marriage, she said to him: 'spread the corner of your garment over me' (Ruth 3:9). In Biblical language, this means 'please marry me'.

We can see God himself using this metaphorical language in Ezekiel 16:8 when he speaks to the nation of Israel, saying to them: 'Later I passed by, and when I looked at you and saw that you were old enough for love, I spread the corner of my garment over you and covered your naked body. I gave you my solemn oath and entered into a covenant with you...and you became mine.' This is a clear image of a husband taking a wife (remember, the church is the bride of Christ). So when a man 'spreads his garment' over a woman, and takes her on as a wife, he is covering her vulnerabilities – she is no longer exposed.

As women, we need this covering. Being exposed to the elements is exhausting and scary. We need a good man who will look after us, protect us, and ensure that we are treated with dignity and respect. We need a man who will stand up for us and fight for our honour. **It is not wrong to want this.**

Feminism has shouted at us for so long, telling us, 'You don't need a man!' 'The future is female!' 'Girls rule the world!' But this is incredibly unhelpful. Trying to look after yourself is just so exhausting. Not only do you have to work to provide for yourself, you have to protect yourself as well! It's like trying to hack through a bush with a machete, while holding a shield in one hand to ward off the attackers. Not exactly the kind of thing that enhances the feminine spirit. The thing is, we do need a good man to 'cover' us, and to do the hard work of looking after us.

When you are young, this man is your dad. When you leave your dad's covering, you need to enter someone else's covering – ideally, your husband's. But if you leave home and enter the world as an independent, single woman, you may eventually find yourself with that untethered feeling. (You may have also experienced this feeling if you lost your dad in your childhood or youth.) You do get used to it, and might think it's normal – but I think it carries with it a constant, underlying anxiety and tension. And it's when something bad happens that you realise how much you need that man in your life, and you will run back to the best man you have. This could be your dad, grandad, an uncle, brother, brother-in-law, cousin, pastor, mentor, boss, colleague, friend, or even an ex-boyfriend.

Think of the last time something happened that you couldn't face on your own. Maybe your car broke down. Maybe you lost your job. Maybe someone broke into your house and stole all your stuff. Who did you turn to?

Let me conclude these thoughts with a really important point: it is normal and okay to want a man to 'cover' you. You don't have to be the strong one.

In the meantime, I have two pieces of advice:

1. Remember that God is always there for you. He covers you and he is strong and powerful. Although you can't see him, he is working in your life, and if you let him, he will keep you safe. But you do need to take his advice and do what he recommends! If you didn't have a great dad to teach you the ropes, you will find everything you need to know in Scripture. So dust off those Bibles and get studying.

2. Stay in contact with your parents or 'covering' family members. Tell them what is going on for you, and let them speak into your life. Don't think that you know best all the time! If you don't have a good relationship with your parents, or they live far away, find a good, stable couple in your Christian community who can be surrogate parents for you. Ask them to 'take you in'. Go to their place for dinner once a fortnight or once a month. Let them speak into your life and pray for you. Take your questions and hurts to them. Be 'covered' by their reputation, and their relationship with you in the community. (And ask them to help set you up with a good Christian man!)

Note: There may be some girls reading this who don't really relate to the anxious, vulnerable woman I've described in this chapter. Perhaps you are a rare breed of modern girl who comes from a strong, healthy family, and you are still firmly under the covering of your excellent male family members. You may be single and feel the pain of every passing 'single' birthday, but you still feel pretty safe, known and loved. For you girls, I would suggest that you have yet to find any man for whom it's worth 'leaving and cleaving'. I mean, if your own family is still fulfilling your needs for protection, provision and companionship, why leave? And that's your prerogative. But if you do want your own family one day...it might be time to shake things up.

CHAPTER 2

How will I survive the wait?

I used to think that I could handle being single *if only* I knew that one day I would be married. If God would just tell me, 'You're single now, BUT you will be married within five years', then I could rest easy, take a breath, and get on with my life. But of course, that didn't happen. Like you, I just had to pray and hope that one day, it would happen.

It's kind of a freaky place to be – not knowing the future. So much of a woman's potential and purpose is centred around marriage and motherhood, and this is normal, right and proper. Don't feel ashamed of wanting to be a wife and mum. As we know from the Biblical creation account (see Genesis 2), **it's the natural desire** and 'fit' for a woman to partner with a man, to be his strong helper and have children with him (if you're reading this book, I know this resonates with you).

So I get how scary it is to wonder if this will ever happen for you. I wish I could tell you that it would, and when. But I can't.

In the meantime, **how will you live?** What routines and habits can you build into your life to become a healthier person? Which relationships will you seek and nurture in order to fill your love tanks? There's no point dwelling on your situation and becoming more and more depressed with each passing birthday. Keep your joy, keep your faith, and stay positive. Here are four ideas you might like to weave into your life in order to survive the wait.

1. Maintain your physical and mental health

Getting to a state where you feel mentally, emotionally and physically healthy and 'balanced' is a wonderful feeling. Health looks different for everyone, but you will know when you are in a good place, because you will feel energised, positive, and ready to face the world. How do you think you can best achieve this in your own life? Perhaps it's a case of improving your physical health – finding the right 'size' for yourself, and improving your energy levels. Or maybe you need to work on your mental health, taking more time out to journal, meditate, pray and 'defrag' your mind. Perhaps you are an emotional rollercoaster, addicted to drama and the big highs and lows – maybe some time off work, finding closure for past hurts, and concluding toxic relationships is what you need to do. Take a moment to think about what might help you in your particular situation.

Without your health, you are just a shell of yourself. Speaking from experience, if you are struggling with either physical or mental health problems, you may be finding it hard to cope with everyday life, let alone be bright, cheerful and active in the dating scene.

If you do have health issues, my heart goes out to you. It's very tough to deal with the daily grind of chronic health issues, particularly if you don't have the emotional/financial support of your parents and also have to continue working and maintaining a social life to survive. **Please take some time out to focus on getting better.** Don't ignore what your body is telling you.

It does concern me that many Christian girls these days are **burning out** left, right and centre. Working a full-time job, studying, doing church leadership and service, and/or doing a very taxing job like social work, pastoring, professional sport, communications, medicine, law, nursing or teaching (for example) can really take it out of you. Please check in with yourself and make sure you're not overloading your delicate feminine constitution. (You're not as tough as you think, by the way!)

Chronic fatigue, adrenal fatigue, thyroid problems, fertility issues, anxiety, depression, and so on – these issues are rife among women these days, and our stressful lifestyles certainly don't help.

If this is ringing a bell for you (even in the far-away recesses of your mind), I urge you to **take stock and to cut back** on your commitments, both physically and emotionally. See a doctor or a naturopath, get a battery of blood tests and/or hormone tests, and check that all your levels are ok. You might need to start a round of supplements, a different diet, an exercise regime, counselling, or even some medication to help balance out your brain chemistry. You might need to reduce your hours at work, or change things up so you don't have a long commute. It's really important that you address any issues you have before they get out of hand. **Ignoring them won't make them go away.**

And please, don't take on the shame and guilt that may be put on you by well-meaning Christians, if you choose to take some time out to rest and recharge (or change your lifestyle altogether). It can be disconcerting for other people in your ministry team if you up and quit. They might give you some spiritual platitudes or just tell you to 'go hard or go home', or compare you to the Apostle Paul who gave up everything for 'the cause'. This is unhelpful, insensitive and frankly can be very damaging. *You know yourself best.* Trust your gut and do what you need to do to look after yourself. And remember, women are different to men. In general, we are more vulnerable at certain times of our lives (menstruation, anyone?) and generally do have a higher sensitivity to emotional stress. Trying to operate on the same level as the men in your church is not going to end well.

So overall, when it comes to this topic and to our demographic, the main thing you probably need to do is to *do less*. Cut a few things out of the schedule. Quit a few teams. Cancel a few commitments. If you have to get up at 4.30am to fit in a gym session, before your meal prep, commute to work, a full day's work, another commute, grabbing dinner, squeezing in an hour of study or a quick boxing class, and leading a church meeting at night – then doing it all again the next day – don't you think something is a bit out of whack? Although this is kind of normal these days – *it's not normal.*

It's actually okay to get 8+ hours of sleep a night, to linger over a morning coffee, to saunter into work on time (not early or late) without having perfect hair and makeup, to leave on time, and to go home for a snack, a rest, an evening stroll, and a night curled up with a good book or a phone call to a friend. And if you feel that you don't deserve this kind of free and relaxed life – you might need to get some counselling on that, because it's an issue. I'm telling you now – you're worth it!

2. Dwell in community

Life was not meant to be lived alone. In today's Western world, it's normal for people to move out of home while still single, and to live alone or in a small or large share-house, or college dorm. Then it's very common for people to partner up and to cohabit for any length of time, without necessarily getting married (if you want instant and long-lasting anxiety, try this!). People don't really talk to their neighbours anymore. Houses take up entire blocks of land and there are no backyards for kids to play in. Young and older adults don't talk to their parents that often, and festive holidays can be pretty lonely and depressing for many. Families are small and friends scatter. So what's going on?

We have lost the 'village' culture, due to a bunch of sociological and moral factors. Urbanisation is a big one, with all the young people leaving their small towns in droves to head to college in the big cities. More concerningly, and I know this is a sweeping statement, the introduction of the contraceptive pill (1960's) and the no-fault divorce law (1970's) have contributed to **sexual promiscuity and the break-down of the family unit.** We also have a society that is in some ways culturally 'led' by kids and youth – their 'rights' and freedom of opportunity are paramount, and honour for **key stabilising groups** such as elders, mothers, and men has dissipated at an alarming rate. Young women at school and college are being pushed to have careers and are not really encouraged or even informed about how to become wives and mothers. So lots of women just don't really get around to it, or don't know how to do it.

These days, once you hit 25 and leave your young adults church group, and all the vibrancy and fun and future and 'calling' that was your language for your youth has passed on to the next generation, you may find yourself a little bit out to sea. (Because what's left after young adults?) You might feel unanchored. Lost. Lonely. Drifting. Trapped. Confused. Tired. Unseen. (Pick a word that suits you.)

If you are single, and you feel lonely, *that means you are normal.* We are not meant to live alone! It's not weakness or immaturity that makes you feel sad when you don't have anyone who checks in on you, or takes you out for a birthday brunch, or remembers to buy the bread you like. **It's healthy to feel a longing for someone to care.** We are built for relationship, and we can't get away from this.

However, the older you get, the more you may become hardened to deal with your loneliness. Have you ever heard about how older singles become 'set in their ways'? This really happens. It just means that living for yourself for too long creates a bit of **a crusty shell** around your heart, and cracking it open is just too hard. *This* is what you want to avoid. You need your heart to stay supple and open so that the man of your dreams can 'get in'.

The solution to <u>keep loneliness and crustiness at bay</u> is to dwell in community. What does this mean? For starters, *I strongly urge you not to live alone.* It's not good for you. I know it's annoying to keep moving house, to have to keep finding new roommates, and to put up with new ones who aren't tuned in to your ways. Trust me, I share-housed for 16 years with about 50 different girls, in many different houses. At times it was hard, frustrating, depressing, and got super annoying when I was like 31 and they were all around 20. (Not ideal.) You may have to work hard to find flatmates that will suit you. Do it. And please, live with Christian girls if you can. I *really* don't think it's appropriate or helpful to live with men, even in a mixed share-house. (Not just because of the dangerous sexual dynamic that can fizzle under the surface, but because a man in the house with you will most likely become your 'pseudo-covering', filling your love tanks, which is okay...until he moves out one day and you realise you're 45 and still single!)

If you have the opportunity to live with family, then do that. It's fine for a woman to continue living with her parents, or a sibling or relative, if you get along. Remember, women need to be under a covering. They need to be protected, both physically and emotionally, from the harshness of this life. We are different to men. **A man can live in his car. You can't.**

As well as living with others (and I mean *living* with others, and not just hiding out in your master suite without ever interacting), it's important to be **part of the wider community**, where people know you and care about you, and you have a role to play. This could be your church, a Bible study group, or a sporting team or other type of group, such as a charity, community centre, choir or theatre group. It doesn't really matter what it is, but it does matter that you are *seen* and *loved*.

Try different churches and groups until you find one that has the right vibe for you. (And remember, bigger is not always better.)

Let me give you a quick overview of what 'community' actually is. It's a real buzzword these days, but in fact, a lot of churches and groups aren't actually very communal. A community is not a place where you are just a cog in the machine, or a number in the crowd. A community is a place where you are seen, known, respected and heard, and where there is (at least on a micro level) some group flexibility and adaptation to cater for your particular needs, idiosyncrasies and dysfunction.

M. Scott Peck in his brilliant 1987 book *The Different Drum: Community Making and Peace*[1] sets the <u>stages of community building</u> as follows:

1. **Pseudo-community**

   This is when everyone is fake nice to each other and talks about superficial topics.

2. **Chaos**

   This is when conflict arises between persons in the group, and tensions get high.

   Now there are 3 options: The group dissolves or explodes, or certain people just walk away from the group. Or the group moves backwards into pseudo-community again, because they are in denial of the truth and can't handle the tension. Or the group enters the Silence phase, which requires self-reflection and honesty.

3. **Silence**

   This is that awkward time when everyone goes away to lick their wounds, think about what's happened, and grieve/forgive/repent etc. Then people adjust their views, behaviour or distance in order to maintain relationship within the community. (Change for the sake of harmony.) As Pastor Danny Silk asks in his great 2015 book *Keep Your Love On*[2], 'Are you willing to change to protect your connection with the one you love?'

4. **Community**

    If the group members are 'big' enough to face their issues, repent and forgive, change and adapt to each other, and own their own stuff, then the group can come back together and it becomes stronger. This 4-stage process will keep cycling through and the group will get stronger and stronger = true community.

One of the best share-houses I lived in was with 4 other girls, and I put a post-it note with the 4 stages of community on the fridge (yes, I was that girl). Whenever we got into an awkward discussion about money or cleaning, or a full-on heated argument, someone would point at the fridge and say, 'We are in chaos! This is good!' It was a good learning tool to see that conflict can be healthy, and is an important part of moving towards true community. **Because the reality is, you just don't bother doing conflict with someone you don't care about, do you?** The person is just not worth it to you.

So find a community where you are worth fighting for, with people that you could be bothered fighting with in order to maintain relationship. That's a true community.

By the way, if you yourself can't go through the silence and community stages with anyone, you will not be able to sustain a functioning dating relationship or marriage. You have to be able to own your stuff and stay present in the relational tension. If you walk away every time things get hard, or take it back to pseudo-community due to your fear of conflict, you're not going to move forward in relationships. Sort yourself out!

3. Do something meaningful

If you're going to be single, you may as well do it well! Don't waste your life away huddled in your work cubicle, staying late to make extra photocopies for the boss. Get out there and live life to the fullest!

Fortunately for you, we live in a generation and culture in which doing 'big' things with 'big' meaning is highly encouraged for women. Whether it's pursuing further study, climbing the corporate ladder, doing triathlons, hiking Machu Picchu, feeding the homeless, or volunteering in a refugee camp, girls these days are strongly supported to 'follow their dreams' and 'make a difference'.

However, it's important to find something to do that is **meaningful to *you***. It's got to be something you have the <u>time, competence, and money</u> to do. We can't all take a year-long road trip through the USA in a campervan (on my bucket list!) or get a PHD in neuroscience (too hard!). But what's something viable that will provide meaning to your days? Something that makes you want to get out of bed in the morning? Something that relatives will be able to ask you about at the family events, with real interest?

Maybe you are working on writing a book, or painting a beautiful piece of art. Perhaps you are growing a garden, starting a small business, or learning to surf. Maybe you are thinking of joining a local choir, or sporting group, or volunteer group.

Look at your current lifestyle. **Do you find your work meaningful?** In our generation we often expect to have a career that brings us lots of satisfaction. But in reality, this is a pretty rare achievement. My guess is that 99.5% of people around the world just work to pay the bills. To find meaning in your work – this is a blessing on top of that.

So if your work isn't meaningful, you need to find meaning elsewhere. Of course, the long term-goal and (arguably) the primary way that women find meaning is to get married and have kids. But in the meantime, what's something you can do to **spice up your life**?

As a rule of thumb, I think it needs to involve *creativity* and *relationships*. So something on the side you create just to make money, for example, may not be enough to help you feel 'meaning'. It's got to be something that you enjoy, that gets your creative juices flowing, requires you to tap into new places inside yourself that you haven't discovered before, and involves at least some level of relational interaction or pushback, in order to help you grow. And the most meaningful activities make a difference to someone else's life.

It takes a bit of effort to start doing something meaningful. But it's worth it! Get off that couch, log off Facebook and start planning.

4. Seek and submit to surrogate parents and elders

A final thought on helping you to survive the wait of singleness, is to lean on older and wiser community members. This may be a novel idea to some of you, but in my experience, I have found this to be a crucial part of getting me closer to marriage.

So many young women have basically cut ties with their parents these days, and demand an independence they can't really handle. **Women are living for themselves**, by themselves, taking their own advice, and learning how to be 'female' from dysfunctional characters on Netflix and HBO. Not helpful.

Believe it or not, your parents may have **a smidge of wisdom** to share with you, if you would lower yourself to receive it. And when it comes to relationships between men and women, older women have some good home truths that can be pretty useful. Maybe they don't have the perfect marriage or family or career themselves, but **have you ever asked yourself why that might be?** Have you ever considered what moral fortitude they've had to muster up to survive their circumstances?

Has it occurred to you that maybe they made the choices they did not for their own good, but for the sake of others? And no doubt that whatever the case, they've learned some hard lessons. **I guarantee that there is a lot of information behind the scenes that you have never been privy to.** It might be time to have some heart-to-heart chats with the older women in your life.

Women from past generations have often proven to be pretty tough. We can learn from them and try to practice some of the selflessness, persistence, forgiveness and general hard work that they have displayed in life and relationships.

Now if your parents are *really* dysfunctional or absent, then sure, you may like to look elsewhere for the wisdom of the elders. Is there an older couple at your church or in your neighbourhood with whom you can build relationship? You *need* to be under a covering. If it's not your parents, it needs to be someone else.

I think a lot of Christian girls place themselves under the covering of their **pastors** (without realising it), which can be really good or really bad – depending on the pastors. Here are some **questions you could ponder** to decide whether or not your pastors are going to help you flourish, or just take advantage of you:

Do they have your best interests at heart? Are they checking in on you? Are they holding you accountable? Do they give you plenty of time, and listen to you, and let you cry on their shoulder? Do they tell you when you need to pull your head in, or do they just shower you with flattery? *Do they care about the parts of you that have no connection to church life?* Do they stand up for you, and protect you? Do they model healthy relationships and emotional maturity in their own family life? Would you like a marriage like theirs? Do they try to find good guys for you to date? Or are they just using you to do more church work or personal favours?

There are so many benefits to being under the covering of good Christian parents or parent surrogates. **Trust me, it will really help you in the dating scene because it will give you a place to come back to where you can be soft, vulnerable and feminine.** You can take off your daily armour and ball-busting weaponry that you use to survive, and can actually just sit back and let someone else look after you for a bit. This will fill your feminine love tank and keep your heart nice and supple for your next date with Mr Right!

And believe it or not, there are tons of older Christian couples and older ladies out there who would just love to be utilised. They want to pass on their wisdom, and to take the young ones under their wing. **See who's around, and invite yourself into their world.** Be vulnerable, be honest, and be humble. I'm sure they would love to have input into your life.

CHAPTER 3

But will I make it?

Being single for a long time, with no hope on the horizon, is extremely demoralising. Am I right? I know what it feels like to be wondering, waiting, and praying day after day for God to bring a good man into your life…**and nothing happens**. Particularly after the age of 30, it can start to get seriously depressing. And you wouldn't be the only girl out there who is feeling a deep sense of dread and fear about your future.

To be honest, I know of a few girls, myself included, who have voiced the thought: ***What's the point anymore?*** *Why stick around? I'm just sick of it all.* I used to think, *Look, Lord, I've done everything I want to do and there's nothing left except for marriage and kids…so if that's not gonna happen, and you could just take me home right now, that'd be great.* **Have you ever felt like this?** If so, you're not alone.

So what's a girl to do? It gets really tough on the weekends, doesn't it. Those two days are like a yawning chasm of emptiness, offering up nothing but the excitement of a couple of hours at church on Sunday. And I mean, how many more girly brunches can you have, mountains can you hike, and clothes can you buy? **It gets so repetitive.** Setting you and your gals up for the perfect Insta shot, and then hardly getting any likes, let alone any action. It's exhausting! And not having anyone to just hang out with, because all of your couple friends are busy with 'family time' on the weekends and busy during the 'crazy hour' before dinner…it's rough.

Well, obviously **I don't recommend driving your car into a tree** (if you've considered it – please don't!), so let's look at some ways to keep you sane. Your life CAN have meaning, and God has brought you into this world to reflect his image and bring him glory…and you are, and you will.

I think there are **two things you've got to do** to stay somewhat 'normal' during this time, without turning your life into a train wreck.

1. **Discipline**

Ok, let's get the hard one out of the way first. **You have got to discipline your life.** I know that you have times when you just want to throw in the towel, spit the dummy and just go crazy – get skanky and go get wasted at the clubs, date a bad boy, string along 20 random dudes online, max out your credit card on travel or shopping, binge-eat for months on end, bail on your faith, or get a hectic tattoo on a whim (not that tattoos are wrong…are they? But think it through!)

But the key to maintaining **your feminine soul** is to *stay the path*. Stay the path, sister! Now when you are in your 30's, no-one can tell you what to do, right? If you want to have boyfriends sleeping over, turn into a wino, become negative and critical, watch R-rated movies every night, let yourself go, or spend hours exchanging sexual banter in online chat-rooms…who can stop you? But girl – *you* **have to stop you.** That's what maturity is. It's operating from what's called an _internal_ locus of control, rather than an external one. You don't do things (or not do things) because of rules and regulations, but because *you* have decided what is right for you and good for you, and you discipline yourself to act accordingly.

You might think, **Well, who cares?** *What's the point anymore?* For starters – I care. I do. I am praying for you and believing that God will hear your prayers for a husband. And <u>your future husband</u> – he cares. He is looking for a steady woman of **maturity, grace, modesty, patience and strength** (which is what you need to succeed at being a wife). You know who else cares? <u>Your friends and family.</u> They do. Even though they are busy with their own precious lives, they do care about you and would probably try to help you (if you ever let them in). And also – <u>God cares.</u> Do you think he designed you in your mothers' womb with your own special features, fingerprints, personality and spirit just to see you throw all his handiwork down the toilet? No. He values you as his own child, his own special girl. He is watching your journey and his heart aches for you.

Here's a scripture for you to ponder today.

'Someone may say, **"I'm allowed to do anything,"** but not everything is helpful. **"I'm allowed to do anything,"** but not everything encourages growth.' (1 Corinthians 10:23, God's Word Translation).

In this section of scripture, the Apostle Paul is talking to the Corinthians about eating food offered to idols. He's basically saying, *Look guys, just because you feel like it's all good, and God's grace will cover it, it doesn't mean it's the best course of action. It might hurt other people, and it might hurt you.*

I like applying this common sense to all areas of life. You see, even though technically you can kind of do whatever you want, and hope that the Lord 'will understand' – well, regardless of God's grace, you have to realise that not everything is beneficial for your life! Every action has a consequence, and <u>if you do stupid things, you will damage your life</u>. **Where are you going to draw the line and muster up a bit of self-control?** And what are you doing in your life to build and grow your maturity, patience, grace, modesty and kindness? (All those lovely feminine things.)

Did you know that in the Bible, **young women are sometimes referred to as pillars?** In Psalm 144, David sings to the Lord and envisions an Israelite nation (the Christian family) as a righteous people who are blessed by God. This is what he sees: 'our sons in their youth will be like well-nurtured plants, and <u>our daughters will be like pillars carved to adorn a palace</u>' (v.12). How would you describe a pillar? Beautiful, ornamental, picturesque...but primarily – strong, steadfast, holding up the roof, unshakeable, trustworthy, stable. **Would you describe yourself as a 'pillar' right now?** Are you trustworthy and stable? Are you able to hold up any roofs at the moment?

If this is convicting you, **ask the Holy Spirit to refresh you** and to speak to you more clearly – he is your counsellor and your conscience, and will direct your actions if you choose to listen to his voice. **You have to trust that his direction will lead you to a good place, even though the journey can be hard and boring.** You may need to repent of some things, and ask God to give you the grace and motivation to change. You may need to throw out some of your outfits, delete some of your pics or contacts, adjust your language/thinking, wrap up some friendships or relationships, and change your job, schedule or location. Do what you've gotta do. And fill it with good things! Find a friend or two who you can be honest with about your struggles, and who will do the journey with you.

And remember: sometimes you need to say no to things, just because it's not good for you. **You are worth looking after.** *You are worth it.*

2. Self-care

This is the other, very important, side of the coin. A lot of Christians who are trying to stay on the straight and narrow don't realise that

following God's path is *not* about being oppressed, squashed, voiceless and lacking in all freedoms. A life that is 100% discipline can be rigid, perfectionistic, and when out of balance can actually lead to a lot of issues!

It's not about saying 'no no no' to everything, all the time. **It's about learning what to say 'yes' to.** You are worth a yes! And here's where self-care comes in.

Now let me offend the feminists again with a few thoughts. Remember – I'm a previous career-woman, Masters-degree, workaholic, servaholic, outspoken, kind of gal. So I get it. But I do see that because of my personal issues, poor boundaries and lack of accessible wise elders, some of the negative things I achieved from that lifestyle were: burnout, stress, anxiety and depression, heartbreak, betrayal, and a deep soul weariness. So, what did I do wrong? Well, frankly, I was trying to be a man in a man's world.

It's very hard to retain the feminine softness of spirit (which includes **selflessness, receptivity, sweetness and patience)** when you are forced into very masculine behaviours due to your responsibilities. I mean, if you are too submissive and forgiving in your workplace, you might get walked all over by bosses, colleagues and clients alike! I don't know what you do for a living, but maybe you have to dance this really tricky dance of the masculine/feminine combo in order to survive. It's difficult.

And sadly, have you noticed that **girls have become very 'hard' these days?** If you really want to understand, go and hang out with older ladies from some other cultures. Expand your perspective a little bit. You might be surprised to realise that the 'women' you see represented in the western media, the community and even the church are not always the most 'feminine'. The way western women relate to others (including their husbands) is not the only way to do it. We can learn a lot from other people groups – and we must acknowledge that we certainly don't have a monopoly on femininity.

Back to self-care. The thing is, when you're acting like a man, it's exhausting in every sense of the word. You really do lose a lot of your feminine spirit, and you might feel like a **dried-up prune** inside. The answer is self-care. I really recommend Dr John Gray's 2008 book *Why Mars and Venus Collide*[1], which explains how men and women deal differently with stress, and what to do about it.

Basically, Dr Gray suggests that **women need a reduction in testosterone, and a boost of the oxytocin hormone (the cuddle hormone) to get their feminine vibe back.** And, you guessed it, that hormone is not stimulated by yelling across the boardroom table, being stuck in peak hour traffic, or staying late to finish your paperwork. But here are some ideas (thank you, Dr Gray) for getting a kick of oxytocin and remembering that indeed, *you are a woman.*

a. A relaxing bubble-bath, by candle-light.

b. A gentle walk in nature, or by the seaside (not a power-walk!)

c. Patting a pet.

d. Cuddling a baby.

e. Arranging flowers.

f. Lighting an aromatic candle and listening to relaxing music.

g. Yoga, meditation, or similar.

h. Cooking or baking for enjoyment (without rushing).

i. Getting a relaxing massage or facial.

j. Getting a spa pedicure (in a relaxed environment).

k. Catching up with the gals for a good goss.

l. Wandering around the shops with a girlfriend.

m. Reading a book.

n. Trying on outfits at home, or playing with makeup, at leisure.

o. Chatting on the phone to your mum, a female relative or friend.

p. Rearranging your furniture and doing some interior décor.

q. And so on.

Basically, it seems to me that the criteria for an **oxytocin activity** are: <u>no deadlines, no pressure, not results-based, female-oriented, self-focused, fulfilling, comfortable, and *for your benefit.*</u> What's something you can weave into your weekly routine to fill these needs?

And what I've realised is that the main thing you need in order to make all this self-care work, is to actually have <u>a male benefactor</u> – a father or father-figure (and eventually, a husband) – **who will do the masculine work for you.** I've thought about this a lot, and I just can't see any way around it. **To stay feminine in a man's world, you need a man to do the masculine stuff for you.** Otherwise, you have to play the role of man and woman, which not only messes with your head and hardens your heart, but also screws with your hormones!

As a woman, you need someone to take care of you. Self-care is a start, but it is not enough. I mean, it's a bit tough to relax when you're worried about how you're going to move your fridge next weekend! **So go and reconnect with your father, or find a good father-figure in your community who can fill the void.**

In the meantime, ask the Lord to cover you and protect you, as your Father and Husband. He has got your back.

CHAPTER 4

Why does it seem easier for non-Christians?

Sometimes it can seem that everyone around you is getting married – except you. Maybe you've wondered why your non-Christian friends and colleagues seem to be finding partners so easily, some of them even getting married and having kids. Meanwhile, you're lucky to get one date every two years. Talk about frustrating! Now, I don't have any data on this, but let me give you a few thoughts on the matter.

The key issue underlying all this is sex. Truly committed, emotionally healthy **Christians tend to save sex for marriage**. They also tend to be monogamous, family-oriented, and less interested in a promiscuous lifestyle. So Christian guys **tend to get married a lot younger** than non-Christian guys. I mean, most guys are ready to have sex by the age of 15, so it's not a stretch of the imagination to see why Christian guys want to get married young, between 20-25 years old. (Hence why there aren't many left for you to choose from!)

On the other hand, non-Christian guys *may* (and this is a generalisation) prefer to play the field a little, **sow their 'wild oats'**, have a few relationships, and 'enjoy' their bachelor lifestyles until they really want to settle down and take on the responsibilities of marriage and family, often in their 30's. And this is usually after starting a sexual relationship with someone. **I don't know of any non-religious guy who would wait to have sex until the wedding night.**

Christian girls have **much higher standards** of what they want in a partner. That's why your non-Christian girlfriends are possibly finding it easier to get married. *They* want a guy who is kind, funny, has a good job, has a car, and will be nice to the in-laws. *You* want a guy who has all that *plus* loves God, knows his Bible, serves his community, is great with kids, attends church regularly, practices grace and forgiveness, wants to run a Bible study, gives to the poor, is a virgin, won't pressure you for sex before marriage, and doesn't drink/smoke/swear/watch too much sport. Do you see the distinction?

So – not only do you have WAY higher standards, but as I've said, Christian guys get married young, leaving less of them still in the dating game when *you* are ready to find someone. Plus, with the explosion of readily available **pornography**, easily obtainable **casual sex** (even with Christian girls), and the general acceptance of **delayed adolescence** within our culture, there is very little incentive for many older Christian guys to give up their freedom and personal life to commit everything to one woman in marriage. These guys are not worried. They know they can stay single for ages and no one will really care. (In fact, they will be hot property – and that feels good!) And they know that there are still plenty of good Christian girls waiting in the wings to play the leading lady, whenever they are chosen.

Overall, it's no surprise why non-Christian girls have a less difficult time in finding Mr Right. I guess the question for you is – what are your standards and values, and how much do they matter to you?

(And if you're thinking about dating or marrying a non-Christian, head on over to Chapter 27 to get some thoughts about that!)

SECTION #2

Sorting Yourself Out

Sometimes in dating, it can be tempting to think of yourself as a **product**. It might seem that the ideal woman – the one who gets the man – is the one who is gorgeous, well-groomed and flawless, like a Stepford wife. But you are not a product. **You are a person.** It's the make-up of your character, genetics, history, personality, values, experience, motivations, fears and self-management that really defines you – not your perfect hair or practiced punch lines.

A loving, emotionally healthy man does not want a Stepford wife. He wants a loving, emotionally healthy person to be his life companion. I think that an 'emotionally healthy' person would display the following characteristics:

- Mature
- Responsible
- Able to say sorry
- Able to forgive
- Sets and maintains good boundaries
- Able to say 'no' and mean it
- Conscientious (eg. gets to work on time and follows through on commitments)
- Honest
- Able to negotiate to get needs met
- Able to receive

- Communicates clearly (they say what they really think, kindly, with good timing and an appreciation of context)
- Able to be vulnerable
- Humble
- Courageous
- Works towards competence
- Able to self-sooth in a healthy manner
- Able to feel and express both positive and negative emotions
- Able to maintain friendships and professional relationships long-term
- Self-sustaining
- Self-aware
- Open to positive and negative feedback
- Able to acknowledge and accept the tension and suffering of living in a fallen world
- Seeks community and relationship
- Aims to be a productive citizen
- Kind

And so on. That's quite a list! You might be wondering if guys like this really exist. (Keep searching!)

But beyond that, if this has made you realise that there are areas of *your* life where you could improve and become more emotionally healthy, you may benefit from some self-awareness or 'shadow' work (in the language of psychologist Carl Jung). You may need to look at your fear of being vulnerable, or your inability to trust people, for example. The following chapters will outline some ways you could start this journey.

CHAPTER 5

Do I have to change?

I'm sure that many of you are doing your best to go on dates and to meet as many guys as you can, in order to let your future man find you. Good on you! But I'm sure that there are also many of you who are just **too scared** to put yourselves out there.

Perhaps you find it more comfortable hanging out with the same crew after church each week, sticking to your usual mid-week group, and making the same not-so-funny jokes with your one or two male colleagues day after day. Maybe you engage in some romantic connections via Facebook, text or online dating, but when it comes to actually meeting in person, you think 'No…' and bail out.

Do you find yourself wearing worn out, frumpy or plain clothes, even though you can afford new ones? Do you think to yourself, 'There's no point doing my hair and makeup; no-one cares'? Or are you carrying a lot of extra weight – because you're scared for someone to see what's underneath all those layers? There are plenty of psychological explanations for these behaviours, but the bottom line is that you are probably afraid of the big 'V' word: **vulnerability**.

There can be lots of very traumatic events in our lives that cause us to shut down and to be too afraid to try new things anymore. Maybe you've come from an abusive family background, where you were hurt and neglected. Maybe you've been through a terrible break-up, even a broken engagement or divorce. Maybe you've been lied to and betrayed by guys. Maybe you had your heart set on something (or someone) and it didn't turn out. Your hopes have been dashed, your spirit crushed. Maybe no-one has ever looked twice at you, and you feel invisible and worthless.

Did you realise that where you are today is simply the result of a lot of choices? It's true that as children, we have very little power and we are subject to the choices made by our caregivers, and/or by those who abused power in our lives. My heart goes out to those of you have been mistreated in any way, and were not given the start in life that God designed you to have. Those of you who resonate with this – you have some processing and grieving to do, and a few extra hurdles to overcome. But it can be done.

Now that you are an adult, you have a plethora of choices at your fingertips. Perhaps you don't realise it. **Maybe you are living as a powerless victim.** 'But I have to stay late to finish this project…I have to visit my mother every Tuesday night…I have to baby-sit for my step-brother's kids every fortnight…I can't leave this church now, after all I've invested…I can't quit the team; I'll be letting them down…I can't change careers; this is my dream…I can't lose weight; this is just the way I am…' Why don't you have a go at completing the sentence for yourself? *I can't* _____ *because*

_____.

But is that really true?

Every choice we make has a consequence. And yes, consequences can be hard and scary to deal with. But what's it gonna be? You get to decide. What will it take for you to risk something? **If you don't change,**

nothing will change. You don't have to bet the farm – but just try to change one thing this week. Stand up for yourself in that work meeting. Say 'no' to that oppressive family member. Take a Sunday off and lie in the sun instead of going to church. Try doing your hair and makeup in a different way. Go along to a new young adults group. Do something that feels risky (in a positive way) *for you.*

You get the idea. We're not looking for results overnight, but for a new confidence and self-esteem to start bubbling up inside you. You need to start feeling a sense of empowerment in yourself as an independent adult – free of others' pressures and rules. Do you want to end up 45 years old and still living alone with your cat, never meeting any guys and never even getting your hair done, because there's no one to see it? **Stand up for yourself! Grow up! Get out!**

Here's the only equation you need to understand when it comes to change motivation: *the pain of staying the same has to be **greater** than the pain of change.* That's it! If you are not changing, then you're obviously content with the life you now have. (And that's totally fine.) **If it was that terrible, you'd do something different.**

So if you really do want things to look different, instead of whining about your situation and lamenting the problems in your life, CHANGE. Did you know that the greatest predictor of the future is the past? Unless you change something, it's almost 100% guaranteed that your next few years are going to look exactly like your last few years. And stop over-spiritualising it! God is not going to bring Prince Charming to knock on your door with a block of chocolate and your favourite box set (seasons 1-6). Get off that couch and grab that lipstick!

And sure, it'll be hard. I never said it would be easy. Do you think it's easy for an overweight person to join the gym? Do you think it's easy for an introvert to strike up a conversation at church? Do you think it's easy to make new life choices and deal with the hate from family members and friends? NO! But you have to decide if it's worth it.

Here's a good place to start: stop staying 'no' to interesting, fun things, and **start saying 'yes'**! If you are in community, you are probably receiving invitations on a regular basis. It might be for women's events, fellowship dinners, church socials, overseas trips, interesting courses, sporting clubs or events, cookouts and BBQs, or even…dates! You might not realise it, but perhaps you have an automatic 'no' switch built into your anti-vulnerability armour.

The guys at work invite you grab a drink on Friday afternoon…you say no. Your physio invites you to join their team for a charity walk-a-thon…you say no. Your pastor invites you to give a short testimony at church…you say no. Come on, ladies! The thing is, **every opportunity that you wouldn't otherwise have had leads to more opportunities down the road!** Sure, you might think the guys at work are less than appealing, but maybe one of their cool flat-mates might drop by and say hello. You just don't know where or when the connections could happen.

So for now – practice saying 'yes'. (Obviously don't say yes to freaky guys asking you to walk down a dark alley.)

Caveat: If you legitimately cannot pull yourself up off the couch to make any forward movement in your life, it's possible that you are suffering from **depression, anxiety, PTSD,** or something similar. I encourage you to see your doctor and/or a professional Christian counsellor to get to the bottom of your lack of motivation.

CHAPTER 6

How can I learn to trust again?

Many of you reading this book have experienced so much pain and rejection in your history that you feel you can't allow any part of your life to be at risk, to be spontaneous, or to be open to change. Perhaps you are stiff with fear and need everything to be 'just so' in order to feel safe. Maybe new situations fill you with anxiety, and the idea of straying from the beaten track gives you panic attacks. Or possibly, you are the ultimate 'hot mess' and your life is totally out of control – you jump from boyfriend to boyfriend, drama to drama, and push yourself to the limits with your time, money, relationships and sexuality. Is this you?

I'd like to put on my counsellor hat and explore the meaning behind these feelings and behaviours. Do you realise that **your behaviour is the fruit of a root?** (Thanks to my friend Claire for revealing this concept to me.) I wonder what the 'root system' of your life is like. **If you drew a picture of a tree (you) and the roots stretching down into the earth, how would you label each root?** You could think of the roots as being all the significant events and relationships in your history. Each of these has brought you pain or joy (or both). This would be something worth reflecting on at length. (Make a cup of tea, grab the Kleenex and pull out those journals!)

Some of the major painful life events that you may have experienced include the following:

Being separated from your primary caregiver at a young age.
Bereavement.
Poverty.
Divorce in your family (or in your own life).
A relationship breakup.
A friendship breakdown.
A family member (or yourself) 'breaking the family code' – eg. a sibling or parent coming out as homosexual, walking away from the faith, not entering the family business – or anything perceived by the family system as 'wrong' and worthy of being shunned or named as the 'black sheep'.
Incarceration of a family member or romantic partner (or adult child, depending on your age)
Betrayal (or perceived betrayal).
Rejection.
Humiliation.
Major injury, illness or disability in the family (or in your own life).
Major financial hardship or bankruptcy.
Drug and/or alcohol abuse in your family or close community.
Mental illness in your family.
Emotional, psychological, physical or sexual harassment or abuse.
Burn-out.
Loss of job.
Loss of a life-long dream.
Immigrating to another country.
Loss of a home.
War and deprivation.
Etc.

You might have even experienced an event that no-one knows about, such as the break-down of an illicit relationship, a miscarriage or even an abortion. These events can be doubly traumatic, as you may experience 'disenfranchised grief' – grief that is not acknowledged by your community, or worse, grief that is compounded by blaming and shaming by the community.

'Trauma' is generally defined as a deeply distressing or disturbing emotional or psychological response to an event or experience, and the key thing to note is that it is based on <u>your perception</u> of the event or experience. Someone else experiencing the exact same thing might not have the same reaction as you. So when you tell someone about the event and the ensuing pain, they might say, 'Oh that's no big deal. That happened to me and I was fine.' This is incredibly hurtful and confusing to hear. But if it was traumatic for you, it was traumatic. If you are a highly sensitive person, in particular, you may find yourself being hurt more easily than others. And that is okay – that is who you are and you just need to acknowledge it and work with it. (A note to the sensitive types: check out the 1996 book *The Highly Sensitive Person* by Elaine Aron[1] – it might reveal parts of yourself that will finally make sense!)

Once you have identified the events or relationships in your life that have caused you deep pain, it's important to consider whether you have processed the grief of those experiences. Pain doesn't just disappear. You can't just 'get over it'. You really do need to express the feelings and essentially 'cleanse' yourself of the pain as much as you can. This is called grieving.

Many cultures have organised rituals for the grieving process. For example, in Jewish culture when a family member dies, the family 'sit sheva' for 7 days – this is a structured time of mourning when they sit in their home or the home of the deceased, and receive condolences from family and friends. The bereaved person/s are then obligated to go to the Synagogue each day for a year and to recite the 'Kaddish' – a prayer of mourning. At the end of the year, they honour the anniversary of the death (the 'yarzheit') by lighting a special candle. This is a beautiful way of working through the various grief emotions and **actually paying tribute to the fact that a significant loss has occurred.**[2]

There are heaps of other rituals and styles of mourning expressed by various cultures around the world. In some countries you can even hire professional mourners to do the weeping and wailing for you. But in western Anglo-Saxon culture, we don't do grief well (or at all). Often there is no response to people's grief but silence, abandonment and lots of awkwardness or inappropriate rousing remarks, which can completely invalidate the depth of pain you are feeling. Perhaps people fear that if the pain is recognised, you'll fall into a sobbing heap and never be normal again, and nobody wants that, do they? It's messy, inconvenient, time-consuming, expensive and awkward. And, yes – that's grief.

I am quite a sensitive person and have experienced plenty of heartbreak in my life, including relationship break-ups, exiting church communities, health problems, and family dysfunction. Did they cause pain? Yes. Did I have to do a lot of grief 'work' to process these situations? Yes. Am I still sobbing into my pillow at night about the events? No – because my grieving has been done (mostly). And trust me, it took a lot of work. But unfortunately, if you choose to ignore your pain, and ignore the need to grieve, the pain will eventually pop out somewhere.

If you experience a great trauma, for example, and bottle up the pain inside, it will eventually express itself in one or more of a variety of dysfunctions. For example, through eating disorders, obsessive-compulsive disorder, addictions, mental health problems such as depression and anxiety, sleep or other health issues, character incongruences, 'dirty little secrets', or simply a loss of your former 'free' self – you may build a hard shell around your heart and not let anybody in.

You may tell yourself, 'I'm fine; everything's all good; everyone has a few problems; that's just life; I'm just going to be tough and carry on.' This is particularly easy to do when your dysfunction seems to be a positive thing, such as an addiction to exercise, being overly involved in church or ministry, or becoming a workaholic. And if your pain was invalidated by the first one or two people you told, then you might have taken on a feeling of shame and thought you were over-reacting. So now, maybe you never share your deepest fears and joys with anyone. Maybe you rarely give anyone a hug. Maybe you never cry. This is not healthy for any person. Our emotions are a huge part of who we are, and to deny them is to deny a part of ourselves. As humans, we are built for relationship, community and shared experience, and *our emotions help us to forge those connections.*

If this is resonating with you, I encourage you to dig a little deeper, to identify that moment, event or relationship that has caused you pain, and to work through it to find a place of freedom and wellness. In terms of the particular interest of this book – helping you get married – **it's extremely difficult for a man to break through the hard shell around your heart if you are closed to emotion.** Emotions work like a pendulum. If you force them to stop short of the sad end, they'll stop short of the happy end, too. You'll end up with a flat, stagnant experience of life, an inability to be vulnerable, and a lack of joy and appreciation for what a man can give to you. Alternatively, if you are more of a 'hot mess' and out of control, it's very hard for a man to be able to get close enough to 'wrap' you in the metaphorical hug that you need. It's like trying to corral an eight-legged porcupine on crack. Working through your pain will help you to find a more centred place of being, out of which you can feel and express both sadness and joy; you can cry and you can laugh; you can have good boundaries and you can also give people hugs. Do you think you're ready to start this journey?

If you're feeling overwhelmed or freaked out by this topic, you might need to put this book down and come back to it in a couple of months. Take time to process what you've read, and don't push yourself too hard if you don't feel emotionally ready for the work of grief. Additionally, you may not be in a community or context where you can afford the time and energy to do your grief work – perhaps you don't have a safe space in which to break down, or you are in a season of life where you just have to get on with it, or you are in a life situation where unravelling your pain would lead to major lifestyle changes that you're not willing to make. You do need to have time, space and safety to grieve.

Grief is extremely tiring, and as you work through the pain of your past, you will probably become aware of your own blind spots and contributions to the dysfunction of your life, which will cause even more pain! So you have to be ready. But I believe that the rewards you will start to see – the internal freedom you will feel – will make it all worth it.

CHAPTER 7

What does grieving look like?

So, grief. Ugh. Can't we all just lie on the beach sipping Pina Coladas and reading magazines? Sure you can – but if you are consistently single and want to get married, you probably do need to take time out for some 'heart work'. Think of it like doing a college degree. It takes a while, you have to commit to it, and it will stop you from doing some of the things you used to do. Argh. But the results at the end will be well worth it.

In the last chapter I encouraged you to go deep and have a look at some of the painful events from your past that may be causing you to bear dysfunctional fruit. Now if you're happy with the fruit you're 'bearing', then by all means stop reading right now and go hit the beach. But if you are sick of your current status and desperate for change, then get your active-wear on and prepare for some serious emotional exercise.

The first thing to know about grief is that it goes through various stages. It's not always about just having one big cry and then you're totally fine. There's a handy acronym **DABDA** that was introduced by Swiss psychiatrist Elizabeth Kubler-Ross in her 1969 book *On Death and Dying*[1]. This acronym stands for the five stages of grief, which can be experienced in a linear fashion or a cyclical fashion, or in no order at all. This is what DABDA stands for:

Denial
Anger
Bargaining
Depression
Acceptance

Let's put it into a dating scenario. Perhaps you've been dating a guy for a few weeks, and things are looking hopeful. Secretly, you've been thinking about how to split up your share-house and get a career transfer to his city, and have been creating a private Pinterest board for your wedding. (We've all been there.) Then all of a sudden, he calls it off. VIA TEXT.

So here's what your grief might look like:

1. **DENIAL:** It's totally fine. He's just got cold feet. Maybe he's been talking to his divorced brother again! He doesn't really mean it. We are perfect for each other! He said he wanted to take it slow. He's just having a break. This is still happening!

2. **ANGER:** How DARE he break up with me! Via TEXT! He should burn in a swamp of sulphuric acid. NO-ONE should treat me like this. Doesn't he realise HE WAS LUCKY TO GET ME. I am a total HOTTIE and he is missing out, BIG TIME!

3. **BARGAINING:** Maybe if I hit the gym and lose 20 pounds asap, he'll come back. Or was it my hair...I think he said he preferred platinum blondes? That's it; I'm calling Rachel for an appointment RIGHT NOW. Or maybe I wasn't spiritual enough? I'll tell him that I usually go to church twice a week; the other week was just a bad time for me. Should I have gone

further sexually? I suppose most of the girls do. I know, I'll go to his house and wear something sexy under a trench-coat. He'll have to let me in, sparks will fly, and we'll be back together in no time! Or maybe this is a test from the Lord…if I can hold off on texting him for 48 hours, Lord will you bring him back to me? Pleeeeease?

4. **DEPRESSION:** This relationship was never going to work. I can't believe I wasted so much time and energy on it. I'm a complete failure. I can never get anything right. My life is a flat, dry desert. No one will ever love me. I will die alone. Who will pay for my funeral? I better start a savings account for it. Probably no one will come anyway. I'm going to die a virgin. Whaaaaa!

5. **ACCEPTANCE:** Oh well. It was a good learning experience. I suppose there were a few reasons why it didn't work out. I can see how we were both to blame, and we just weren't compatible. It was not cool for him to end it the way he did, but that's his problem. I know that I have something to offer in a relationship, and I'm going to trust that there will be someone out there who will make the effort to get to know me and want to romance me. Sigh. I've got my friends, my family, my work and my health. I can do this.

Can you identify yourself in any of these stages? Maybe you are still in stage 1 - denial. Or maybe your life really is perfect, and you're nowhere on this page! But maybe, if you step back and take a look, you'll notice a few loose ends that need to be sorted (this is called 'unfinished business').

Perhaps you are in one of the stages and you have been there for a LONG TIME. Now it's true that grief has no timeline. And there are many events in life that are so traumatic that you may indeed never 'get over it' completely. But there should be some **movement in your grief**, a new level of acceptance with time, a healthier way of expressing your sadness, new relationships blossoming, and so on. If you are not experiencing this and seem to be feeling the same feelings over and over for months or even years, maybe you are 'stuck' in grief.

Sometimes, being single for a long time and feeling hopeless can leave us in a state of depression, and we really do feel stuck – like we are just **hamsters running on a wheel**, with no progress and no meaning to life. This is a legitimate feeling and can be soul-crushing and terrifying at the same time. I felt like this for some years, and it was terrible. At times it can be hard to drag yourself out of bed. But I want you to know that you are not alone, and that there is hope for your future. **God does have a good plan for your life**. And there are millions of men in the world hoping to find a nice woman to be their companion for life – it's just a matter of connecting with them! Take heart – it's not over yet.

If you are stuck, **you probably need someone to help shake things up** and get the grief process back on track. Ideally this will be with a trained counsellor or psychologist, as discussed in the next chapter, who can help you identify your pain and work with you over time to walk through the various stages. At the very least, organise some girls' nights, head to a women's retreat, or get a great new flatmate – do *something* to get good, wise people into your inner world.

It can feel unfair to see younger, happier girls getting married and making it look downright easy. But maybe they haven't walked the painful journey you have. Maybe they have less obstacles to overcome. Maybe they have other issues you can't see. Everyone has their own journey! **And wouldn't it be great to turn your life into a success story?** I believe you can.

CHAPTER 8

Where do I find healing?

For those of you who have admitted to yourselves that perhaps you do have just a little smidge of baggage, and you are ready to face it – in this chapter I want to show you where to go to get the help you need, to free yourself from the weight of pain and move forward.

There are a few ways to go about this. Remember, **we are made up of body, soul and spirit.** (Our 'soul' is often described as including our mind, will and emotions.) So there are a bunch of ways that your 'you-ness' is expressed, and also a number of ways that pain might be affecting you.

In my experience, it's easy in the Christian world to focus solely on the 'spiritual' part of yourself. Have you ever shared your emotional pain with someone just to be hit in the face with a slew of Biblical platitudes? 'It'll be ok; God works out everything for the good, remember!' 'Jeremiah 29:11 – He knows the plans he has for you!' 'You are an overcomer in Christ!' Now, while all these things are true, they are not always what you need to hear in the moment. And this is where western culture really sucks at grief.

The thing is that invalidated pain *doesn't just go away*. Consider the following scenario:

You: 'I'm so tired and down all the time. I'm 36 and still single. My last boyfriend told me I'm 'unlovable'! I haven't had a date in three years and I'm really starting to worry. I'm so lonely! I don't even know what the point of living is anymore.'

Friend or Pastor: 'Hey, cheer up! You have eternal life! That's better than anything! God can use you as a single person!'

You: 'Oh my goodness, you are SO right! Wow, thank you! I never thought of that before! Suddenly I feel so happy! I can't WAIT to go and be an awesome single and change the world!'

Yeah, right. You can't just make pain go away by pretending it's not there or that it doesn't mean anything, or that it's *wrong*. **Painful emotion is never 'wrong'.** It's just that it makes some people so uncomfortable that they will do anything to skirt around it and cover it up. Not helpful.

Now, if you are in a strong, loving community that accepts you for who you are, where you can express yourself honestly (the good and the bad) without fear of judgment or criticism, where you feel heard, and where people have 'got your back' and want to join with you to help you succeed in your life, chances are that you will heal quickly, through the encouraging and life-giving atmosphere. But this is a rarity for most people. If you can find even one two loving friends or mentors (ideally, the parents or parent-surrogates I've described), you will be able to hold onto them through your tough times, and have a 'safe place to land' when you're sinking towards rock bottom. I encourage you to seek out these kinds of relationships.

But for the average girl reading this alone in your apartment, wondering when you'll next get a text message or a call from someone who cares, let me give you some alternative options for where you can find healing for your pain.

1. **Christian Counselling**

This is the best place to start. The role of a counsellor is to 'join and journey' with you. She is not there to fix your problems, but to listen to you and be the 'container' in which you can express all your grief, rage, depression, anxiety or whatever. She will 'reflect back' to you what you're really feeling, and be kind of like a mirror, helping you to become more self-aware.

You don't need to know what to do or what to talk about – she will draw it out of you. A good counsellor is very skilled at picking up on what the real issues are for you, and will help you identify them and examine them. She takes it from a head level to a heart level. (To truly grieve pain, you need to get to the heart level.)

The main things you will do in counselling will be talking, crying and sitting in silence. It can be a bit strange when you're not used to it. Christian women in particular often find it hard to believe that there is someone who is actually emotionally strong enough and caring enough to literally sit there and listen to your crazy for an hour, without judging you or getting bored. But a good counsellor does this all day long – it's their job. They really are amazingly kind and empathic people.

I would recommend Christian counselling as opposed to secular counselling, because a lot of your baggage is probably tied up with your ideas and experiences around religion, church, God's will, sexuality, and your eternal purpose. A Biblically sound Christian will potentially be able to understand and handle these issues better. They will also be more empathic about the difficulty of reaching your goals without denying your deepest values.

The main priority is **getting a *good* counsellor** that you click with. Look for one with a professional qualification. There are some not so great ones out there, so if you have a bad experience with the first one, try someone else until you find the right fit. I always work off recommendations when it comes to counselling.

I'd strongly recommend a **female counsellor** rather than a male. This is because the counselling environment can get very 'warm' and you don't want to be building inappropriate bonds with a man who can't (and certainly shouldn't) reciprocate. It takes a very experienced and solid male counsellor to maintain proper boundaries with a single female client. Furthermore, I personally think **there are some things that only a woman can understand!**

In our generation, there is now very little stigma around counselling. You'd be surprised at how many Christian women have made regular counselling a part of their lifestyles. Find a good one, and go for it!

2. **Seeing a Psychologist**

A psychologist typically has higher qualifications than a counsellor (and has had to do many more hours of prac). Psychology is usually more expensive than counselling – an average session might be around $150 per hour, but you may be able to claim some of the cost back on your health insurance, or if you're in Australia, see if your GP can arrange a mental health plan for you, which offers subsidised psychologist visits.

The main way that psychologists are different to counsellors (in my experience) is that they are often a bit more intellectual in their approach to dealing with your issues. (Psychologists tend to take a 'top-down' approach, whereas counsellors often prefer a 'bottom-up' approach.) Psychologists may not be as concerned about creating a warm, friendly environment, but are keen to get straight into the nitty-gritty. They will be very evidence-based and may bring more education into the sessions. They can definitely handle you crying and bringing your 'crazy' to the table, but you may not get the full sense that they are *feeling with you*, like you will with a good counsellor. **Counsellors really drill down into your emotions, and are happy to sit in your pain with you for as long as you need, whereas psychologists are more interested in your behavioural and thinking patterns, and are keen to achieve behavioural goals with you as soon as possible.** But both counselling and psychology are generally what would be called 'talk therapy', and you can vent as much as you want.

If you feel like you need a warm grandmotherly hug and some empathy before you build up the courage to do the real work of change, see a counsellor. If you feel like you want someone to just help unravel what's going on and give you perspective quickly, see a psychologist. Again, a Christian psychologist would be best.

3. **Pastoral counselling**

I must tread carefully when commenting on this as a therapy option. The thing is, there are some church pastors or lay pastoral leaders out there who are just brilliant at listening, caring and providing good advice, with no ulterior motive. But these are few and far between. Here are my issues with having counselling sessions with a pastor, and why I don't recommend it:

ISSUE 1: COUNTER-TRANSFERENCE.

There's a phenomenon in counselling called 'transference' and 'counter-transference'. **Transference** is when the client attributes their personal feelings and expectations of someone in their own life onto the therapist – for example, the therapist reminds them of their mum, so they have the same feelings for the therapist as they do for their mum. Counter-transference is when the therapist reacts to this and starts actually acting like their mum, or attributes feelings about their own child onto the client (for example, the client reminds the therapist of their annoying teenager, and the therapist deals with the client accordingly).

Generally, this is not helpful to the therapeutic process and in fact can simply reiterate and solidify the problems already experienced by the client (eg. feeling disrespected and out of control.) Transference can be used on purpose, by skilled professionals, to draw out the issues of the client. But in a pastoral setting, uncontrolled counter-transference is common, and often ends up causing a huge relational mess, as well as an ineffective counselling dynamic. (Remember, most pastors are not professionally trained counsellors.)

The thing is, **any person who is not professionally trained as a counsellor or psychologist is really vulnerable** to falling into the counter-transference trap. A professional therapist is able to manage the difference between connection and building an unhelpful therapeutic relationship with the client. It's really hard to do. And most pastors are **simply not trained** in dealing with this.

ISSUE 2: DUAL RELATIONSHIPS & POWER IMBALANCE.

There is no possible way that your church pastor can be completely neutral on your particular issues. If you are a member of the congregation, then your behaviour will have some kind of effect on them or their church community.

Say you want counselling about a lay church leader that you are dating. You've discovered that he has a porn addiction and want to know what to do. Well, the pastor is probably going to find this really tricky to deal with, as he is good friends with your boyfriend and thinks he's just great (plus he depends on him to run the bus ministry). He might counsel you to let it slide, to just break up with him and move on, or to 'forgive and forget'. He might not want the news to get out to the rest of the congregation, so might counsel you to keep it quiet. This is not a healthy therapeutic approach to the situation and in fact divests you of any power.

Another example is this: your pastor needs you to serve and give to the church. He needs you to like him. **But you can't do therapy with someone who needs something from you.** This will completely affect everything they say to you. They will just keep things superficial and flatter you. You need a therapist who is bigger than you – who doesn't need you and in fact will go home at the end of the day and forget about you until your next session.

ISSUE 3: CONFIDENTIALITY.

Or lack thereof! Pastors are people-persons. They love a good chat. They are always networking and sharing the goss. Pastors simply do not have the same discipline around confidentiality as do professional therapists. They have no ethical obligation to you, particularly as you don't usually sign a contract with a pastor, and usually meet them in a more informal context. You cannot be sure that the pastor won't go spreading your secrets throughout their family, church, or the wider church network. This could even affect your future employment or dating prospects! (God forbid!)

Furthermore, pastors are already incredibly weighed down by the deep, dark secrets of everyone in their church. Generally pastors don't get their own counselling, supervision or therapy of any kind, so they don't have anywhere to download and vent about all the burdens that they are carrying. Hence they may let it slip to an inappropriate person, or might just buckle under the weight of your issues and completely break relationship with you, which could be very hurtful to you.

ISSUE 4: IT'S NOT COUNSELLING.

There's pastoral care, and there's counselling. They are actually two very different things. Pastoral care is great, having dinner with your pastors is great, getting a warm hug and some encouragement from your pastors is great – but this is all not true counselling. It's unlikely that in a coffee session with your pastor that you'll be able to deal with your unresolved issues towards your dad, for example. You might get a shoulder to cry on over the latest break-up, but you won't be able to deal with your obsessive need to control every situation (for example). These are deep issues and will usually only be dealt with properly by a trained therapist.

I could go on, but I think I've made my point. Now if you can't or won't see a professional therapist and really want to talk to a pastor anyway, here are my tips:

Talk to a female, or a married couple. Never talk to a male one-on-one.

Ask her to be clear about whether she can keep your information confidential. If you don't feel you can trust her, then don't share.

Don't expect counselling. Expect encouragement, maybe some good advice, and some helpful modelling of how to interact with life in a more functional way than you currently are. Chatting with a pastor is more like talking to a kind parent – really nice and makes you feel warm and fuzzy – but doesn't get to the root of your problems.

4. **Journaling & letter writing**

If you feel that you're not quite in need of therapy but still have some simmering feelings (eg. anger or sadness), writing can be a really helpful way to express those emotions and get them out of your system. Perhaps you are really angry at someone but you're not really an 'angry' person. Try writing a letter to that person and just let it rip! Use any language you want; write a novel if you want – just get everything onto the page. And DON'T SEND IT. You will find that your anger will start to dissipate straight away!

You might think, 'Oh but that's terrible, I should be a nice forgiving person; it's not very Christian to do that' – well, you can either have the anger inside or you can get it out. Because it's there! (Christians are people too.) And if you don't express it through writing or talking, trust me when I say it will come out somewhere else, possibly in a life-impacting way such as chronic fatigue, depression, self-harm, critical talk, eating disorders, workaholism, addiction to drugs, alcohol or shopping, or even in the form of a super-religious and rigid puritan lifestyle.

On that note, have you ever noticed that religious women often have a lot of internalised anger, maybe more than non-religious women? Christian women are usually socialised to never 'feel' or express anger, because it's 'unspiritual' or 'not gracious'. But that's impossible – sometimes life throws some horrible things at you and the normal response is anger or even rage. **These are valid feelings.** (Just look at King David throughout the Psalms…he was a rollercoaster of emotions!) It's extremely important to express these negative feelings. I'm not saying you should *act* on your anger and go and throw rocks at your ex-boyfriend's car, but that it is okay to *feel* angry and to acknowledge the reasons for that feeling. Therapy is a great place for this, and journaling or letter writing can help a great deal. And by all means, pray for God to help you forgive the people who have hurt you, so that you don't have to carry all that anger around forever. But there's no benefit to denying that it's there.

5. **Art Therapy**

There are tons of variations of therapy, so go nuts finding what suits you, but let me mention art therapy. You don't have to be artistic to do it! Art therapy is so cool – you just let your emotions come down out of your body and through your fingers onto the page. You will be stunned by what comes out of you. That's the amazing thing about therapy – you actually don't know what your subconscious is feeling, so you enter the therapeutic process to actually discover what is going on deep inside. You don't need to go into therapy saying, 'I have control issues and need to work on them' (although you can). In art therapy, you don't have to speak at all! The therapist will direct you. So it's a great option for those of you who simply don't feel ready to put your trauma into words, or are afraid of opening up to people.

Well, there are a few ideas about how to start your 'self-improvement' journey. **How do you know if *you* could benefit from therapy?** Answer these questions: do you have repeated negative patterns in relationships? Do guys always dump you, or string you along? Do you attract guys you don't like and don't want? Do you never get asked out? Do you self-sabotage your relationships? Do you avoid relationships like the plague? Are you unhappy with your life? If any of these are you, maybe you could benefit from therapy. You might wonder if it's worth the time and money. But if you commit to it for say, a year (maybe about ten sessions or so, spending a total of around $1000), your life could literally be changed. If someone told you that if you spent ten hours and $1000, you could be married within the next few years, would you do it? Heck yes!

CHAPTER 9

Why do people take advantage of me?

It's common for single Christian girls to find themselves in a pattern of always being the ones serving, giving, leading, helping, and fixing everyone else's problems. Sound familiar? If this is you, perhaps you could be someone who is a **'people-pleaser', 'approval-addict', or 'doormat'**. And these girls often stay single for a long time.

Think about **the last three conversations** you had. Were they characterised by any of these features?

1. The other person talking about themselves, and you listening;
2. You feeling like the other person *still* knows nothing about you;
3. You offering to help with their problems, giving them advice, or apologising for their situation;
4. You feeling a little bit 'switched-off', empty, anxious or angry inside;
5. You feeling frustrated afterwards because you feel like you keep having the same conversation with that person and they don't change;
6. You feeling like you weren't good enough, or you were rejected in the exchange;

7. When you reflect, you realise you were feeling negative feelings towards this person, and yet you only communicated kindness and warmth.

These are classic symptoms of a people-pleaser (PP). It's a tricky thing, the old PP syndrome. **The problem is that it actually gains you a lot of social capital, especially in the church.** That means that people say nice things to you, like 'Oh you are so servant-hearted.' 'You are such a giver.' 'Lucky we have you around!' 'Don't worry, Sally will take care of it.'

This is nice for awhile, but has **two major issues:**

1. Once you get stuck in this identity, it's hard to get out of - and people start taking advantage of you.
2. It's hard to get to know the 'real' you.

When it comes to dating, **being a PP is not going to work in your favour.** You might think that men would be drawn to a woman like you, who is always giving her all, burning herself out for the needs of others, and is always available. But on the contrary, men like women who take care of themselves, and who have space and softness to *receive*.

Remember, **it's the man's job to <u>give</u>, and the woman's job to <u>receive</u>.** (It's right there in your biology!) If you're always giving, where does he fit into your life? There needs to be room for him to input to you – to help *you*, and to minister to *you*.

This will only be possible for him if you start to **reveal some of your vulnerable areas.** <u>These are areas where someone (him) can make a difference.</u> The obvious ones are practical, like helping you move house, or picking you up if your car breaks down. The more subtle ones are you sharing some of your fears about life, or your sadness about a friendship breakdown. I'm not talking about becoming a whiny Whitney – but sometimes you have to give people at least **a little glimpse** of your weak spots. Usually a PP won't have the opportunity to do this, because they're always washing up or stacking chairs, always trying to help and never getting to talk about themselves, last to leave church and always missing out on getting a ride to the coffee bar with the cool crew.

The other issue about being a PP is that you usually **fill all your free time** with other people's problems. This is very common if you are part of a thriving church community. I bet you're on loads of teams and committees, and are a 'crucial member' of the body. In actual fact, and I'm speaking from experience here, you are probably trying to fill a deep void of **loneliness and insecurity** with all your volunteer roles and the accompanying social capital that you get from them. Perhaps you don't feel that you are worthy of doing something just for yourself?

Go and look at your **weekly calendar.** Cross off everything that is being done for someone else's benefit, with very little long-term personal reward (if you're honest). Do you end up with some big chunks of empty space? If so – does that freak you out? **Gaps are good.** *This is not a message you will often hear these days.* Usually the common theme at work, church and even in the media is: 'Hit the ground running!' 'How will you make a difference this year?' 'Go the extra mile!' 'Make every hour count!' You don't hear many leaders saying: 'Take a break. Nurture your creative side. Listen to your inner voice. Stop serving so much. Go out and get a life!'

And when it comes to dating, the thing is, a guy can't really approach you **unless you have gaps.** Where is he going to fit? I have actually had people tell me that years ago there were guys at church who were interested in me, but didn't approach me because I was too busy, and I looked like I was totally sold out to my career and/or ministry. I just didn't have any gaps.

So make some gaps. You won't fill them with dates straight away, so I suggest you fill them with things that are good just for *you*. Here are some more Dr John Gray-esque ideas[1]:

- bubble bath night
- a new TV series
- wine and chat night
- call your mum/Aunty/grandma/bestie
- late-night shopping
- a fellowship/worship group (that you *don't* lead or serve at)
- flicking through magazines
- gardening/flower-arranging
- cooking or baking for fun (not in a rush)
- craft/scrapbooking/collage/painting/drawing/sculpting/writing
- art class/pottery class etc.
- yoga/walk/run/swim (for relaxation and enjoyment)
- join a sporting group
- etc.

As opposed to 'people-pleasing', this is called 'self-care'. Self-care is doing something that is **just for you**, that won't directly benefit anyone else. People-pleasers can find it very hard to do self-care, as it brings no external benefits or kudos from other people. So you need to practice it. It may make you anxious at first, but over time, you will start to enjoy it, and realise that the world will go on turning without you, and that you are worth it! (And here's a tip for self-care beginners: *don't* post about it on social media. The whole point is to reconnect with your soul, your inner person, in a way that is private and low-key – *not* to perform for the outside world.)

These good vibes + the actual gaps in time will make you far more accessible to men.

If this chapter resonates with you, it's possible that you have a bit of a people-pleasing style. If so, I really recommend you check out the following books: *Approval Addiction*[2] by Joyce Meyer, *Codependent No More*[3] by Melody Beattie, *Love is a Choice*[4] by Hemfelt, Minerf and Meier, and *Keep Your Love On*[5] by Danny Silk.

And look, I understand that Christians are called and encouraged to live lives of generosity and service. There's nothing wrong with doing 'good works' and trying to help other people (and don't worry, once you're married with kids, your life will become a lot more service-oriented). But I'm guessing that you're **still single** because you haven't spent enough time on finding and developing an intimate relationship. And unless you have someone out there arranging your marriage for you, you'll have to put in some hard work yourself to get there. So don't feel bad about stepping back from other people's problems for awhile, in order to work on your own!

CHAPTER 10

Why do I keep getting dumped?

I have a good friend who is kind, caring, servant-hearted and forgiving. For years, she would pro-actively date various men, most of whom had a few issues to iron out. **She would spend months** helping them with their problems, encouraging them, and putting them on the path to wholeness and success. And then, after she had poured out all her love and care on them…they would dump her. AND they would marry the next girl they dated. What the?

She called herself '**the one before the one**'. It was a brutal time.

Has this ever happened to you? Perhaps you have poured your soul out in an effort to 'fix' a man, to help sort his life out, to reconcile him to his family, to get him a better job, to clean up his act, to help him lose 40 pounds, to introduce him to church life…and what do you have to show for it? **I bet you that the relationship is over.** And even more galling, I bet that HE dumped YOU. Ouch. (Don't worry, this happened to me numerous times. You're not alone!)

If you are the kind of girl who is always picking up '**broken-wing' boyfriends**, let me share something with you that could change your life: *if you become a man's mother, you will never be his wife.*

A man who is **still a little boy inside** needs a mother to help him with certain things:

- laundry
- eating right
- money
- health
- hygiene
- social life
- lots of ego-stroking and 'poor baby' soothings
- heavy limits and boundaries to discipline 'bad' behaviour
- lots of prodding to get him moving in a productive direction
- you get the point.

If you are helping a man in these areas – you are being his mother. You might be scratching your head thinking, **'I love him, but I'm not *in* love with him'**. What's happened is that your maternal instincts have kicked in. Your nurturing spirit has a job to do, so you pour all of your energy and love into putting groceries and homemade pasta bakes into his fridge, making sure he has fuel in the car and reminding him to call his sister for her birthday. You know who does that kind of stuff? Mums. Are you his mum? No! (Many wives eventually find themselves doing some of these things for their husbands, and some of this is right and good – but it depends on whether the man is playing his part in taking on the manly responsibilities of the relationship. It can't be a one-way street. This is all part of the complexity of marriage, and every couple has to figure this 'dance' out for themselves. But you *definitely* shouldn't be doing it regularly as a girlfriend or date!)

What's he doing for you, may I ask? Does he remind you to service your car? (Or better yet, book it in and take care of it?) Does he take you out for a nice meal every now and then? Does he go shopping with you and buy you a new outfit? Does he check in on you after your important work meeting? Does he attend your Grandma's 80th with you and chat happily to the family? Is he aware of what's going on between you and your bestie at the moment? Because he should! This is the man's role. *He gives, you receive.* He should be taking a deep interest in every aspect of your life, giving you support, counsel, encouragement and practical help. *He should care about you and not be focused solely on his own life.* (Side note: you need to be vulnerable enough with him so that he can actually *have* information about your life, to take an interest in! And when he does offer his concern and care for you, receive it!)

Do you know how men feel around their mums? Soft, squishy, lazy and greedy. They love their mums, they want their mums' food, they give their mums lots of hugs – but **do they want to marry their mums?** Heck no.

Here's the worst part about being someone's mother figure. A mum's job is to ***raise her child to leave home.*** Once the child is raised – he leaves. So once *you* get little Johnny back on his feet, successful at work, with his closets finally organised and his hair neatly trimmed, you know what's going to happen? <u>You're about to be royally DUMPED.</u>

If you want the guy that you're into, or your current boyfriend, to actually make more moves and take it to the next level, you have to pull back. Don't be motherly. If he needs a mummy, **let him run back home to his warm milk.** <u>You want a man who has *already* left home</u>, and is looking for a WOMAN.

You can't fix a boy and turn him into a man. Only his parents or a mentor can do that, as he takes a journey of self-discovery and grows from boyhood to manhood. (You can't engineer that, by the way. It has to come from him, in his timing.) But you *can* **inspire** him to become a man, so that he can win you. You are not the *mother*, you are the **prize**. Act like it! And <u>if he really wants you</u>, he will push through the 'birth canal' of maturity (what an image) and emerge on the other side, ready to face the world and to man up, just for you. So sit back, see what he does, and save your maternal instincts for actual children.

CHAPTER 11

Why am I intimidating to guys?

In our culture these days, it's become common for women of all ages to feature in direct leadership roles across all industries. We don't think twice about a woman being a CEO, school principal, or politician, nor do we think it unusual or wrong for a woman to lead men in a professional setting.

This has of course infiltrated **church life**, with many women holding lay leadership positions that require them to lead groups or teams of both men and women. It's quite normal for young women to be organising men of all ages in arranging events, recruiting volunteers, and scheduling rosters.

Furthermore, the buzz words of our generation are centred around leadership, and regularly invite women to assess their **'ministry gifting'**, **'leadership style'**, **'personality type'** and **'calling'**. Particularly in school and college these days, women are strongly encouraged to forge their own paths and to try to rise to the top of every field. So women these days have no problem 'manning up' and taking the reins.

But when you throw a romantic relationship into the mix, the cracks can start to appear. **It's not easy** for a woman to lead herself and lead others 24/7 for years on end, then all of a sudden to have to 'clock off', get out of the driver's seat, and stop bossing a man around (let alone let *him* lead *her*).

If this resonates with you, perhaps you *are* a girl with a 'leadership gifting'. This probably just means that you are **experienced in life, highly intelligent and have a strong personality type and/or moral convictions, with decent social skills – and, you're single.** (Often, married girls are more content to take a back-seat at church, as they get plenty of attention at home – and they are too busy working, cooking, cleaning and raising kids!)

Think about it – if you think faster and more practically than most, can see the big picture due to your experience and knowledge, are charismatic and inclusive, outspoken, and care deeply about something – chances are, you are going to end up being some sort of leader.

This is a bit of a **poisoned chalice** for a single woman. For starters, if you're like this, every man in your context sees you as a boss – a ball-buster, a schoolmarm, or a mother. These do not inspire romantic feelings in any man. On top of that, and possibly worse, is that you may have developed a sense of **entitlement, self-sufficiency, and pride.** For example, do you and your girlfriends sit around commenting on specific men you know, with disdain and contempt? Do you run around cleaning up after certain men that you lead, because you feel they are a bit useless? Is everything in your life about you, emphasised with high drama all the time? Do people tell you that you're cynical, and too picky? Do people suggest certain men in your world for you to date, and you give a mocking laugh and say, 'Oh please.'

What's really happening here is that you've had to (or learned to) rely on and trust yourself so much, that you no longer want to risk being vulnerable. When you're young, you are vulnerable and you can't do much about it. You have very little social capital, you're probably poor, and you're not that smart. But when you're older, you've got a lot more social status and confidence in yourself. (Sometimes, you're more arrogant.) And you may have a lot more to lose. Risking all that on a relationship with an unknown man who might turn out to be a dud, is really scary. You'd probably rather 'keep your options open'.

But if you eventually want a relationship, you have to choose to take that risk. You have to choose to be vulnerable again and to jump in to dating and relationships with both feet. Sure, it's terrifying. So is sky-diving. But if you don't try, you definitely won't succeed.

Vulnerability in this area is about **stepping back down the ladder of power** that you've been climbing. *Stop using your status as a shield.* Just give a guy a chance, even if you're a university professor and he's a tradesperson. Are you hiding behind your big titles and huge income? Do you regularly brag about your exciting travel history, to prove to yourself and others that you are worthy? Do you treat guys like disposable hand-wipes, to make yourself feel better than them? Well…I would suggest to you, girlfriend, that you are just *scared*. You are scared to be weak.

Sure, you act strong. You are smart. You have big dreams. You're picky and tough and you don't want to 'settle'. So be alone, if you want. But if you want a partner, you have to learn how to be weak again, in some ways, and to be a heck of a lot stronger than ever, in other ways. (Marriage is super hard and requires a great deal of maturity, wisdom and diplomacy. That's strength!)

Here's the bottom line. When girls say to me, 'I'm such a strong person; how do I let a man lead?' Well, by doing exactly that: *let* him lead. **Surrender something.** Because you know what? Maybe you're not 'strong', but brittle. You look tough, but you're afraid to crack. Sister, you just have to take yourself down off the pedestal you've created where you are God's gift to man, humble yourself and realise that you're just a normal person like everyone else. **Let someone in.** It's actually a <u>conscious choice</u> to allow a man to gently invite, encourage and provide for you. That sounds lovely, doesn't it? (And terrifying.)

To reiterate, the deeper question these girls are asking is: 'Can I trust him not to let me down?' **It's a trust issue.** I'm pretty sure that a lot of you reading this have been let down by your dad (and/or your mum), or another important parental figure in your life. Your trust has been broken. You've been vulnerable before, and been burned by it, and **you don't want to feel that way ever again** – hence the walls you've put around your heart, and the measures you've put in place to ensure that you're never left hanging or humiliated. Well - I'm so sorry that happened to you, and it is tough to come back from those kinds of situations and history. But **you can get healing**, and it's up to you to work through your trust issues.

Because here's the thing - in a relationship, you will need to *choose* to trust a man, and he will still let you down. He is human. **You just have to decide what level of 'letting down' you can live with.** Does he forget to empty the trash, every now and then? Or does he cheat on you every couple of years? There's a big difference!

You're not going to get the perfect man – there's no such thing. So what can you give up, what can you live with, and what can you not live without?

For example, I once dated a guy who was chronically late for everything – because he was extremely social and helpful, and was always busy chatting or helping someone fix their car. Was it annoying? Sure. Was it a deal-breaker? In retrospect, not really – **I could have adapted** to work around his lateness. (There were other deal-breakers for me though, so that was a non-starter.)

Another time, I had a couple of dates with a guy who seemed to be a decent, hard-working guy, but lacked emotional intelligence, was boorish and unsophisticated, and had no idea how to treat a lady. That was a **deal-breaker** for me. I didn't want to be married *that* much!

The first guy I was totally 'in love' with turned out to be a complete player. He had a lot of good qualities, but at the end of the day was not a respectful or trustworthy person. (I guess he just wasn't that into me!) So thank goodness that didn't come to anything. You definitely don't want to be in a relationship without **respect and trust**. Major deal-breaker!

And with all that said, I think **the REAL issue at the very bottom of everything** is that perhaps at the moment, *no-one is offering to lead you anywhere*. If a man is pursuing you, he's taking the lead. Full stop. All you have to do is **give him a chance**, and figure out your deal-breakers. But if no-one is pursuing you, then of course you don't feel led. If you are always initiating things with men, waiting for them to respond, trying to analyse their (few) messages, looking for signs that he's about to make a move, prescribing the way he should talk to you and interact with you – well, I'm sorry, but it's not that he's intimidated by you - *he's just not that into you*.

That's why I'm so adamant about dating rule #1: **let him initiate**. (Check out the rules in Chapter 21.) Unless a man is pursuing you, you have ZERO CHANCE of being led by him! You might say to yourself and your friends (as I did for many years): 'I guess I'm just intimidating to all guys because of my strong personality' or 'none of these guys are strong enough for me' – but the truth is simply that **'none of these guys are into me enough to want to break down my walls'**.

It's amazing how a man who seems shy, meek, insecure and lazy can all of a sudden rise up and pull himself together when he meets a woman he is really into, *even if* she has a strong personality. It's totally possible, and it happens all the time. It's just not happening for you, YET.

Prior to meeting my now-husband, in most of my dating relationships I'd tried to 'dumb myself down' and play the role of gentle, sweet, docile girlfriend (which is just not my personality). It was exhausting. By the time he came along, I'd had enough of pretending to be someone I wasn't! So although I was still well-presented, well-mannered, and appreciative, I didn't hold back my intelligence, my opinions, my sense of humour, and my leadership skills. I was just my own relaxed self – but I didn't take on the leadership *role*. I gave him a chance to show me what he was willing to offer, and I didn't 'manage' the relationship or tell him what to do. I just sat back and enjoyed the ride.

What surprised me was that unlike the other guys I'd dated, he didn't run away at the first sign of my strong personality or challenging thoughts. He was secure enough in who he was to not be thrown off by that, *and* he liked me enough to take on the challenge. Talk about a breath of fresh air! And because he was interested enough to stick around, I was able to let down my guard and actually let him in, over time. That was a relief. So regardless of what kind of woman you are, it is possible. You just need to be found by a man who really likes you, and make yourself accessible to love.

How do you show the men in your context that you want to be chosen, pursued and led? **How do you show them** that you aren't the ball-busting schoolmarm they see you as?

1. Act like a lady. Be feminine. Wear lipstick. Smile. **Let men take care of you.** Don't tell them what to do! (Talk less.) Stop crushing them with your snide comments and cynical banter.
2. Appreciate their gestures of caretaking and leadership. Admire them, thank them, and encourage them.
3. Don't act like you have it all together. (Because you don't!) When asked, share some of your fears or weaknesses. Allow a man to find the places in your life and heart that he could help to fill and to heal.
4. When they try to lead, follow. Then say thank you.
5. Feel the fear, *and do it anyway.*

CHAPTER 12

Why do I never get a second date?

Perhaps you have worked on your issues, you've gotten out there, met guys, and finally procured yourself a real, live date! You text all your friends, shave your legs, dress up, praise the Lord, and get ready for your future to truly begin. You feel that you are on your 'A game' on the date, and are scanning the man for all his redeeming features. His company is tolerable but that's hardly relevant, as he is the right height, about the right age, goes to church and even gives to charity! Swoon! He pays at the end, kisses you on the cheek, and you think that your future is sealed.

And then…nothing. No texts. No calls. No flowers arriving on your desk at work. No tags on social media. Nada. He's vanished! Your dreams are crumbling, you're having panic attacks, and you're madly scrolling through all your past communications for clues. What's happening?!

If this is a common scenario for you, it's time to step back and dissect what's going wrong. I find that in the older, single Christian women demographic, this is often because you are **just too desperate**. Men can smell desperation a mile away. And when you're 35+ and that clock is ticking, who wouldn't be desperate? <u>But you have to hide it</u>. You have to play it cool. You must remember that you are a catch, and that *even if you think you're not*, men want <u>what they can't have</u>.

This is a high-stakes game, girls. You have one chance, one date, a couple of measly hours, to get his attention and to entice him into a mystery that is more compelling than any of the other twenty desperate girls at church who are throwing themselves at him. How do you do this? You *play it cool*. Try some of these ideas for next time:

* **Prime yourself before the date** – talk to a friend on the phone to get all your words out prior to the date. Go silly and say whatever you want; get it out of your system! Go for a run or do some aerobic activity to shake off some of your anxiety. Have a warm shower, exfoliate your skin and lather on the moisturiser, so that you've had some 'physical touch' prior to the date. Eat something nutritious beforehand, so that you don't get hangry or stuff your face with food. Try to fill up your various love tanks as much as possible, so that you're less desperate when you get there. Don't go into a date cold!

* **Let him initiate**. See what he does. Do NOT instruct him in any way (eg. 'Aren't you going to open my door for me?' 'Didn't you realise they don't have undercover seating?' 'Here's a menu; I recommend the pasta.' 'Will you say grace, or should I say it?') Just look after yourself and if he offers to do something to help you - like pass you a menu, open the door, or offer you his jacket - calmly accept and say thank you, without making a big deal of it.

* **Let him run most of the conversation**. He knows that he needs to step up to the plate on a date, and to interest you with his (hopefully) fascinating life. Listen to his stories and laugh at his jokes. When appropriate, share a similar anecdote or thought from your own life. I strongly recommend you avoid talking openly about your political views, childhood history (especially if it's bad), past relationships (or lack of), fear of the future, body image problems, health issues, how much you hate your boss, or your expectations of a husband. <u>Keep it light!</u> Talk

about mutual friends, favourite books, interesting travel you've done, hobbies you have (if they're not weird), fun moments in your workplace, what music you're enjoying right now, and how much you love the restaurant he chose. This is not the time to reveal anything negative, controversial, or depressing.

A lot of Christian girls these days take the approach of 'lay all the cards on the table'. Well – **that doesn't work in card games, and it doesn't work in dating**. If you do this, you're shooting yourself in the foot, big time! And don't give me that 'authenticity' spiel. It's just not good manners to dump all your baggage in front of a complete stranger and expect him to sift through the pieces. What's appealing about that?

You need to employ some sales tactics. Reveal just a little bit at a time. Present your best self. Be genuine but be classy. Don't sell yourself short!

* **Don't act too spiritual.** If you are super passionate about God, church, the Bible, Godly living, purity, evangelism, etc. – that's great. I hope you get lots of treasures in heaven. But how do you think a man feels when the woman in front of him is basically Mother Teresa, his Sunday school teacher, and the Pope, all rolled into one? <u>He feels like he is not good enough.</u> He wonders if he will be able to maintain or even match your seemingly insatiable craving for spiritual activity. He is freaked out by how much you are crushing on various Christian leaders. And he is turned off by your puritan ideals. All he wants to know is: is this girl cool, will she be faithful, will she act respectfully towards me, will she be a willing sexual partner, does she know how to love and raise kids, and can she make me a sandwich every now and then? Men are simple. They want to have a laugh with you and not feel like they're at church every time they're with you.

On that note, **can you even enjoy yourself doing non-spiritual activities?** If not, there's something wrong. It's okay to go to a concert, to the movies, out for brunch, shopping, hiking, camping, or whatever – without making it an evangelical event. You need to learn to live your life in the world. So chill out on the Christian chat during a date. <u>Stop being so intense!</u> Take the lead from the man and don't overwhelm him with your spiritual passions. Match his tone and his topics, and later on you can decide if he's spiritual enough for *you*. (Side note: I've observed that sometimes the most 'churchy'-sounding guys are the biggest players of all, and the most normal, average, hard-working, seemingly boring guys make the best husbands.)

So overall – chill out, hold your tongue, let him lead, and most of all, try to go on lots of dates, so that you're not so desperate!

SECTION #3

Where are all the men?

This is a short section, but one of the most crucial. You can be totally ready for a man, but if there aren't any around, what's a girl to do? It's a desperate situation these days, and I think there are two main reasons why Mr Christian Right is nowhere to be found.

Firstly, if you're reading this book, you've probably missed your ideal dating 'window'. Most Christian guys start looking for their partner at a young age, say in their early 20's, and they look at girls aged about 16-25. So if for whatever reason you didn't get any dating traction in those years, and you are now 32 (or 42), there are very few Christian men left. And unfortunately, the older and smarter and more successful you become, the *less* appealing you are to many men. (Remember, a man wants to be able to make a difference in your life. Plus men generally prefer women who are innocent, hopeful, and keen to have a man's influence in their lives.)

Secondly, the world is not operating as it should be. Due to 'the Fall' in the Garden of Eden (thanks a lot, Adam and Eve!) humans are walking the wide road to sin and death, unless they are redeemed through salvation by faith in Jesus Christ. As a result, the world is really screwed up, with lots of sinful humans making a huge mess of dating, sex, relationships, marriage and family.

So if you feel like you're banging your head against a brick wall, not getting anywhere, and constantly failing in the dating department, it's partially because the whole system is broken.

Read on to find out how to overcome these very real problems.

CHAPTER 13

Why am I surrounded by losers?

I guarantee that every Sunday morning or night at church, you scan the crowd to see if any new guys have decided to dwell in the house. And I guarantee that with a frown and a sigh, you realise that nope, it's still just the same old duds who fit into the categories of:

    a. Ugh
    b. Meh
    c. I'd rather die alone.

So your options are quite limited. (Although there seems to be a strange phenomenon…whenever a new young blonde girl starts coming along, all of a sudden one or two really eligible guys seem to come out of the woodwork and attempt to sweep her away. Where were they hiding all that time?)

In this chapter I want to address two main questions on this MAJOR issue you are facing.

    1. **WHY is this happening?**
    2. **HOW ON EARTH can I overcome it?**

Firstly, let's look at the why. Obviously, there are no good guys left. Right? Or at least, not good enough for you!

Psychologist Dr Jordan Peterson talks a lot about a widely accepted social construct called the 'dominance heirarchy'.[1] Basically that's a fancy way of saying that the 'best' (most highly resourced) people are at the top of the social hierarchy, and the 'worst' are at the bottom. Ok, so that's obvious. Think of the power couples at your church or work. (There's always a cool crew!) Clearly, the higher up on the heirarchy you are, the more appealing you are to the opposite sex.

You might have heard of the term 'social climber'. This is a person whose origins place them on a lower rung initially, but they work hard to improve their social status in order to achieve a higher position in their community. It's generally frowned upon as desperate behaviour, but to be honest it's pretty smart (if you can do it without being too obvious). Think of all the leading ladies in the Jane Austen books. Their whole goal in life was to move into more popular circles, in order to increase their chances of attracting a higher quality man for marriage.

But while Elizabeth and Jane Bennett top the charts for marrying way out of their league, let's take a look at what's happening with modern women today, who aren't spending their time attending debutante balls and receiving gentlemen callers.

It's important to realise that there are different hierarchies for men and women. And the crazy thing is, that because feminism has been screwing us around for decades and selling us outright lies, girls like us have been putting all our energies into climbing the wrong hierarchy. Rather than focusing on improving our feminine appeal to be more attractive to the opposite sex, we have focused on improving ourselves to become more like the men we admire. And our culture seems to applaud us when we become smarter, faster, richer, louder, more successful, more demanding, more famous, with more stuff and more cool stories to share at the bar (or coffee house) every Friday night.

Women of our generation don't dream (or at least don't talk) about baking our husbands a roast and knitting by the fire while our children play at our feet. (You should practice talking like this, because it might attract some guys!) Usually these days, **we dream about climbing Everest**, saving the children, rescuing the homeless, having the biggest and best Bible study group at church, working in NYC, getting a PHD, buying a house, backpacking around Europe...and so we put all of our time, money and emotional energy into those goals. And we often succeed (and have tons of fun along the way).

Unfortunately, while those **'markers' of success** are very attractive *in* a man, they are not particularly attractive *to* a man. Uh oh! Girls with this lifestyle have actually been rising on the MALE hierarchy! So compared to the successful guys out there, sure, we are on par with them. We can hold our own, and in fact do garner their respect on many levels. **But they don't want to marry us.** Plus, how much valuable dating and child-bearing time have we wasted working our butts off to buy a house, trek around Europe, or finish our Masters degree? Eek!

The female dominance hierarchy has a completely different set of markers to the male hierarchy, particularly in the Christian world. What a Christian man wants most in a woman is **beauty, fertility, vulnerability, innocence, conviction, virtue, kindness, respect, loyalty, and hope.** A man desires a woman with these characteristics because **they will best fit with what he hopes to offer her** – protection, provision, adventure, leadership, and strength, most likely in the context of Christian family life. A man who properly operates in his masculinity wants a woman who will essentially reflect his masculine glory, by her femininity (1 Corinthians 11:7).

All that to say, if you want to attract a man (who is ideally high on the male dominance hierarchy), you'll need to pay some attention to working on your own feminine features. And sure, I know this doesn't sound very spiritual. Shouldn't a man just love you for your inner goodness, respect you for your achievements, and be impressed by your commitment to church activities? Well…it doesn't work that way.

I'm aware that some of you might be offended by this discussion. It's definitely not 'PC' and isn't what you're being taught in school or college, and unless they're from the old school, your mums aren't teaching you this either. Plus, you haven't really heard men talking like this, so what right do I have to assert these confronting ideas?

But here's the thing – men don't talk like this around women anymore (depending on where they live), because they'd probably be lynched. **But deep down, men are as simple as they have always been.** They want a nice, pretty girl to talk to at the end of the day, to hug them when they're down, to bear them a few kids, make them hot dinners and keep a lovely home (and provide a spicy bedroom). Trust me.

So a man isn't really that interested in your successes, your degrees, your titles, your wealth. These mean very little to him, if he's pursuing you for the right reasons, and in fact they can be a real obstacle to you actually attracting a man. You may be getting confused reading this, because *bosses at work* and *pastors at church* **do** often want you to have these qualifications and skills, so that you can serve them with a higher level of autonomy and competence. But a man who is looking for a romantic relationship does *not* look for these things. Sure, he will probably want a woman who can participate in an intelligent conversation and enthusiastically engage in his hobbies with him, but he's not necessarily looking for a high-achiever.

No man wants to romantically pursue a woman who is like a man, or worse, a woman who is more 'masculine' than he is! (Please go and watch the movie *Act Like a Lady, Think Like a Man*[2] by Steve Harvey. It's 100% truth!)

And if you are high on the masculine dominance hierarchy, *you may actually attract men who are high on the feminine hierarchy!* Weak, shy, immature or sweet mother's boys who need you to take charge of them and lead them. Not cool!

So basically, YES, all the men who are high on the dominance hierarchy are already taken. Why on earth would they be single at 30 or 35? They are the cream of the crop! **They would have snapped up a nice girl a long time ago.** And YES, this means that *generally* there are only the less appealing guys remaining; those at the bottom of the hierarchy, immature and stuck in the birth canal of adulthood, or poorly positioned in life due to genetics, place of birth, family issues or misfortune.

(Please hear me – I'm not saying these types of guys are of less value to God or have less right to enjoy life to the best of their ability, or that you can't make a relationship work with a man like this. But the reality is, when it comes to relationships, we naturally look for the men who are the most highly resourced – and best suited to meet the needs of our personal context.)

If you're worried that you've missed the boat and that there aren't any decent guys left…there is hope! There are a few viable guys out there who are **late bloomers.** They may have been hurt by a previous relationship, so are very slow at testing the waters again. Or maybe they've been working in an isolated job for many years, and are finally re-entering society. Or perhaps they've had their head down studying for a very long time, to reach their professional goals. (Or maybe, they've come out of a divorce relatively unscathed – see Chapter 30 to read my considerations on this type of man.) Thankfully, they still have all the raw material for being a really good husband. If you see a guy like this, do what you can to attract his attention, although be aware that he may still not be ready to choose and to commit. These guys work on their own timeline and there's nothing you can do to hurry them along.

And, you can always date **someone a bit younger.** Nothing wrong with a bit of cougar action. (But be careful that you don't become his mummy!)

Let me conclude. Basically, there are three things you can do to overcome the 'no guys left' situation.

1. **Get off the male dominance hierarchy!** Start breaking down your masculine attitudes. You need to make spaces in your life that a man can come into. (The man initiates, the woman responds. The man enters, the woman receives. You get my drift? It has to work that way for him to feel like the man.)

   If it's causing you to be tough, emotionless, burnt out and too independent, sacrifice your big titles at work and/or church. Heck, quit your job if you can and do something a bit more feminine, with less responsibility and less stress! If you've moved out of the city and away from the action, move back into a fun-loving and vibrant share-house in town where you have more chance of meeting people. You've got to go where the men are! And **be a woman.** Don't become like a boring, grumpy old nag whinging about taxes, health check-ups or the price of gas. No guy wants to be with a woman like that.

   Return to the covering of your dad or another trustworthy, older man. Show yourself to be a woman who knows how to be sweet, receptive and vulnerable – a woman who allows a man to protect her and to provide for her. Don't be all Miss Independent – it's not attractive.

Stop spending *all* your money on investments and sensible purchases, and **invest some cash** into bright and appealing clothes, a fresh sexy hairstyle, and some good quality makeup. Invest your money where it will give you the returns that you want. (Do you want financial security, or do you want a husband?) And let me make an important point here about money – the reason women are marrying less these days is because they are too economically independent. **Girls aren't getting married…because they don't have to get married.** If you're financially secure in yourself, why would you join yourself to a man who is, after all, just a man?

You might think that guys these days just aren't worth it. (And to you, maybe they're not. I hope you like being single.) But when you look at history, do you really think the men were 'better' back in the good old days? Not really! (Many men in the western world are probably more emotionally intelligent, respectful of women, highly educated and health-conscious than ever before.) Women in the past had to marry men who were pretty average (or 'less well-resourced', to be more politically correct), just because they were unable to earn their own living (and many women wanted their own children). And they had to be grateful that they had a provider and protector, and had to make it work as best they could. Am I saying this is right? Am I saying this is good? Am I saying this is easy? Not necessarily. But it's just the way it is. Ponder that!

In terms of femininity, you do need to focus on your inner *and outer* appearance. (Not very spiritual, but still true.) Quit your after-work scrapbooking class or book club and join the gym instead. Remember, when it comes to outward appearance, **age is not your friend.** This is not the time to be embracing your wrinkles and getting comfortable with 'the real you'.

Seriously, hit the gym, get a makeover, wear heels and learn to flirt! You need to become less man, more woman! Again, I know you think that a man needs to love you for your inner self, and eventually, he will. But he needs to be attracted to your outer self first, otherwise he won't even get a chance to know the real you, will he?

2. **Change your expectations** regarding the type of man you want. In fact, instead of thinking 'what do I want', think 'who wants me?' Because frankly, guys aren't exactly beating your door down, are they?

   If you've been thinking, *Ok, I want a guy who is successful, rich, owns his own house, respected at his job, in leadership at church, taller than me, good-looking, well-dressed, from a good family, kind to children, romantic, well-travelled, sophisticated…* Well I'm sorry, but you're probably going to end up dying alone. First of all, this guy doesn't exist, and secondly, he is already taken!

   Psychologist Dr Jordan Peterson suggests that women like to marry men who are higher on the dominance hierarchy than they are, and about five years older. (And men often like to marry women about five years younger.)[3]

   He also says that for women, the higher your IQ is, the less likely you are to get married. (Probably because you are too picky.) **So if you are old and smart, your chances are not good.** *You're going to have to compromise.* This doesn't mean that you are low on the female hierarchy; that you are a dud, or you are unlovable. What it means is that you have unfortunately missed your optimal window for dating and mating, which I think is probably between age 16-25. **So you have to make some compromises.**

Do you really have to marry someone who is well-travelled? Do you really have to marry someone who has the same missional dreams as you? Do you really have to marry a man who is a leader at church? (Do you have to marry someone from the same church denomination?) Recently I suggested to two of my friends the idea of marrying a white, Australian plumber. They were both like, 'Ew'. These girls are looking for someone more exciting, more cosmopolitan, more 'spiritual'. But interestingly, they are both white Australians themselves. Now I ask you, <u>what's wrong with a nice local plumber?</u> At least they make decent money and will be home every night for dinner.

Girls, you're going to have to change your ideals. Last time I checked, a man's role was to **pursue, protect and provide.** Not to offer an exegesis of the book of Romans in the original Greek. Not to be a regular volunteer at the local soup kitchen. Not to give you emotional counselling for three hours after work every day. **A man is a man if he PURSUES, PROTECTS, and PROVIDES.** So if there is a man who is offering that to you – take it!

3. **MOVE.** This is the obvious strategy and has been known to work for countless desperate and dateless women. If there truly are no potential men in your circle or your wider community, then you need to move to a different community. I'll discuss this more in Chapter 19.

CHAPTER 14

What's wrong with the world?

Before I got married (at 34) I spent many, many years wrestling with questions about my single (or recently dumped) status. *Why, God? Do you want me to be single? Is this some cruel joke? What's wrong with me? Where did I go wrong? What's wrong with guys these days? Why isn't anyone helping me? Should I buy a cat and be done with it?* And so on. Perhaps you resonate with some of these. And if you're like me, as you approach your mid-30's (or beyond) the reality of your situation may cause you to become angry, anxious, terrified, bitter, depressed, cynical, empty, promiscuous, crazy, or a whole lot of other emotions. Totally normal. And totally understandable.

The thing is – *it's not you.* You might be banging your head against a brick wall with the frustration of not knowing why you just can't seem to get traction with a man, even though you are pretty hot property, if you do say so yourself. And yes, I've been there. It's so exasperating!

So what is it? Why is there a generation of fairly awesome Christian women who seemed destined for loneliness? I'll tell you – it's sin. Yep, that old chestnut. It helps if you think of the world, your country, this generation, our culture and so on, as bigger than you. We live within a huge ecosystem of humanity; a massive heaving organism of souls interlinked in space and time by myriad connecting factors. And when that organism is diseased with sin, everyone suffers.

During my Bible reading one day, I came across a passage in Isaiah that literally made me tremble. In chapter 3 and into chapter 4, through the prophet Isaiah, God says to Jerusalem and Judah (His people) that because of their wickedness, bad things would happen to them. Their 'wickedness' encompassed things like turning away from God, forgetting God and taking His leadership and blessings for granted, engaging in sexual promiscuity, not following His laws, and so on – particularly the sexual promiscuity bit. What struck me was how some of the consequences laid out for these sins *are happening to our society right now*.

Here are the verses that apply to our particular area of interest:

The Lord Almighty is about to take from Jerusalem and Judah...the hero and warrior, the judge and prophet, the soothsayer and elder, the captain of fifty and man of rank, the counsellor, skilled craftsman and clever enchanter...I will make boys their officials; mere children will govern them...A man will seize one of his brothers at his father's home, and say '... be our leader...!' But in that day he will cry out, 'I have no remedy...do not make me the leader of the people'....

In that day seven women will take hold of one man and say, 'We will eat our own food and provide our own clothes; only let us be called by your name. Take away our disgrace!' (excerpts from Isaiah 3-4)

(I encourage you to read the commentary found in the reference list at the back of this book[1], which is both illuminating and terrifying.)

So in answer to the question: **where have all the good men gone?** Well – although there are tons of great men around who are doing their best to hold things together – it sure seems that real men are hard to find (especially single ones), and maybe it *is* due to the sin of the whole society. Sometimes it can feel like the men in charge are like children;

young men and women are leading everything; elders are few and far between; and women are desperate. Sound familiar?

Your problem is bigger than you.

So what's a girl to do? Well, apart from applying everything in this book to increase your chances with the few decent men remaining, there is a spiritual response too.

First of all, **it's okay to grieve**. Our culture has seriously messed things up, and unfortunately, you have to suffer for it. We have committed a grievous sin towards the Lord by throwing aside his commands and living like the world – letting feminism, promiscuity, pride, lust and greed motivate our choices. Our sin is on our own heads! It is right and proper to feel the pain of this sin, this collective sin, and to grieve the great damage it has done to our culture, and the effects it has on your own life.

Secondly, **you need to repent and commit to righteousness**. Get on your knees and cry out to the Lord for his deliverance. If you have areas of your life in which you have turned away from the Lord, particularly in terms of idolatry and promiscuity, you really need to repent and do whatever it takes to get that stuff out of your life. This is serious.

And third, **ask God for His help**. It's a crisis, and you need supernatural intervention! Before I met my husband, I had recently gone through yet another break-up, and was so exasperated with the whole dating scene. I felt like I had tried everything, and was getting nowhere. For three days I cried and prayed to the Lord (outside of work hours) and petitioned Him to come through for me. But seriously, I was a mess. I put all my cards on the table and invited God to split me open and lay my soul bare – to reveal anything that was holding me back. I reminded Him of my faithfulness to Him and my friendship with Him. I repented for my sins. I brought to his attention the answered prayers of the Biblical women who had difficult requests – Sarah, Hannah, Naomi, Esther, and so on.

Afterwards, I didn't feel heaps better, but I had made my case and what else could I do? There was no way I could take any other path. I was committed to the Lord, 100%, 24/7, and that was that. He was my only hope. And a few weeks later, I met my now husband.

There isn't much more you can do. **Don't give in to the temptation** of living a secular life – it's not better or easier, and it won't give you the satisfaction you crave. Sure, it might seem like the quick escape route – but nothing can change the fact that you are a daughter of God, and that's a relationship you want to keep. You need the Lord on your side, big time! He should not be trifled with. And may I also suggest, don't shut down and give up hope. You don't need to throw out your hair straightener, buy a brown cardigan and adopt a cat. Get your hair done, buy a red dress, and subscribe to a dating site! Don't give up!

If you stay on the righteous path and get a little bit more proactive, I believe that in time, the Lord will deliver you from your singleness (maybe in a way you didn't expect – be open!)

In the meantime, check this:

*Dear friends, do not be surprised at the painful trial you are suffering, as though something strange were happening to you…If you suffer as a Christian, do not be ashamed, but praise God that you bear that name…So then, those who suffer according to God's will should **commit themselves to their faithful Creator and continue to do good.*** (excerpts from 1 Peter 4:12-19)

Just keep going. He loves you and He sees you!

SECTION #4

A Good Man

So, you've dealt with your issues, you've grieved and repented, you've got your hair done, and you're ready to be a bit more 'open'. Should you tread carefully, be somewhat picky, and be precise? Or should you just give anyone a red hot go? Well – a bit of both. There are various types of 'men' out there, and you want to end up with the right kind of man – a real one! This section will deal with some of the specific nuances of identifying decent husband material.

CHAPTER 15

What should I look for?

My heart really does go out to all 30+ single Christian women in this day and age. It's super hard to find any decent guys who are single, and then to actually have them pursue you, and to turn out to be mainly issue-free? It's like finding the golden ticket. Very, very rare.

So what's a girl to do? Well, as we've discussed and will continue to look at, there *are* things you can do to increase your chances. But it depends how much you want it. If you are fairly happy the way you are, pretty satisfied with your current social group, moderately pleased with your position in life, and still optimistic about your romantic future, you will probably want to keep rolling along the way you are. But if you are sick of your situation and are willing to do whatever it takes to get to the holy grail of marriage (and children, please God!), then here are some tips for you.

Okay, so first of all you *do* need a basic idea of the kind of guy you want. Now I'm not talking about a crazy long list of features that combine Thor, Billy Graham and Richard Branson into one imaginary and non-existent freak of nature. What you actually need to do is to figure out who *you* are. This will then give you an idea of what type of guy will be the right 'fit' for you.

I was at a marriage seminar once where local counsellor Peter Janetzki taught us a really cool acronym that has always stuck with me. The acronym was described as a way to define the core elements of yourself, which can be applied to see if the person you are dating is indeed a general 'match' in these five areas:

Body
Emotions
Intellect
Neighbour
God.[1]

Your **BEING** is who you are. It was suggested that if you want to put these in order of importance, you should start at the bottom and work your way up. I would tend to agree. Here's what they really mean:

God: your faith, and your maturity within your faith. Your commitment to your faith and the level of importance it has in your life. *You need a man who has a similar level of commitment to the (same!) faith as you.*

Neighbour: your ability to be friends with this man. The level of your 'neighbourliness', your goodwill, your ability to shoot the breeze with this person and to enjoy being with them. *You need a man who you can talk to, and who is your friend.* Having a fun and flourishing friendship with your husband is one of the nicest things in life!

Intellect: your level of intelligence, your IQ, your smarts. *You need a man who is on par with you intellectually, or at least knows how to make you laugh. This is very important for a smart woman! You must be able to respect your husband – and it's not always easy to respect a man who is not as* *bright as you (unless he excels in another area that makes you admire him). He may not have the same IQ as you, but he needs to be sharp enough to challenge you. Also, note that this trait will probably have a major influence on your entire lifestyle – the kind of work he does, your combined income, his social group, where you live, etc. So it's a biggie.*

Emotions: your temperament, personality, conflict style, expressiveness, and so on. *While you don't need someone who is exactly the same as you in this area, you do need a man who can handle your emotions and who you can 'mesh' with when it comes to communication, conflict and romance. This is really what 'chemistry' is about. NB. You don't want a 'sensitive' man in terms of <u>him</u> being sensitive about everything. You want a sensitive man in terms of his sensitivity to <u>you</u> and your needs.*

Body: your looks, height, health, fitness, the way you dress, how much priority you put on physical exercise and sport, etc. *You need a man who thinks that YOU are beautiful! (Very important.) Guys are visual and they need to think you are just the best thing that ever happened to them. But don't marry someone who you think is repulsive. You have to want to have sex with him! You need a man who you are not embarrassed to be seen with in public. And remember, while women want men to change and believe that they will 'help to fix their man', usually men don't want to change. What you see is what you get. Don't think that marriage will change his ways!*

This **BEING** acronym is a really handy rule of thumb to use whenever sizing up a potential date or boyfriend. Of course no one is perfect, and these five elements do not take into account other important things like culture, baggage or character, but they are a good place to start in reflecting on what type of guy would be a good fit for you. Only you can decide which areas you are happy to compromise on. In your situation, you will probably have to make some compromises somewhere. But don't lie to yourself – go in with your eyes wide open. If there are flaws and major differences, be honest with yourself and really reflect on whether you could live with them. Then grieve them, accept them, and move forward with the relationship!

So, let's assume you are a fairly intelligent woman and you are happy with your appearance, you are a strongly committed Christian, very extroverted (perhaps a little on the strong side), a big talker, and love sport. Well, where are you going to find a man who would suit you? Hm. You need to look at the culture of the places you frequent. Do you only have access to super intellectual geeks with weird hobbies that you don't enjoy? Are you surrounded by non-Christian businessmen who are all married? Is your Bible study group filled with women and no guys? Take a moment to reflect on this.

Perhaps you are always complaining 'There's no guys in my church.' Well, what are you going to do about it? Having the knowledge is not the same thing as *applying* the knowledge. You have to change up your context in order to 'widen your net'. If you want to hunt bears, go to the woods. If you want to hunt pigs, go to the bush. You know that old saying, 'There's plenty more fish in the sea?' Yeah, well you have to actually go to the <u>sea</u>, to where the fish are.

Look, I'll be the first to admit there's a very small pool of available guys whose BEING is similar to yours. But there is a pool. You just have to find them!

If you want a really bookish, intellectual guy, start going to lectures or seminars, or hanging out at university cafes. (Move to a university town!) Attend some book launches. Join a course or start going to the more intellectual events at church. Go to that party hosted by your really nerdy friend. Don't hang out 24/7 with guys who've never heard of Freud, Nietzsche or Tolstoy.

If you want a sporty guy, join some sports teams! (Seems obvious.) There's tons out there. And don't just join netball, which is filled with women. Duh. Get onto some mixed teams. Sign up for free weekend running clubs, or whatever local public sporting event is out there. Join a mixed gym and do a few classes. Maybe you'll have a moment with a special someone at the water cooler!

If you want a really committed Christian or someone in ministry, don't just bank on the Sunday services at church – start going to the midweek prayer groups, different Bible study groups, training nights, missionary dinners, and so on. Go to your local mixed-church events, conferences and worship nights.

And here's one to make your elders turn in their graves – **change churches**! Church-hopping gets a bad rap, but if you're 30+ and single and your pastor is not introducing you to a new guy every week, well you have to take matters into your own hands! There are no *rules*, remember. You're not employed by the church (or maybe you are ha ha.) There's no *contract*. You ARE allowed to leave, you know! I met my husband after changing churches *twice*. (You gotta do what you gotta do.) No regrets!

You get my drift. There's no guarantee that you'll meet THE ONE at the first different event you attend, or sporting club you join. But if you didn't get a job from the first interview you had, would you give up? No! You just keep on putting yourself out there *until you get a job*. Yes, it's tiring, time-consuming, expensive and emotionally exhausting. Well, so is climbing Everest. **How much do you want it?**

And may I finish with an important side-note. I've noticed that a lot of **chronically single girls** only hang out with other, chronically single girls. May I suggest that you start spending more time with mixed groups, dating couples, married couples and families. Most connections after the age of 25 end up being through 'a friend of a friend' – so you need to be regularly in the world of men in order to actually *meet* men. Plus, you obviously need to change up your thinking and behaviours a bit, so you'd be better off hanging out with people who actually challenge your perspective on dating and men, and help you expand your horizons (not girls who will agree that all men are duds, and will only sit on the couch with you watching TV and eating ice-cream). And did you realise there's nothing more intimidating to an approaching man than a bevy of desperate 35-yr old women? Eek! He'll run the other way. Most of the time it's best to cruise around by yourself or with one other friend. You have to be approachable!

Remember – your friends might not want to do the new activities you want to do to find a man. So if you can't find a wing-woman, you might just have to go by yourself. Be brave! And who knows – a man might take pity on you if you're alone, and start a conversation. Perfect.

CHAPTER 16

What does a real man look like?

I bet you and your friends are constantly lamenting the lack of 'good guys', 'real men' or 'decent blokes'. And yep, I totally get it. We now live in a society in which men wear makeup, or live with their parents until they are 40 years old (or both). Eek! No one is suggesting you should be walking down the aisle to these guys – and let's face it, they are not the marrying types anyway. (And, the guys that are the most appealing and 'normal' seem to be afraid of commitment! What's that about?)

What you want is a *real man*. But what IS that? Every girl is attracted to a slightly (or hugely) different type of guy, aren't they? And across cultures, there are tons of differences…so is there a way to define a 'real' man?

Well, yes. And it's summed up in this one word: **responsibility**. A real man takes responsibility for himself, and then takes on the responsibility for others.

Let's break it down.

Baby: totally helpless.

Child: somewhat capable but naïve and lacking in judgement, physically too small to look after self, can't work to look after self.

Teen: somewhat capable but naïve, lacking in judgement, massive risk-taker, ego-centric, hormonal, sometimes big enough to look after self, sometimes able to work to provide for self.

Emerging man: physically able to care for self, works to provide for self, is self-controlled and stepping out in a productive direction. No longer reliant on parents or the community to sustain him.

Real man: Cares for self physically, financially, spiritually, is self-controlled, productive, and *looks to care for others as well*.

This is why it's hard to find a real man – they are busy looking after themselves, and have already committed to being responsible for more people, usually in the context of marriage and family.

Now let's throw in some **anomalies**. As outlined in the brilliant 2010 book *Being a Bloke*[1] by Michael Knight and Peter Janetzki, typically there are three types of men whose masculinity has been stunted in some way, and they are *passive, fearful,* or *arrogant*. Let me put my own spin on how I've experienced these three types in the dating scene. Can you relate?

Man-child (arrogant): fully grown, provides for some level of self-preservation, but is ego-centric, critical, a true 'bachelor', makes dating all about him, and will discard you as soon as you pull him up on his shortcomings. He may have missed out on having his dad or father figure pass on to him what it means to be a man, so he's latched onto unhelpful stereotypes of masculinity - and he is constantly looking for affirmation from 'da boys' (and hot girls) that he really is 'the man'. (Think Ross from the hit 90's sit-com *Friends*[2].)

Peter Pan (passive): fully grown, often quite attractive and hyper, sweet and fun, sponges off everyone else for everything they need (but in a cute way), always hangs out with girls (particularly younger ones), never seems to get into a romantic relationship (but may be sexually promiscuous), is unable to lead, doesn't seem to have gainful employment but rather is always 'hanging out'. He's like a kid in the playground. Peter Pans love church communities because they often offer a high level of socialising, tons of adoring and naïve young women, and a low expectation of maturity. (Think Joey.)

Weakling (fearful): fully grown, usually has a regular job (but nothing exciting), never takes risks, low self-esteem, wants to date but is too scared, doesn't believe the good life is for him, may be still attached to his mummy for security, second-guesses himself, doesn't think you'd be interested in him, and sometimes comes across as very 'blah'. No one really notices much about him, as his behaviour is usually inconsequential. (Think Chandler.)

I don't know about you, but I've encountered plenty of these in the dating world. When you date a Man-child, you become his surrogate counsellor and ego-stroker (exhausting!) and when you date a Weakling, you spend all your time reassuring him that you are interested, and urging him to take some risks with life. And you probably have a crush on a Peter Pan, but will never know what it's like to date him, because he doesn't really do relationships.

Should you avoid these anomalies? Will they ever change?

Well, until you see proof of change – don't waste your time. However, be encouraged by the fantastic 2013 movie *The Secret Life of Walter Mitty*[3] which tells the story of a Weakling who finally digs up enough courage to take a risk, have an adventure, and reach out to the woman he loves. (Yay Walter!)

Walter battles through his fears to become the fourth type of man – the **Hero**. Every man struggles with the three hero antitheses from time to time (arrogance, fear and passivity) but a real man does whatever it takes to break through and become a hero, whose behaviour can be defined as *'strength in action, with character'* (from *Being a Bloke*).

But it all comes down to **responsibility** in the end. So with the guys you're crushing on, dating, or hoping to date: do these words resonate when you think of them?

Responsibility
Strength
Action
Character

If not, it's time to go where these kinds of men hang out. Stop hanging with the Peter Pans and the Weaklings and the Man-Children. Because even if they float your boat, they're probably not going to marry you in the end. They are just too immature. **Go to where the Heroes are**, the men who take responsibility. (Think about where that might be in your community or context.) It's not success, wealth, fame or even popularity that you should be assessing him on – but *is he responsible?* He could be a CEO or a garbage-collector – but is he responsible for himself, and does he care enough to be responsible for others, to put strength in action, with character? *That* is a real man.

CHAPTER 17

How do I know if he can lead me?

I want to start this chapter by saying: **God loves you**. He wants you to be cared for, protected and loved. God designed marriage so that man wouldn't be alone – he made Eve especially to suit Adam, to be his helper, his friend and the mother of his children. God made women for men. (1 Cor 11:9)

So it's ok to want a man to ride in on his shining steed, save you from your life of drudgery in the cellar/tower, and give you a happy reason to get up each day. And the good news is, men are biologically predisposed to do this. They *want* to face a challenge, to conquer, and to win the heart of a beautiful woman. **They want to look after you**.

Well then…where are they? A valid question. Hold that thought.

First of all, let's look at **what it means** for a man to want to save you and look after you. We've discussed the concept of **responsibility**. But now we need to look at the idea of **leadership**. The issue of leadership is quite pertinent to you, my lovely readers, as I'm sure many of you have strong personalities, powerful professional roles and big responsibilities as lay leaders in church.

Some of you come from dysfunctional families where the men were, quite frankly, useless – and you've had to 'man up' yourself to survive. For obvious reasons, you are tired of men who can't find their way out of a paper bag, let alone know how to woo and win you. And the whole point of marriage is so that you don't have to call all the shots, earn all the money, and fix up all the messes, right? **So you probably want a man with some leadership abilities.**

Perhaps we don't fully understand what it means to be led by a man. When you think 'strong leader', who are you thinking of? What traits does he have, and why do they appeal to you?

Leadership in marriage is not about having a domineering husband who is inflexible, bosses you around and does whatever he wants. Some men are more commanding than others, and you have to work with that – but **the generic idea of a 'good leader' is extremely superficial**. It's not about being tall, loud and popular. In fact, a man doesn't even need to have followers in order to be a good husband. He only needs **one follower** to start with – you!

And therein lies the answer. <u>Marriage and family can *make* a man into a leader, over time.</u> No guy is perfect overnight, and a lot of the guys you probably idolise as 'great husbands' didn't start out that way. (You don't see what happens behind the closed doors of a marriage, remember.) But it's certainly a gamble, knowing whether or not the guy you like has what it takes to eventually grow into a great husband. How can you know for sure? Well, you can't – **but you can assess a few of his current qualities to see whether he's got the raw material for greatness.**

When you're looking at a guy and wondering if he can lead you, what you need to be asking is this:

1. **Does he love what he does?** If so, this will probably mean he is secure in himself, is competent and productive, and actually working or realistically has the potential *and a plan* to parlay his passion into a viable job. (A job is essential, but jobs come and go, so you need to be really wise but also a bit flexible in your expectations here.)

2. **Is he kind?** The trait of kindness is consistently rated as the most important factor in the success and happiness of a relationship.[1] I'm not talking about him being a martyr, a doormat, disingenuous or having false niceness – but true kindness. A truly kind man is worth his weight in gold.

3. <u>**Does he want to lead *you*?**</u>

   Here's the thing. A man might look like a complete deadbeat until the woman of his dreams walks in. Then something inside him turns on. He is able to step up, make a move, and become the hero. As dating coach Steve Harvey says, **Any man <u>can</u> change, but he <u>won't</u> change unless he's really into you.**[2]

   It's not really about his personality type. **If he likes you, he'll lead you.**

   And for you strong girls with big personalities, lots of college degrees, and high expectations, you know what? When a man comes along **who is really into you,** *if you chill out and let him take the reins,* he will treat you in such a way that you can eventually end up trusting him and letting him lead you.

<u>So, here's what you need to do.</u>

When a man shows interest in you, **give him a chance.** Don't write him off immediately because he doesn't fit your perfect profile. Sit back and see what he does. If he offers to open the door – let him. If he offers to buy you a coffee – let him. If he takes an interest in your work – tell him about it. He has to ease his way into your life, and slowly build your trust with small things, one at a time. Give him time and opportunity to do that. He's not going to look like a hero in the first five minutes.

Stop taking the lead when you're around men. It may have become a habit for you, and we all know that you're probably way more efficient and smarter than they are – but you have to just chill out, humble yourself, and let them take over. **A man will have no interest in a woman who doesn't need him around.** Why would he? Men want to be needed. They want to be able to make a difference. (This is the issue with getting married later in life. You become so independent and competent that sometimes, having a man can seem a bit redundant! This is why I think it's best to get married while you're still young and needy.)

I have to ask: if you say you need and want a man, well, *do you really?* What do you want and need him *for*? Take a good hard look in the mirror and answer that honestly. Maybe you have it all together and your life is functioning quite well, thank you very much. That's fine. You can be single if you want! But if you want a man around, you'll have to make space for him.

Let him make mistakes. No one is perfect, and no man is going to be perfect when he doesn't know you, he's trying to impress you, and he's nervous and may be stressed about stuff going on in his own life. Dating is pretty hard for guys, you know! Cut the poor man some slack. You need to decide what your **deal-breakers** are, but you also need to be **realistic**.

Are you really going to dismiss a guy who is kind, really into you, and loves his job, just because he's an inch shorter than you? Is it worth giving up on a decent fellow because he can't recite Romans 8:28? Do you really expect a man to be the perfect date, every time, and not lose the keys, forget where he parked the car, or have the wrong time for the movie? (These things happen.) Eventually, once you are aware of his idiosyncrasies, **you can actually help to fill in those gaps.** Maybe he's a terrible navigator and always gets lost driving to the restaurant. Well, that's where you can start to help him and do the navigating. That's what a marriage relationship is – <u>teamwork</u>. But let him woo you in the beginning – let him show you what he's got and do a bit of the hard work at the start. Just sit back and enjoy the ride.

Let me conclude with a final thought on leadership. If you have a strong personality and a 'leadership gifting', then I have good news for you. **You will be able to lead yourself.** The best leader is someone whose own life is in order. I'm not talking about being rigid and controlling. I'm talking about **maturity**. Have a think about the various areas of your life, and see if there are places where you could be leading yourself better. You just worry about you, and when the man who is into you comes along, he'll want to worry about you too.

And although the 1950's image of marriage is kind of appealing in some ways, at the end of the day you are two grown adults who should be able to lead yourselves. So you don't necessarily need a man who can *lead* you – you just need a man you can respect, and who is capable of challenging you from time to time. (Besides, most of the issue comes down to you learning to stop being <u>selfish</u>, having to <u>have everything your own way</u>, and <u>taking over</u> all the time. Yes, I'm talking to you!)

CHAPTER 18

What kind of man do I want?

It's normal to visualise your ideal future, and this can be really helpful in understanding whether or not you are suited to a certain type of man. Do you picture yourself as the corporate wife, hosting fabulous parties, attending lots of social events, and maintaining your home and appearance to really make your husband shine? Are you planning on living a life of travel, moving from place to place and exploring the world, working with different people groups and living out of a backpack? Do you want to settle on a homestead and raise five kids, keep chickens, and be a stay-at-home mum baking cookies and home-schooling? Are you a career woman, expecting your husband to support you as you pursue a Masters degree and then a PHD, involving years of research projects, stress, travel and a low income?

Of course, no one can know what the future holds, and you might change your vision of the future if you meet a man who is different to what you were expecting. But it's important to be realistic about what type of lifestyle you imagine for yourself, and whether this particular man is going to be able to provide it. <u>Because when you get married, you're not just signing up to a particular life partner – you're signing up to a certain kind of life.</u> However, flexibility is key! You are never going to get everything you want in a man or in your life. That's just reality. So you need to figure out what are your deal-breakers and preferences, and weigh that up against how much you don't want to be single!

For example, I'm a massive extrovert, love spending time with people, having people close for physical affection, and collaborating and chatting all day long. So I knew that I just couldn't handle being married to someone who would work away from home for months of the year, or work long shifts with strange hours (like long-term night shift). If I don't have my husband around a lot, I get antsy, looking for community and fellowship opportunities elsewhere (and as any wise person would tell you, this can become dangerous emotional territory). You need to know yourself, and know what you need.

That said, obviously as your options get more limited you do need to be as flexible as possible. And there are all sorts of marriages out there. There are all sorts of combinations when it comes to living arrangements, work-life balance, lifestyle choices and long-term or seasonal family commitments. Many people around the world do not have the 9-5 white-picket-fence lifestyle. And the thing is, none of these combinations is necessarily 'wrong' or 'right', but you must realise that depending on your personality type, personal needs, family history and life goals, you may or may not be suited to a certain type of lifestyle. So be wise!

As you get older, it's common to experience more and more parameters around your life. For example, you might be locked into a career path, or you might be a key leader in your church group, or you might have purchased a home and so are locked into mortgage payments and staying in a certain geographical area. It is tempting to want the man you are dating to fit into <u>your</u> parameters. But this is a huge issue for girls dating in their later years. The truth is, <u>a self-determining man does not want to fit his life into yours</u>. He is not an accessory, a flatmate, a toy-boy, or a personal assistant. He wants to bring *you* along on *his* adventure. He may not necessarily want to move into *your* house and help pay off *your* mortgage, join *your* church, and attend *your* social events. (If he does, I'd be curious. Does he have a life of his own?) He does not want his life to be completely dictated by your schedule. Where is the room for him to wow you, to woo you, to excite you, to invite you into something new, something of his that he has put together just for you? Doesn't he have any vision for his own life?

It's a fine line for girls in their mid-thirties onwards. You don't want to just be sitting around doing nothing, waiting for Mr Right. You feel you need to get on with your life, and make something of yourself! But you do need to consider that if you have created too many parameters in your life, then how will Mr Right get access to you? Where is the fertile soil in which he can plant his seed? Are there any untouched areas of your life that he can impact? Do you have any vulnerabilities that he can protect? Do you have any needs that he can provide? Are you able and willing to up and move if he invites you across the country?

Remember, above all else <u>a man needs to be needed</u>. This is the fuel to his masculine engine. You must maintain a space in your life for a man to meet your needs. If you are meeting them all yourself, then the only guys who will fall into a relationship with you are the passive ones who need a mother figure to keep taking care of them, and don't have the inclination or ability to even try and serve you. Alternatively, it could be someone looking for a sugar mama to pay his way while he lives the easy life and gets it on with someone else. No one wants this kind of husband!

Now it's true that in this modern era, marriages can look more like equal partnerships than they ever did before. And that can work, to some extent, for a time. It would be unrealistic to think that a woman in her 30's or 40's wouldn't have her own thing going on – her own hobbies, friends and work, for example. When an independent woman marries an independent man, for a time they can keep rolling along with their own lives, while living in the same house. But there has to be some sort of 'meshing', don't you think? For a marriage relationship to become strong, it needs to become **interdependent**. The man and woman need to need each other. Otherwise, you're little more than flatmates.

There are two common life events that often throw a spanner in the works of the 'partnership' marriage. The first one is when each party has a major goal they want to achieve, but the goals conflict. Eg. You want to take a huge promotion at work which requires a move to a different city, but your husband has just started a business that requires him to build up a local clientele. What's going to give?

The second event is having children. As soon as a previously independent woman has children, she realises how dependent she now is – on financial support, help with the kids, ongoing community, and so on. This can be really challenging for her when she sees her husband continuing to live his normal life and achieve his own professional goals. But it's just the way it is.

In both cases, in what I believe is the design for Christian marriage, the wife takes a step back and allows the man to fulfil his biological drive and mandate to provide for his family (with the sweat of his own labour). And the child-bearing wife needs to humble herself, realise that motherhood is a great and a noble calling, and accept that she is indeed now dependent on her husband and others to help her raise the children as best as she can.

My point is that while you may have a strong vision for your life at the moment, professionally or in ministry (for example), when you get married you may need to shelve some of your goals for a time, or forever. If that's the case, will you be satisfied joining your husband on *his* journey? Rather than think – *will he fit into the vision for my life?* You need to think – *where is a man with a great vision that I can enthusiastically join in with?* You'd be amazed at where wives end up. I know of many women who never thought they'd find themselves being the supporter and partner of a husband whose life took them into missions, business, ministry, the armed forces, education, sports, large family life, home-schooling, being on the move, living overseas, being super wealthy (or very poor), living in the bush, or myriad other options! Life has a way of unravelling itself over the years, and as your husband's wife, you will be obliged to go with him on the adventure (and help him succeed). The more willing and able you are to do so, the happier you'll be.

I would also suggest that **personality** plays a huge part in dictating whether or not you 'fit' with a certain type of man. It's pretty unlikely that you'll end up with someone who has exactly the same personality as you. But it's worth understanding how you differ in temperament, so that you know which behaviours to chalk up to 'personality' and which to assign to 'he's a lazy slob'.

The personality tests based on psychological trait theory have at their foundation the 'Big 5' traits, which are used to measure individual temperaments. I'll give you a very brief overview of the 'Big 5' traits here in layman's terms, but I suggest you go and take Dr Jordan Peterson's 'Understand Myself' test at www.understandmyself.com.[1] (It's worth paying for.)

The Big 5:

- Neuroticism - your level of anxiety and predisposition to psychological stress.
- Extraversion/Introversion – how much you enjoy and are good at being around people, and whether you are energised by people or by being alone.
- Agreeableness – a mixture of your politeness and compassion; your tendency to be compliant or resistant.

- Openness – ability to think outside the box, to accept difference, to be comfortable in the 'grey' areas, to enjoy novelty, and to be creative.

- Conscientiousness – how important it is to you to follow rules and instructions, to follow through, to be organised and dependable, and to be diligent.

Personality traits can have a big impact on the success of a blossoming relationship because they direct a lot of our behaviours. For example, if you are very extroverted but your boyfriend is very introverted, you might be constantly offended by his disinterest in going out in a group with your friends, or coming along to every family gathering. But perhaps he just doesn't have that kind of social energy. You will need to decide if you can handle being with someone who won't come to every event with you, and who may need you to skip a few exciting parties to stay home with him and watch movies on the couch. Or, if you are highly neurotic, he might get sick of your anxiety-driven behaviour and obsessive planning – but if he's made aware that it's just your temperament to think ahead and be super organised, maybe he'll be able to go along with it a little more easily.

If you are highly conscientious, you may find it very hard to break the tiniest rule, such as 'no talking in the library'. But your very low-in-conscientiousness boyfriend might find such rules to be pointless, and disregard them at every opportunity. Maybe he's the kind of guy who thinks nothing of driving without a license, or keeping $50 that he finds on the pavement. These kinds of things might really bug you. Imagine this magnified over a thousand different things for 60 years…it would get pretty frustrating!

Another thing to consider in terms of your **suitability** to a certain man is whether or not you're passionate about the same things. Most of marriage is work and talking. Mostly, when you're not working, raising kids, and doing housework, you'll be supporting and talking about your husband's work or passions (or yours). So, are you interested in what he's passionate about? (Is he interested in what you're passionate about?) Will he be talking your ear off about concrete, the surf report, technology, fitness, finance, theology, or people – for the next 50 years? Whatever it is…I hope you want to hear about it. Again and again and again.

Having similar values is obviously key, but so is having similar interests. That's why it's important to be yourself when you are being pursued by a man. There's no point pretending you're completely captivated by fishing if it actually bores you silly. (Let him go fishing while you go shopping. But make sure you do have something in common!) Be honest about your interests, and <u>consider whether or not you have enough overlap</u> with a man in order to have enough good conversation for the next five decades!

So it's best to go into any relationship with your eyes wide open. **Know yourself, and know your man.** Be prepared for major differences, and get ready to accept and adapt as necessary. It's hard work!

I suggest you check out a very informative YouTube video by Dr Peterson on the pitfalls of being *too* different. Just google: *Jordan Peterson on Relationship Compatibility and Personality Traits.*[2]

SECTION #5

Action Stations

In this section, I'm going to hit you with a bunch of different topics and the accompanying tips that will give you a much larger toolkit for dating success. Some of these ideas might seem really unusual to you, but I encourage you to try new things and see what happens. Remember – the goal is to get married to a decent Christian man who loves you (and has a job), while maintaining your integrity and self-respect. Sound challenging? Sure – but who doesn't love a challenge?

CHAPTER 19

What are my options?

I'm picturing a lot of the girls reading this – you've been single for a while, you're not getting asked on dates, you're pretty much a total catch, you've been praying hard, online dating is not really getting you anywhere, and you're starting to feel despondent (or worse).

I feel your pain and I know **it's such a battle**. It's a really hard season and when you see your other friends getting married, having kids, and being 'happy', it can really start getting you down. Everyone's busy talking about God's call on their life, and their new renovations, and their overseas family holidays, and you're just nose to the grindstone at work day after day, seeing the same 'ugh' guys at the gym, pretending to enjoy all the weddings, engagement parties, and baby showers that you have to go to (and spend lots of money on!), watching the collagen in your face and arms and hands start to lose its elasticity…it's rough.

So. What's a girl to do? As far as I can see, **you have a few options**. Which one you choose will depend on your age, circumstances, amount of $ you have, family ties, job, personality, and so on. **Only you can decide what risks you want to take, and whether or not it's worth it for you.** (This is called the 'cost/benefit ratio').

Option #1: Do nothing.

Stay where you are, doing what you're doing, and believe the Cindarella/Rapunzel story that 'one day your prince will come'. Possible – but unless you're young and gorgeous, and in a huge dynamic community - not very likely. (Sorry.) In fact, if you choose this option, you have to be okay with the idea that you may *never get married*. It's not a given, you know. There are lots of women out there who just **missed the boat**, so to speak. They are making good lives for themselves being professionally successful, awesome aunties, members of the community and the church, and looking after others. That's great, and we must esteem and include those women. But be aware that this may be in your future, unless you take action.

Option #2: Date like a fiend.

Get online and get dating. Join a bunch of dating sites. Be open to all sorts of guys. Go on dates with different guys every week (I wouldn't recommend every day – that is REALLY an emotional workout). Petition your family, friends and colleagues to connect you with any potential (single and Christian) guys they may know. Look around for speed dating events. Go for coffees until you can't handle any more caffeine. Get a few date outfits at the ready in your cupboard – date on the go! This is the 'it's a numbers game' approach. The more men you meet, the more likely you are to meet someone who suits you *and who is into you.*

Option #3: Go church-hopping.

I'm a big fan of this because it worked for me! I changed churches twice before I met my now-husband. I was initially at a church for about 15 years, dated a few guys there, realised it was time to get serious, so went to another church for eight months, no luck there, then went to another church and was there for about six months before I met my husband. Now to make church-hopping work for you, here's what I recommend:

- **Go to large churches, if you can.** If you go to a small church (say 20-100ppl), after a few weeks you'll be able to see at a glance how many available guys are there (if any). And unless they pursue you within a couple of months, I doubt you'll get any traction after that. (Guys are different to girls. Getting to know you over months and months of small group and experiencing your various baked goods is not going to make him eventually fall in love with you. If he hasn't pursued you within a couple of months, he's not going to.) Small churches aren't ideal for husband hunting (let's be honest; that's what this is), because you need lots of people to get to know. Remember, every person is connected to many other people. So the more people you meet, the more people you meet!

- **Get involved.** If you just attend the service, particularly if it's the dark, smoke-filled, concert-style atmosphere, it's extremely hard for anyone to even know you're there, let alone get to know you. You must get involved in some sort of small groups, serving teams, and so on. And join teams that have single guys in them and are quite dynamic (always changing). There's no point joining the knit-for-Siberia group if it only consists of 70-yr-old ladies! Try sitting in different areas of the church sanctuary – change it up. And attend regularly. You need to become *seen and known*.

- Let yourself become **known by influential people** in the church, and let it be known that you are looking for a good man. In my case, people who met me actually said to my now-husband, 'Hey, you should meet this girl Ruth. I think you two would really get along.' And people said the same thing to me!

Honestly, if people hadn't said those things to us, I don't think we would have ended up connecting.

- If a guy does ask you out, and you don't know much about him, **ask one of the leaders or stalwart members about him.** I always preferred to date with references. In my case, when my now husband asked me out, and I barely knew him, I texted one of the main pastors asking whether or not this guy was legit. He responded in the affirmative. Result: marriage. But if I hadn't built relationship with that pastor or become a respected member of the community, I may not have been able to do that. I wouldn't date just anyone, and if you don't know a guy from a bar of soap, it's best to ask around about his reputation. Unfortunately, there are some 'wolves in sheep's clothing' in churches, looking to prey on girls.

- **Join the para-church ministries.** Your church may have some sort of charity attached to the main church itself. Maybe it's some sort of community service, youth service, school program, or whatever. This is a great place to meet new people, including Christians who don't necessarily go the church itself.

- **Don't stay forever.** If it's been a year or so and you've given all the single guys a once-over, and no-one is pursuing you, then I would move on. You don't have that much time to waste!

Option #4: Change your expectations.

Maybe you've always pictured yourself marrying a corporate-type guy. Or a church leader. Or an outdoorsy woodsman. Maybe you've pictured your married self living overseas, or having the white-picket-fence soccer mum life, or living near your family. But maybe you need to expand your vision a little. The *main* thing you need is to be found by *a Godly guy with gainful employment who loves you.* That's pretty much it. If he ticks those three boxes, will you give him a chance? Even if he's older, younger, shorter, poorer, less educated, less sophisticated, of a different culture, widowed, divorced, lives far away…? Only you can decide what you can live with, of course, as we discussed in the last chapter. But your options are limited. A lot of girls say, *but I don't want to lower my standards or settle for second best! I know God has the best for me!* Well, sorry, but what does that even mean, and where does it say that in the Bible?

I mean, heck, look at Tamar in Genesis 38 – her first husband was wicked and died, her second husband refused to give her children and died, her father-in-law refused to give her a third son to marry and basically shunned her, so she dressed up as a hooker and manipulated her own father-in-law to sleep with her so that she could bear a son and finally gain some cultural status and provision. WHOA.

Or how about Esther. She was basically kidnapped off the streets as a teenager to join the King's harem, probably had to deal with major jealousy and hate from the other girls in the harem, became the King's wife (he was probably way older than her, of a different culture, and maybe even ugly), was threatened with having her whole race killed off, approached the King for favour and in doing so risked her life, then got a guy killed basically in order to survive. Brutal.

Or how about Ruth. Her first husband died, along with her father-in-law and brother-in-law (talk about family trauma), so she and the other ladies were basically childless and destitute. So her mother-in-law takes her to a new land and culture where she becomes a beggar and literally begs a total stranger to marry her. (Fortunately, he was quite a catch.)

So that's a little history lesson for you. The point is: life's not easy, and **sometimes you have to make the best of a bad situation**. It's not about 'lowering your standards'. It's about 'being realistic'. If you think that you're going to end up married to a tall, rich, handsome, muscular, smart, sophisticated, romantic, emotionally intelligent, popular, super-Christian guy who is great with children and animals – well, good luck to you. Tell us where they hang out and you'll have a lot of happy girls on your hands!

Take a look around at your friends' husbands. There may be one or two gold nuggets there, but for the most part I guarantee that they are just average guys. And remember, you don't see them at home in their stinky man-caves, or have to wash their dirty underwear. No one is perfect. So, does he love you, love God, and have a job? Give him a chance.

Option #5: Change your context.

This is the most scary but probably the most productive option. You need to move. Maybe you can start small by just changing churches, changing up your living situation, or changing jobs. If that doesn't open anything up to you, you might need to do a big move. Move cities. Move countries! When I was 33 and single and feeling completely hopeless, I was going to move to another country to serve in a ministry environment. I figured I might meet someone over there! I even applied for leave from work and started the process of looking at visas. Then my husband came along, thank goodness! But you do need to keep moving.

Where could you go and do something where you'll meet a whole different batch of men? Now don't get stuck on a six-month mission trip with 10 other ladies and no guys. You need to make it count. Go where there are guys! If you want to start small, try moving cities first. You don't want to waste too much money on flights to visit your family! And do consider the impact of cultural differences on a relationship. I'll discuss this further in Chapter 33.

Overall, it's super tough and scary, but I advise you to do something if you are in your early 30's or older. And all of these things won't work out unless you're really working on being in a healthy place, physically and emotionally. As I've said before, without counselling to sort through some of my issues, I don't know if I would have been able to get married. I just didn't give off the right 'vibe'. So get yourself to a good place, then start looking at visas!

CHAPTER 20

How do I improve my chances?

Let me reiterate what I think are your two best options for success. They are both pretty simple and very hard work. Are you ready to take the plunge?

1. **Change your context.**

I know I keep harping on about this, but it is absolutely crucial. If you've been in the same church, the same social group, the same workplace, the same team and so on, for a long time, why do you think that all of a sudden something different is going to happen? It is extremely unlikely that Mr Right is going to swoop in out of nowhere and make you the luckiest girl in the world. I know, miracles can happen – but trust me, waiting for Mr Right to turn up while sitting back in the same threadbare pew is going to cost you a huge chunk of time – a commodity you don't have.

Visit other churches. Join a different Bible study group. Start hanging out with other social groups (but don't ditch all your friends). If you are 30+, I would suggest that you need to switch things up about every 6-12 months. If you've been in a setting for this amount of time and no good guys have asked you out, then it's probably not going to happen. The thing is, in most cases a guy only has to meet you a few times to decide if he's into you. Getting to know you on a deeper level over a few years is not going to make him more attracted to you (that's not how guys work).

I know of two separate guys, both Christians, who saw attractive girls working in retail settings, and literally walked up to the counters and asked them out! They didn't even know them! Now they are married to those girls. So it doesn't take a guy long to know if he's into you. Sometimes it's just one look or one conversation. Thus, if you've been talking to a guy for months and he hasn't started pursuing you, chances are he's not going to. MOVE ON.

As I've said, you might even need to move to another city or country. **How much do you want to get married?** (If you do move overseas, perhaps think of somewhere not too far away. You don't want your kids to be too far from their grandparents!)

2. **Improve your appeal.**

You need to ensure that you are putting forward your 'best' self! Your best self is your healthiest, happiest, most vibrant, colourful and engaging self. It is not frazzled, burnt out, cynical, drab, or scraggly. You have to realise that guys are visual. And let's be honest, we are too! (You don't want to date an obese guy with bad breath, yellow teeth, greasy hair, and frumpy clothes…do you?) Guys are the same. They want a woman who looks nice.

Quick tips for the older single – for those of you who like specific advice:

- Get to a healthy weight for your size, and try doing some strength training (eg. pump class, squats and weights, cross-fit, etc.) to tone those muscles. It really does make a difference to how you look in a nice dress.

- Buy some new clothes – bright, patterned, trendy, with a bit of 'wow' – but still you! A couple of pairs of good jeans, some basic good-quality T-shirts, a denim or leather jacket and a well-fitting coloured blazer, funky leather flats and boots, a pair of good heels, fun jewellery, a couple of bright tops and one or two well-fitting dresses = success! Throw out anything that is faded, has holes, is obviously no longer trendy, is worn, or is drab.

- Educate yourself in what colours suit you. Apparently, I have a 'winter' skin colouring, so I look best in jewel-tones like ruby red, emerald green or sapphire blue. I look terrible in pastels! And if you are determined to dye your hair blonde (often men do like blondes), make sure it suits your skin tone, and that you get it done professionally. Fake blonde hair doesn't suit everyone!

- Get a good handbag – preferably in leather, not 'pleather'. Black, brown, or white always works. Or it could be a trendy patterned or textured one. And if it's a big one – please don't jam it full of everything you need for the next two days, including the kitchen sink. Big hefty bags scream 'bag lady'. You want to be cool, collected and streamlined. No fuss, no mess! On a date you should only carry a small clutch purse, not a 'mum' bag that's overflowing with all the bits and bobs you might need in a crisis. (On a date, you want to be cool and mysterious!)

- Get your hair done - don't stick to the same old look all the time. Change it up! Look at fashion magazines and ask your hairdresser what new style and perhaps colour would suit you. And 'do' your hair every day, or at least every time you go out to church, a party or an event. Invest in a hair straightener – and learn how to use it. (Or if you have crazy, curly hair – get a good diffuser and some decent products.) Well-kept hair makes a major difference to your appearance, so it's an important investment.

- Wear some jewellery – but not too much. I like to wear big, colourful earrings or silver hoops. They're a bit of a trademark. What's yours?

- Wear make-up. Especially as you get older, a bit of natural-looking makeup is imperative. Foundation, blush, neutral eye-shadow, eye-liner, mascara, and lipstick is all you need. And don't go cheap – cheap makeup is for teenagers who already have glowing skin. I recommend getting a good quality foundation, at least. Women lose their 'colour' as they age (hormones!) so you need to brighten up and smooth out your face a bit. At the very least, some mascara and tinted lip gloss will go a long way. If you don't know how to wear makeup well, get some lessons. This is crucial! Cancel your Netflix subscription and invest in some beauty tutorials instead. (Remember, what are your priorities?)

- Get braces and whiten your teeth. This is an expensive thing to do, but if you have bad teeth, it's vital. You could try Invisalign, which is a bit less intense and obvious. And teeth whitening strips or gel are really affordable on eBay. Having a nice smile will make a HUGE difference to your appeal.

- Wear good perfume. A nice scent can go a LONG way with a man. My favourites are Coco Chanel Mademoiselle, Romance by Ralph Lauren, and La Vie Est Belle by Lancome. But try some different scents to see what smells nice on you – nothing too cheap!

- **Extroverts:** If you find it hard to stop talking, you need to rein in your anxiety a little bit. (Prime yourself beforehand and use up some of your words before the date!) Give the man some space and some opportunity to prove himself to you. If you have to respond, just smile. It can be really off-putting if you dominate the conversation all the time. Watch for the wandering eyes, the yawn behind the hand, the checking of the watch, or re-positioning of the body language. This means you are talking too much! *Just* *give a little at a time*, and give the poor man time to respond in his own way. He might be thinking about how beautiful you are – why interrupt? As an extrovert you may be surprised to hear this, but with the right silence, space, questioning, and topic, a quiet person can reveal themselves as really interesting! Furthermore, he should be intrigued by you, your mystery, your history, your deepest passions and dreams…don't give it all to him in the first five minutes. As 'The Rules' says…always leave him wanting more![1] (More on 'The Rules' in the next chapter.)

- **Introverts:** Use your internal processing to your advantage by learning how to be a really great listener. (Being quiet is not the same as listening, by the way. No one wants to talk to a statue!) Use 'minimal encouragers' – like smiling, nodding, raising your eyebrows, saying 'mmhmm', and 'wow' to help him feel like he's engaging you, and make a few returns in the conversation by sharing some relevant anecdotes or thoughts on the topic. Laugh at his jokes. <u>Search for agreement, rather than disagreement</u>. Be a pleasure to talk to; be a good 'receiver' of someone's personal information. As an introvert, particularly if you are shy or a bit wary of people, your face may be quite inexpressive, giving nothing away. And sure, that protects you. But no-one wants to talk to someone who doesn't 'let them in' – there's no relational reward. A conversation is like a tennis match. You hit a ball to them, they hit one back; you hit another one, they return it. You can tell if you're a good listener because the other person will keep talking, and will become happy and animated. If they shut down or the conversation falters, maybe you need to work on learning how to draw people out and to help them feel that their information is special and valued by you, the listener.

So – what do you need to work on?

CHAPTER 21

'The Rules' is everything

As an older single, you may have started to realise that there is indeed a dating 'game'. It comes down to the fact that most people in your age bracket are actively looking for a life companion. When you're young, you may fall into a friendship with someone that turns into marriage, or you may date casually just for fun and find that it leads to something more. But getting older means getting more serious about it. It's not so much about enjoying a man's company and then both realising, 'Hey, we are great together! Let's keep doing this forever!' It's more like, 'Ok; he fits the demographic…no wedding ring…I hear he's a Christian…I'm interested!' And as much as you hate to admit it, 'the game' begins.

Why is proactive dating a 'game'? Well – because it has winners and losers. Traditionally, we are okay with the idea of men fighting for a woman's affections - *swoon* (may the best man win.) But these days, due to the sociological factors I've pointed out in other chapters, the whole thing's turned on its head, and we now find women pulling out all the stops to attract their man of choice (before he chooses Becky from marketing). It's a simple fact of **supply and demand.**

Now I realise it makes you cringe to think that you have to actually put yourself out there, try new things, look good, and humble yourself to have something appealing to a man. It feels a lot better to say, 'Heck no! I am who I am! I am woman; hear me roar! I'll do what I want, when I want, how I want!' (So why are you single, again?) Or alternatively, you might like to lean into your faith, sit back, and hope and pray that the Lord will send you the right man at the right time. And I certainly do believe that God's intervention in your dating life can be part of your relationship story. But you know what? Sometimes, there are natural solutions to spiritual problems.

If you honestly want to jump into the dating game and see success, it might help you to start playing by the rules.

In 2001, Ellen Fein and Sherrie Schneider published the accidental best-seller *The Rules*[1]. It outlines a bunch of tried and true tips and strategies for winning the heart of Mr Right. And you know what? IT WORKS.

Here's the thing. There are natural 'rules' girls who already know how to play it cool, how to be feminine, how to use boundaries usefully, and who just happen to draw men like moths to a flame. (Those girls are all married now.) And then there are the rest of us that for some reason – family dysfunction, personality type, feminism, geography, social anxiety, or whatever – have just been clueless and/or unsuccessful when it comes to men and dating. So I like to think of *The Rules* as a framework for how to change the way you interact with men. It's not about joining a weird dating cult and commanding men to fall in line with your new regime – it's about learning some new social patterns that will help you appeal to men, get asked on dates, *and* get asked on second dates!

So, step 1 – go and read *The Rules* right now, along with the 2013 follow-up edition *The New Rules - Dating Dos and Don'ts for the Digital Generation*[2]. They could change your life!

Now, I'm going to give you <u>my own version</u> of the dating rules, based on scripture (I knew you'd love that). Call me crazy, but **the Bible seems to have some fairly legitimate life advice** that tends to prove itself every time. And if you apply these rules, like a scientist in a lab, I guarantee you will see a difference in your dating life. But like any game, if you fudge the rules, the game breaks down. You have to follow them to the letter! Just try them for awhile and trust me, you will get results.

> **Rule #1: Let him initiate.**
> Proverbs 18:22: *He who finds a wife finds a good thing.*

It is **the man's job** to select, pursue and attain a wife. This is in the male biology – the desire to hunt and to conquer. When a man takes this role, he feels powerful, in charge, and like he has something to contribute (this is how you want your man to feel). It is not the woman's role to hunt for and pin down a man. Men who allow women to do this are often weak, passive or not really that into her…but they are too lazy to say anything. It will not end well.

Letting a man initiate relates to every aspect of the initial dating relationship – approaching you online or across the room, asking for your number, asking you out, picking you up, choosing a restaurant, paying for your meal, following you up later, calling you regularly, asking you to be his girlfriend, proposing to you…you get the picture? It's important that the man does these things, because for men, action is everything. <u>It is only by their actions that you can truly know how they feel about you.</u> So sit back, relax, and see what they have to offer.

> **Rule #2: Be modest and discreet.**
> Proverbs 11:22: *Like a gold ring in a pig's snout is a beautiful woman who shows no discretion.*

One of the most appealing things about true Christian women is their old-fashioned values. You might be surprised to learn that (emotionally healthy) men are not that keen on overly made-up, fake-looking girls with mini-skirts and cleavage. They may be physically *attracted* to such women, but when it comes to choosing a wife, a good man wants a woman he can trust. That means he wants a woman who has a certain level of personal privacy, discretion, and modesty. He wants a woman who will reveal her beauty and the delights of her body to him *in private, in marriage* – not to every man walking down the street.

Modesty refers not just to clothing choices but also to how a woman speaks and acts. Would you describe yourself as 'modest'? Are you gentle with your words, kind, soft-natured, and humble about your achievements? Are you able to let a man 'shine' around you, rather than put him down or make sarcastic jabs at him? Do you sit properly and use your manners, or do you sprawl your legs everywhere, talk about your bodily functions, and pile your plate high with food at social functions? I know it's hard to do, but having a certain level of class in your behaviour will go a long way to making yourself more appealing to a man.

> **Rule #3: Be known for your good works.**
> 1 Timothy 2:10: *Women who claim to be devoted to God should make themselves attractive by the good things they do.*

A consistent theme throughout the Bible is that a Godly woman will be known for her good works. Not for her high achievements, powerful career or huge bank account. Not for her good looks, her social status, or how great her parties are. A Godly woman is known by her good works. These would include things like helping the poor and needy, caring for children and animals, serving in the church and the community, raising money for good causes, and loving people who are awkward or uncool. Are you known for your good works?

I don't suggest you should pretend to be Mother Teresa just to get a man's attention, if that's the only reason why you would do good things. But if you consider yourself a Godly woman, these activities and attitudes should naturally flow from your life. If you don't know where to start, start with kindness – there's always room for more of it in our world. And gradually, as you die to yourself and start getting used to being a blessing to others, you will find yourself becoming a more appealing woman.

(I know I've written earlier about not getting burnt out with church commitments, which may sound like a contradiction. But that's because these days, church involvement can go a bit overboard, particularly when it's combined with a busy job. Women in the Bible didn't have 'careers', so they were possibly more free to serve the community in other ways, without burning out. You need to find a balance.)

This rule is more about making space in your mind and heart to be kind to others in small ways. It could be just saving a seat in the lunchroom for that cringe-worthy work colleague, making pancakes for your room-mate's birthday, or visiting your grandma in the nursing home more regularly. These actions are good for you, good for others, and appealing to guys!

Now I know I've also been emphasising the importance of looking your best, and how men are attracted to women who are beautiful and well-presented. This is true, and maybe is the area you need to work on. But if you've been spending all your time at the gym, and obsessing about your appearance, it might be time to think about how to fit some 'good works' into your life…and your heart. Again, it's about finding a balance.

Rule #4: Be prudent in dating.
Proverbs 22:3: *The prudent see danger and hide, but the simple go on and suffer for it.*

To be 'prudent' means to think ahead with wise judgement, and to discipline and govern yourself accordingly. So, it's basically the opposite of 'follow your heart' or 'live in the moment'. (All these modern slogans are completely unbiblical and pretty stupid, actually.) The Bible tells us that our hearts are deceitful (Jeremiah 17:9) and that we shouldn't lean on our own understanding, but rather trust God for his direction (Proverbs 3:5). Our hearts cannot be trusted, particularly when they are rushing with hormones and the desperation of *still* being single.

So what does **prudence** in dating look like? Well, it means to step back, look at the situation, and count the cost. It means to ask God for wisdom, and to seek guidance from Scripture, wise counsel, and experience (yours and others). Humans are all pretty standard – I mean, we all act in pretty much the same ways in response to the same stimuli. That's how stereotypes are created. And I have found that generally, men in the dating scene do fit into certain categories. So it's useless to think, 'Oh, even though everyone is warning me about this guy, my experience will be different.' No, it won't!

For example, say you are casually dating a man who has been fired from his last three jobs, isn't in touch with his family, has asked you to help him pay his rent, and blames society/family/the economy/etc. for his problems. The prudent thing to do would be to step back and think: 'Is this guy marriage material? Can I trust him? Will he be a good father? How will my family feel about him?' *And be honest with yourself.* A woman without prudence would throw caution to the wind and think, 'He has so much potential! I can help him! Deep down, he is a beautiful soul!' Well, that may be true in your idealistic, bohemian fantasy world, but I can tell you now, this guy is currently a deadbeat. Run! He will *not* make you happy in the long term (or short term!)

Don't waste your time on relationships that are going nowhere, or are making your life worse than it was before. Ask God to give you prudence and the gift of wisdom.

Rule #5: Don't be promiscuous.
Proverbs 6:27: *Can a [woman] scoop fire into her lap without being burned?*

Although it's hard to accept, the laws of the universe do apply to you, too. Your choices and your behaviours will have consequences. So if you 'let yourself go' sexually, and engage in sexual interactions with your dates/boyfriend/s, it *will* hurt you (and them). Plus it's a massive turn-off to guys looking for a marriage partner. You might not see it at the time, but this is one of those areas where you need to trust that God knows best. And if you're wondering how far is too far, check out Chapter 39.

Rule #6: Use your words wisely.
Proverbs 14:1: *A wise woman builds her house, but a foolish woman tears it down with her own hands.*

The book of Proverbs has a lot to say about the power of the tongue, and I personally think that 'hands' in this verse is really referring to a woman's greatest 'tearing down' implement – her words. **The tongue is the most influential part of the body.** And as a woman, your greatest power is in how you communicate. Think about it – when boys in school want to punish each other, they get physical. When girls want to punish each other, they don't talk to each other, or they spread spiteful rumours. They use the tongue as a weapon. The tongue is a very powerful instrument, literally able to bring about life or death (Proverbs 18:21).

I personally believe that a lot of the divorces in our community today are caused in part by wives not being able to speak graciously and kindly to their husbands, and constantly criticizing and nagging. It wears men down and it wears the relationship down. Women seem to think they have the right to say whatever they want, in whatever way they want, without thinking about how it will bear good or bad fruit in their own lives. And ironically, while men are often willing to put up with a lot of flak from their wives, the wives poison their *own* minds with their own negative talk, and lead themselves right out of the marriage!

Men are people too, you know, and they like and need to be treated with respect, honour and dignity. (Remember the old saying: *you catch more flies with honey than with vinegar!*) So when you're in a relationship, learn to hold your tongue. There is a right time and a right way to bring up complaints and issues with your man, and you have the responsibility and prerogative to do so – but there are times when you are just not going to get your own way or have everything the way you want it. So do you want to tear down what you're building with him, through a few cutting comments, or do you want to play the long game and act with prudence in the words you speak to him? I suggest you learn and pray for wisdom.

> **Rule #7: Be busy doing good works for your household.**
> Proverbs 31:27: *She looks well to the ways of her household, and does not eat the bread of idleness.*

A Godly and attractive woman is not one who lounges around on the couch all day eating chips and watching TV. She does not spend her weekends propping up the bar, bitching to her cronies about her annoying boss. She is not one to spend all her money on herself, thinking only of her own wants and needs. A Christian 'Rules' girl looks after herself and her home, first of all. So how are things looking for you at the moment? Are you eating proper meals, and keeping to a healthy schedule? Are you keeping the place clean and tidy, and jazzing it up every now and then with some nice décor and fresh flowers?

Secondly, she looks after those in her home. If you have siblings or flatmates living with you, are you accommodating them in a balanced way? Or do you ignore their existence and never take an interest in their lives?

And finally, are you busy or idle? A Godly and attractive woman has productive projects on the go – creative pursuits, gardening, community groups, renovations, cooking, ministry service – whatever it is for you, your efforts should result in good fruit for your household. A guy will be watching how you live, when he starts dating you. Put your best foot forward! And besides, this kind of lifestyle is great practice for marriage.

> **Rule #8: Be trustworthy and be a blessing to your husband.**
> Proverbs 31:11-12: *The heart of her husband trusts in her…she does him good, not harm, all the days of her life.*

A man wants a woman who will be his support and strength when he faces hard times. Whereas woman usually have a solid community of female relatives and friends to confide in, men usually don't let many people into their inner lives. That's why it's crucial that you hold his vulnerabilities with great care and great respect. When you are in a relationship with a man, he is watching to see if you are trustworthy with his private information and the deep desires of his heart. If you break his trust in even a small way, it's possible that he will not be willing to continue a relationship with you. So be very, very careful.

There are many ways you can 'do good' for your man. These include practical things like cooking and baking for him, helping him with clothes shopping, listening to him after a hard day, and giving him a hug when he is down. Other ways to support him would include standing up for him in public, putting your best foot forward when meeting his boss, friends and family, allowing him to give you advice, and asking for his forgiveness when you have hurt him. And a big one is to try and look nice as much as possible.

It's hard to get it 'right' all the time, and no one is perfect. So don't work yourself up into a tizzy trying to be the perfect girlfriend. But do be discreet with your 'chat', learn to be respectful when you don't feel like it, and maintain a soft and teachable heart when you do get it wrong. He will be so grateful for you.

If you apply these eight rules to your dating life, I guarantee your chances will improve. But the Bible has so much more to say. Make it a daily priority to 'wash yourself' with the Word of God; to pore over Proverbs and the New Testament, which give tons of practical advice about how to live a Godly life. God's ways are best, because they actually do provide the best outcomes. Learn the scriptures, apply them, and watch your life transform.

CHAPTER 22

What's flirting and how do I do it?

This may sound like an awkward topic – but it's actually a pretty key area of dating that can make or break an initial introduction.

Whether you are introduced by a mutual friend, bump into someone accidentally in a coffee shop, or are seated next to someone at a conference or on a plane, **the first moments are crucial.** Whether or not you hit it off will depend on the level of 'social lubricant' brought to the table by both parties.

Social lubricant is exactly that – it breaks the ice, it eases the tension, and provides a way into a conversation. If you're an extrovert, this will be easier for you – but you have to be careful not to overdo it, especially if you are really anxious or nervous. (Introverts – check out Chapter 23.)

In a romantic sense, social lubricant is basically flirting. If there's chemistry between you and the guy, you might start flirting with each other straight away. Or if things just start off in a friendly manner, you might work your way up to flirting (a bit of light flirting is a good way to show a guy you're interested, without giving yourself away).

You may think that the following advice is going overboard – practicing your smile, for goodness' sake? But some of you *really* need these tips. I invite you to try them out.

So, what is flirting and how do I do it?

The main goal of flirting is to **leave a man wanting more.** You want to make him interested enough to pursue you, but not overwhelmed with information so that he wants to run away. <u>A little bit goes a long way.</u> Here's a flirting breakdown for you, paraphrased in part from the excellent book *The Rules*[1]:

1. Let him initiate. LET HIM INITIATE. He might say 'Hi', or 'Excuse me' (if he bumps into you) or 'Nice seats we've got here' or anything. If he follows it with eye contact and a smile or a laugh, that's an invitation. Let *him* invite you into an interaction.

2. Smile. This is dating tip #1! Keep it smooth and measured. You don't want to give a huge laugh or massive toothy grin. **Just keep your mouth closed and smile, while making *a little* eye contact.** *Then look away.* Make sure your teeth are nice and white, check for spinach, and ensure you always have fresh breath! Carry mints in your bag at all times.

3. Keep it brief. After he initiates conversation, just smile, make eye contact, and perhaps say something *short and sweet*. Here's an example: he says, 'Hey, they always put me in the front row at conferences!' and looks at you and laughs. You can then laugh (just a little), and say 'Yeah, smart people at the front!' Then smile again while making eye contact. Make sure that whatever you say is *short*. One sentence only! <u>Let him continue a conversation</u> if he wants to.

It's typical for Christian women, particularly those who are used to serving and leading, to want to care for the other person. **This means**

you might find it hard to allow the tension of the moment to build.
You might want to 'save' him by filling in the silence, or be 'kind' to
him by asking him heaps of questions about himself. And you might
just generally love people and be curious about him. But you are not
his mother. You are not his chaplain. You are not his counsellor. You
are not his best friend. STOP TALKING. **Close your mouth, smile,
and WAIT.** It's not your job to make him comfortable. He needs to
feel a little bit of nervous tension in himself, to get excited about the
interaction. Let him sweat!

4. Use your eyes. Your eyes have a lot of power. They show a man
if you're interested or not, and they draw him in. Let him initiate eye
contact, and always look away first. Looking down is more coy and more
attractive than staring up into space like an idiot. **Either look down,
or look down and then away, while smiling.** This sounds simple but
is very alluring! (Eyes are crucial – that's why it's important to get your
eyebrows neatly plucked and to wear eye makeup well. We don't want
any smudged mascara!)

**5. Let him run the conversation, but give him something to
work with.** <u>The only way you can know if a man is interested in you
is if he pursues you.</u> This means that he continues to talk to you, while
looking at you. If he's looking around and obviously more interested in
something else, excuse yourself and slip away. He doesn't deserve your
attention, and by leaving you might interest him more! (Men always
want what they can't have!)

Now, **don't just stand there** like a stunned mullet and make
him come up with all the conversation topics, nodding and smiling
like a puppet. Try to use some witty repartee, or add *a little* personal
information, an interesting anecdote, or some topical news to the mix.

But let him lead. Let him interest you with what he has to say. (If he's not interesting, why are you interested?)

6. Graciously accept compliments. A compliment is a great way for a guy to start a conversation with you. Here is the correct response to a compliment: **'Thank you.'** Or **'Thank you, that's very kind.'**

Incorrect responses:
'Oh, no I actually hate this jacket, I only wore it cause my other one has a hole in it.'
'Oh please, don't be giving me all that flattery! I can't handle it!'
'You're joking, right? This was $5 at the outlet! Got it in the sale bin.'
'Oh, that was the worst presentation I ever gave. Usually I'm way better!'
'Oh, please. Oh, you are just SO nice. No one ever compliments me!'
'Oh no, YOU did such a good job up there; I was SO impressed...'

The man initiates, the woman follows. **The man gives, the woman receives.** That's how it's got to be! So receive! *Give less, less, less.*

It's also important to **graciously accept** if he offers you something nice (and appropriate). For example, if he asks you if you'd like a drink, rather than saying, 'Oh no, really you don't have to! Here, I've got money! Take this $5 note!' or 'You DRINK? I thought you were a Christian! I can't believe you actually drink alcohol – man, I am so surprised.' Just say: 'Oh, I'd love a lime and soda [or whatever]. Thank you.' Then when he gives it to you, give eye contact and a smile, and maybe say thank you again. That's it. **You see, the more he invests in you, the more he will feel connected to you and the more he will care about you**. You need to let him start making 'deposits' in the bank account of you!

If he offers you a lift, *and you feel safe taking it* (eg. he's a well-known colleague, *not* a stranger) say, 'Oh thank you, that would be so great.'

Don't offer him petrol money, or get him to drop you miles away from your front door. Encourage him to go right to your house, if he offers. Show your value! If he has offered something, he wants to give it.

7. The main language is body language. What is your body telling this man? If it's saying something like, 'I am desperate and lonely, please pick me!' then he will pick up those vibes and it will be a huge turn-off. Even if you haven't had a date in years and no one ever gives you much attention, you need to act as though being chatted up by a nice guy happens to you every night. Be cool, be chill. This comes from having an inner peace and confidence in yourself.

You need to know that you are a wonderful, valuable woman, and that **any man would be lucky to have you!** Do whatever you need to do to get your love tanks filled up before you go somewhere you might meet a man. 'Prime' yourself beforehand with some retail therapy, chatting to your girlfriends, a bubble bath or a glass of wine. If you feel good about yourself, it shows.

In practical terms, you want your body to be 'pointing' towards him but not fully square-on facing him. **Allow your body to be 'open' but not exposed; invitational but not aggressive.** Try to avoid folding your arms (too bro-ish), having your hands on your hips (school-marm/bossy), and touching your face and hair (nervous). Just relax. It's nice to show some arm and to wear a nice bracelet and have your nails painted. It will help you feel more elegant, and therefore act that way. If you're seated, pay attention to how you sit – are you sitting like a college boy in a frat house, or an elegant woman being cared for by a gentleman? **Act the part, and the reality will follow.**

8. Dress for success. Your outfit will communicate **your intentions** for the event. If you are dressed in a manner that is too worky/casual/

frumpy/etc., he won't think you are there to pick up, and will treat you immediately like a friend or colleague. To invite some romance, you need to communicate that through your clothing, hair and makeup.

Rule of thumb: be a touch more overdressed than necessary. You want to stand out, and men love shiny things. Girls might look down on you for being the only one wearing red heels at a party when everyone else is wearing Doc Martens – but trust me, you'll stand out to the men, in a good way. ***Dress for men, not for women.*** Don't be afraid to show off your sexy self!

9. Leave the conversation first. So you've flirted, you've had some banter, you've accepted some compliments. *As soon as* you feel the conversation rolling to a pause in momentum, make your excuses and leave. Eg. 'It was great chatting.' Smile, walk away. Or 'Good luck with the lunch queue!' **Smile, walk away.** Do *not* suggest a later meeting, ask for his number, offer your number, say 'I hope to see you again soon' or anything of the kind. *Let him do all the work.* If he's interested, he will find you.

Remember: flirting is for the initial introduction and the first few times you chat. You don't have to keep it up forever – it's just to develop his interest in you!

CHAPTER 23

I'm an introvert – help!

As a committed extrovert myself, I can't fully empathise with the extra difficulty experienced by introverts in the dating scene. But I do have a few close introverted friends, who assure me that certain parts of dating are really hard, like flirting, making small talk, and having the confidence to meet a stranger on a blind date.

If this sounds like you, take heart! All is not lost. Let me point out the salient pitfalls, just to put into words what you can't quite put your finger on, and we'll also look at some possible ways to overcome those hurdles.

Issue 1: Introverted girls are often attracted to extroverted guys, because they can keep the conversation going. Extroverts help to bring out the fun side of introverts, which makes any introverted girl appreciate herself more (and have more fun). The issue is that extroverted guys usually marry off pretty early, as they are confident, meet tons of girls, and enjoy being in a relationship. So there are none left.

Solution A: Expand your horizons to include introverted guys. If you find a guy who has similar passions to you (eg. orchestral music, hiking, cooking or whatever), you can potentially parlay that interest into a viable point of connection. You both may have to work a little harder to bring each other out of yourselves, but that doesn't mean you can't have a loving relationship.

Solution B: Expand your horizons to include extroverted guys who have been burned and are on round two of the dating game. They are out there! A guy who has been chewed up and spat out by the extreme extrovert scene may now be drawn to an introverted girl who is more peaceful, calm, and less demanding than other girls.

Issue 2: It's hard for introverted girls to meet new people.

Solution A: It *is* challenging to meet new people, and for introverts this can be really, really hard. Unfortunately, there's no easy answer but to try and push yourself a bit more. Join a new church, club, sporting team, or work department. Sit with a different group of colleagues at lunch. Sit in a different place in church. Go to the mid-week Bible study that you usually avoid.

Solution B: Online dating. Done from the privacy and comfort of your own home. And when it comes to actually going on dates, ring a friend beforehand to psych you up for the big event!

Solution C: Swallow your pride and ask your friends and family to connect you with any single guys they know of. Again, push yourself a little more.

Solution D: Reconsider that guy who's always liked you, who you put in the 'friend' category – but are really comfortable with. Maybe he could be the One?

Solution E: Take a 'wing woman' with you to events and parties, preferably an extroverted friend who can help you strike up conversation with new groups of people, and provide a safe place for you to come back to when you have taken a risk and talked to someone new.

Issue 3: Dating is excruciating.

Solution A: Be more selective about who you meet for dates. Don't waste your energies on guys who you know you could never marry. Introverts have less emotional energy to spend, and burn out more quickly, so you need to be careful to 'spend' it where it really counts. Don't waste months or years talking to guys online who you know just aren't viable options for you.

Solution B: Gently suggest to the man who is asking you out that you'd enjoy a date including some activity, like going to the markets together, watching a band, or taking a cooking class. That way you don't have to scramble for conversation and you have something else to interest you both. (This is called 'the third object'.) Even going for a scenic walk is a simple but excellent plan.

Solution C: Work on your conversation and flirting skills. Some people are good at this stuff; some people aren't. It's up to you to improve yourself. Start with the updated version of the classic 1936 book *How to Win Friends and Influence People (for the Digital Age)*[1] (2011) by Dale Carnegie and associates. No doubt there are masses of other books and YouTube videos out there about how to learn to connect socially. Back in the Jane Austen days, this was part of a woman's developmental training – learning how to make polite conversation and to use social graces. We have really lost this in our modern, feministic culture, and it shows. (You could always take yourself off to a finishing school in France…I'm sure they still exist!)

The thing is, dating is an extrovert's game. It certainly is easier for an introvert to stay at home and continue a small rotation of friendships with safe people, enjoy her own company, and spend free time pursuing solitary activities like running, baking, watching TV, or talking to family on the phone. But if you want to get married, you'll need to make a few adjustments to your social proclivities.

Here's something to ponder. Imagine your life as a married woman…with your own home and family to manage and nurture…a warm body next to you in the bed at night…someone to make you a cup of tea, bring you flowers and listen to your problems…this is worth the hard work.

Now, imagine your life as a single spinster, wondering if you will ever have children, wondering if you will make your mark on the world, getting depressed about a long, lonely future…is this what you want your life to look like?

Yes, it's very hard to be an older, single, introverted woman in an extroverted world. And there is no pressure or obligation for you to step out of your comfort zone, if you want to stay there. But if you do want to get married, and you're not having any success in dating, perhaps you might want to make a few courageous tweaks to your strategy. I believe in you!

CHAPTER 24 (PART 1)

Online dating - where do I start?

Eek, online dating? Isn't that only for losers and desperados? No! We live in an online society these days, and everyone is more geographically scattered due to urbanisation and globalisation. Everyone is busier and people don't want to waste time and muck around (when they are looking for a serious relationship.) So, online dating is a super-efficient way to put yourself out there to a wide variety of people. And lots of people really do get married to someone they have met online. However, you will need to wade through the time-wasters and the duds and connect to someone who might be right for you. It's worth a try!

Where to start? Here are my three top tips for getting your profile off the ground and taking the leap into online dating!

1. **Ask around** about which sites are good, or read reviews online, and join accordingly. Don't be afraid to be on a couple of sites, but don't be that girl that's literally on every single dating site out there. Maintain at least some mystery! Sometimes the Christian dating sites are the worst. They can be too restrictive with their algorithms, and also often have a lot more women than men represented. But that doesn't rule them out – go with what seems

to work for you. I'd definitely recommend going on some of the non-Christian sites, as there are sometimes Christians on those ones too.

Some sites have a large registration fee, and some are free for the first five messages, or similar. Consider how much you want to invest in this venture. Put some money towards it, if you're serious, but I'd play around on the free sites first to get a feel for the whole online thing, before you make a large financial commitment to one site.

Consider how wide you want to spread your 'net'. Is the site just for your own region, country, or international? Which filters will you choose? If you're planning to engage in conversations and dates with guys who live overseas, for example, think it through. Do you really want to have a long-distance relationship with someone via Skype for two years, then move to another country for life if you get married? If you're not keen on that – **don't start what you can't finish.**

It's inevitable that you will 'run into' other people online who you know in real life, maybe even guys from your own church. That's just one of the hazards of online dating, and you can't do much about it. You don't need to be ashamed of being online. It's a totally legitimate form of meeting people, and you don't need to be embarrassed about wanting to meet someone. Just suck it up and get on with it. And be respectful of people online. Don't go gossiping with your girlfriends about who you saw online and how terrible their profiles are. Have a bit of class and be discreet about it. (I think it's called 'the golden rule'...)

2. Use a great **profile picture.** You have somewhere between 0.5 and 3 seconds to impress someone with your profile, before they click/swipe/scroll to the next potential candidate. And unlike

women, men do not spend much time reading through your bio, cross-checking you on Facebook or Google, calculating the distance between their home and yours, wondering why you wear a ring on your middle finger, and so on. They look at your picture, and either think:

a.   Hm, I find her attractive…

          or

b.   Not interested.

Every guy will have a different concept of what is attractive or interesting to him. And being generically 'hot' is not necessarily a predictor of success (even if you are super 'hot', a guy might immediately think he has no chance of 'getting you', and keep scrolling. Or he might think you are a bit of a loose cannon.) The main thing is to do your best to look interesting and appealing in some way. You don't want to look intimidating, but also don't want to look sloppy. And the absolute key is to SMILE.

Men are VERY visual, so what you look like in your photo is of paramount importance. But avoid showing too much cleavage or skin. (Please try to not look like a stripper.) You want to have a bit of class; be the kind of woman he wants to take home to meet his mum, not the kind of woman he'll meet for a quick romp and then forget.

I suggest a headshot that includes your shoulders, possibly down to your waist. And then maybe two or three other photos including a full-body shot (relaxed and classy, NOT posing on the bed in your lingerie!); a shot of you doing something you love, such as exercise, pottery, walking your dog or whatever; and a shot of you laughing – that is very attractive to a man.

I'd also recommend you're wearing something feminine (maybe with some colour, a pattern, cool jewellery or a headscarf) and trendy. Definitely avoid wearing anything that makes you look frumpy, boring, intimidating or old. And be wearing something different in each photo.

Men love hair, particularly long hair, so make sure it's clean, styled, and preferably out – loose tresses say 'I'm fun, relaxed and womanly' whereas a tight bun says 'I'm stressed, severe, and don't even think about interrupting my schedule'. Take off the sunglasses so that he can see your eyes. If you wear glasses, make sure they don't hide your face or create too much glare in the photo. You might include one photo without your glasses. This is the ideal time to enlist the advice of a couple of friends – male and female. Ask them to help you select your best images.

3. Keep **your bio** short and fresh. It should be brief and upbeat. This is not the place to give a life history, a psychoanalysis of yourself, or to make a list of demands in the kind of guy you want. Lots of women's profiles end up sounding quite bitter – not what you're going for!

Example of a <u>bad</u> bio:

I'm 35, single (obviously) and ready to meet Mr Right. I can hear my biological clock ticking so whoever you are, please show yourself. I'm an accountant and work long hours in the city – I'm very committed to my job and I'm also thinking about starting a Masters degree. I don't really have much time for fun, as I get home quite late and I'm usually tired. I live by myself and spend most of my time watching Netflix (fave shows are Downton Abbey *and* The Bachelor*) and sorting out the drama between my mum and dad (newly divorced) – they need a mediator sometimes, so I guess I'm it. I'm a 'melancholy' personality type and I do enjoy my alone time with a cup of tea and my life-long bestie, my cat Heathcliffe. He's a purebred Siamese with blue eyes, which is very rare. I would like to date a* *man who is between 34-36, at least 6'3", Caucasian, well-dressed and with a good job, preferably in business or finance. I am a Christian so I expect to be properly courted and introduced to his family before embarking upon something more serious. Of course, he must be a committed Christian and a regular church-goer. I don't want to waste any time communicating with someone who does not meet these criteria.*

Okay, so hopefully I don't need to point out everything that is wrong with this bio. While this information may be true, it's certainly not appealing. It's depressing and way too restrictive. Remember, a man has no obligation to pursue you, let alone love you. <u>There's got to be something in it for him!</u> What appeals to a man are the following: femininity, mystery, kindness, innocence, fun, sweetness, beauty, and *space* – room for him to move into your life.

Example of a <u>good</u> bio (same person):

Hi there! I'm a happy and confident professional woman who loves to check out a concert, try a new tapas bar, and have an intellectual conversation! I'm a committed Christian and am part of a vibrant Baptist church in my local area. Apart from church, I usually spend my weekends meeting friends for brunch, enjoying the sunshine, and catching up on my shows. I love my life but I'm ready to meet that special someone and to build a loving future together. ☺

Ok, so let's break it down and look at what this woman is implicitly communicating here, *in a positive and non-demanding way*:

- she's looking for a serious relationship (marriage and kids)
- she's giving him ideas about what kind of things she likes doing (important so he can see if they have common interests, start a conversation, and then plan a date)

- she's a committed Christian and probably has the attached values
- she has time/space for a relationship
- she is happy. (This is majorly attractive to a man.)

Besides looking for a girl who is attractive, a man wants to find a relationship in which he can *make a difference.* He doesn't just want to be a sperm donor, or be used for his money or social status. He subconsciously wants to be able to improve a woman's life on a heart level, and to be someone's knight in shining armour. So when this woman says *I'm ready to meet that special someone and to build a loving future together,* he sees that as: this girl is serious about relationships, is ready to invest emotionally, and is looking for a man who can sweep her up into a life-long adventure of love and family. (A bad place to start would be: *I need a man to impregnate me before all my eggs die.*)

Notice that the bio is fairly short and doesn't give too much away. This is good – it's up to the man to decide whether or not he's curious enough to initiate contact and to find out more about you. You don't want to give it all away. Make him curious! And remember – 99% of his interest is going to come from the photos. PHOTOS ARE KEY.

I have a friend who got married at 33 to a man she met online. Her entire bio existed of a nice photo, and a description: 'bubbly and outgoing'. That was it! And it was enough to attract her now husband. So you really can keep it simple!

You need to think about about presenting your information in a way that is appealing <u>to a man</u>. Think like a saleswoman. You don't force or badger a potential customer into buying a product because 'it's the right thing to do' – you *entice* them into giving it a try. Present yourself in the best way possible, and don't give it all away.

CHAPTER 24 (PART 2)

Online dating – how to succeed!

Have you tried online dating, only to find you end up in some drawn out, complicated and emotional conversation with a man that just **drags on and on**, without it eventuating into an actual date, let alone a relationship? This is very common, but if it's happening to you, it's *your* fault and you *can* stop it!

I've heard stories of girls who have been in **online pseudo-relationships** for *years*…with men they have never ever met! Can I just say – ladies, you don't have time to muck around. There are a LOT of lonely, isolated men online, just looking for a kind and caring woman to hear their sob stories, tell them 'aw, poor baby' and be there for them whenever they happen to log on. These are *not* the men you want to connect with online.

When it comes to conversing with men on an online dating site (or in any context at all), <u>less is more</u>. To bring it down to brass tacks, really you want a relationship in which a man pursues you and locks you down, then goes out to work to bring home the bacon, and lets you cuddle up to him and talk his ear off for the rest of your life. That's marriage 101 right there.

I seriously doubt you want a relationship in which the man spends 90% of the time talking to you about himself, and then when you start to tell him anything about you he suddenly vaporises. Or when you suggest meeting in person, he either offers you a booty call, or again, vaporises. ***Don't waste your time with these time-wasters.*** And don't blame the 'system' of online dating. No one is forcing you to talk to these men. So don't!

Before I was married, I gave online dating a red hot go, and learnt a few valuable lessons. Once I started making it work for me, over the course of about 6 months I ended up going on maybe 5-10 actual first dates with different men who I thought might be ok (I got offered a lot more dates but turned them down – no point wasting time with duds). I also ended up with two legitimate boyfriends (not at the same time!), but neither of them turned out to be compatible with me and both relationships ended in a mutual parting.

So having experienced the whole thing, here are my **3 golden rules** for successful online dating:

1. **Let the man initiate contact.**

    The man is the hunter. You are the prey. This is biological and nothing can ever change that (not even feminism). Besides, do you want a man who is a feminine little wimp and just follows you around like a puppy, looking for pats? Ew. <u>Do not hunt a man!</u>

    I repeat, let the man initiate contact.

    This is crucial. He <u>has</u> to be attracted to you enough to want to reach out. *If he is interested, he will reach out.* Some dating sites require one person to pay money in order to begin a conversation. This should be him. Do NOT feel bad that he has to shell out $5 to chat to you. Don't you realise that you're after a man who will one day shell out a few thousand for an engagement ring? He better be able to lay down $5!

If *you* initiate contact, and continue to do so, you might get a date, hey, you might even get a relationship and may even get the guy to marry you – but maybe…he won't be that into you.

2. **Limit your online presence.**

    What increases your 'value' to a man looking for a date is your level of (un)availability. You want to be available, but not too available. When you are online 24/7 and you respond to messages within minutes, a man will very quickly get bored with you and move on to someone else. (You might think, *but he's still chatting to me, right?* Well, I would bet that he has another five girls on the go at the same time. And anyway – do you really want a guy who has no life?) Even if he was attracted to you initially, as soon as there is no need to chase, he will lose interest. Men are hunters. Give them something to hunt!

    I suggest you log on once a day *at the most*. Think of online dating like a community noticeboard or post office. You go there to check things out and to do your transactions, then you leave. You don't stay there for hours chatting to all and sundry. Get online, answer your messages, and get off. Do not initiate contact. Do not send a second message to a guy who hasn't yet responded. Do not answer any message within the first 24 hours of it being sent to you. And try not to have your messages sent and therefore tagged at awkward times, like 1am. It's not healthy to be online at 1am.

    If he is online at the same time as you, at a reasonable hour, you can engage in some chat, but follow the rule below. (Tricky!) **Best to leave the chatting to a face-to-face situation.** And if you're in a rush, you will end up saying things you haven't thought through, or becoming too emotionally intense too quickly. Eek! (Remember, you *literally* don't know this guy.)

And switching to text messaging does not mean you're going to another level. You may think that because he's texting you via the message app as opposed to the dating app, you're suddenly besties with some sort of secret relationship blossoming. Um, not really. **Until he's your boyfriend, he's not your boyfriend.** So don't be texting all day long – it will backfire.

Online dating is more like sending notes back and forth in class. They don't include much info – they're more like, 'Bike sheds, 1pm! Be there!' This is what you want your online dating messages and subsequent texts to be like – *moving towards* a face-to-face.

There's a phenomenon in online dating I like to call '**the two-week ghosting**'. This has happened to me and girls that I know countless times! You're engaged in a great deep convo with a guy online, he seems keen, he's telling you his life story, checking in on you each morning, acting all romantic, and things are looking good. Then, at the two week mark – he vanishes into thin air! If you're lucky, you'll get some sort of excuse, like, 'I've got a lot on at the moment, so I might not be available for awhile'...and if not, you'll get nothing. Just an empty inbox, day after day. It's super frustrating and confusing, like that feeling you get when you can't find your phone. (Okay, it's way worse than that.).

The reason for the two-week ghosting is that surprisingly, men can get emotionally intense faster than women. Sometimes this is because they are so relieved to have someone to finally share their heart with. But after laying their soul bare for two weeks, they suddenly freak out and realise how exposed they have become. So they pull back. It's different for women, because we are generally making ourselves vulnerable with various friends and family members all the time. Getting close doesn't necessarily freak us out (if it does, you need to work on building closer community and finding trusted girl-friends).

The only way to avoid the two-week ghosting is to *slow the pace.* You need to be in control of the conversation by pacing it out a bit. Don't invite him to tell you everything all at once, and keep the conversation light. It will take discipline, but it's the only way to keep him interested. We are looking for a slow burn, not an explosion!

3. **Engage in a maximum of 3 interactions with a man, then bail out.**

Did I really just say that? Yes. 'But I haven't had time to tell him about my life-changing moment in 9th grade and how my brother's illness changed my view of God and how I was thinking of becoming a chef but then I decided to be a personal trainer…' Yes. 3 CHATS THEN BAIL.

Why do I say such harsh and surely unrealistic things like this? Let me tell you. **As soon as a man sees your picture, he decides whether or not he's keen. Then he contacts you to see if you are crazy or normal.** (That's all he really cares about. He's not really that interested in your job, your dreams, your family, your hobbies, or even where you live.)

In a face-to-face chat, it takes less than *one second* for someone to make an assessment of you.[1] When it comes to communicating online, it doesn't take much longer. And while he is assessing you, you are of course assessing him. You have to realise that it's not really *content* that is the main point of interest – it's *tone.* It should be fairly irrelevant to you whether he is an accountant or a teacher. What matters is his character, his availability, and his level of interest in you.

After exchanging a few sentences, you can probably start to tell whether the man is respectful, kind, competent, mature, experienced, egocentric, fearful, cynical, lazy, still married (!) or just a downright tosser. You can also tell from his writing style whether he is sophisticated and educated, chivalrous or rude, blue or white collar, rough or kind, and/or speaks your language. Some of these things will make a difference to your feelings about him, I'm sure. (And that's ok.)

Don't worry about what he is thinking about you. This is his chance to engage *you*. So just be yourself – but only show him about 5% of yourself! Keep it simple and always remember that LESS IS MORE. Maintain a bit of mystery. Definitely say *less* than him. Answer his questions (not in detail), but don't pepper him with questions.

When to bail: after you've had three solid interactions (not including his 'Hi, I'd love to chat with you' etc.), and you can sense that the conversation is going to keep going indefinitely with no date in sight, say something breezy like: 'I've really enjoyed chatting with you, Marcus. I might log off for awhile now and get back to my pottery/studies/yoga/etc. :-)' This is an age-old dating rule called 'end the conversation first' (make sure you go back and check out *The Rules* discussed in Chapter 21). It also applies to real conversations at church, work, in bars, or at the gym. (And it actually works.)

Then, if he is into you, he will freak out a bit and quickly ask you on a date, which is your goal. Eg. 'Hey Kristy, I don't want to stop chatting. :-(Maybe we can meet in person sometime soon?' To which you can respond (after 24 hours) 'Sure Marcus, that could be fun. :-)' Then *he* should respond and set up a time and date. (Don't give him a list of every single availability you have, and a Google doc link to a variety of your favourite restaurants, with vouchers. Please, just don't.) If he is *not* into you, he will either not respond at all, or be really mean about it, or give you another long sob story. You don't have to respond to these.

The point is, **you have to let him do the work**. Guys these days have become super lazy and have certainly lost some of their dating skills, because girls are throwing themselves at them and metaphorically letting them sit on the couch and eat pizza while they are running around doing their work for them. This has to change! Eventually, if he's into you and *if you hold back*, a guy's inner biological drive will rise up, he will dust off his skills, and ask you out properly. All guys know that this is what is supposed to happen. But guys are pragmatic – they'll only do what needs to be done. So don't do it for them. *If he is keen, he will do it for you.* Plus, the higher the value you put on yourself (and the less heavy lifting you do online), the more a man will value you. See what super famous quirky psychologist Dr Laura Schlessinger has to say about it - just go to YouTube and search: *Dating roles haven't changed.*[2]

CHAPTER 25

How should I use social media?

Did you know that over 2 billion people use Facebook? That's nearly a quarter of the world. And the largest demographic of people who use Facebook are men aged 25-34.[1] So, chances are that any guy who is remotely interested in you is <u>definitely</u> **scoping you out** via your humble Facebook page.

Now, I get it. Instagram is by far the more glossy, appealing, scroll-worthy gallery of stylistic shots designed to make you look as sexy, urbane and on-trend as possible. So your Insta is potentially pretty decent (I hope? – I also hope it's not too lewd? Modest is hottest!) But today's question is: how's your FB profile?

I've noticed some **concerning FB habits** employed by many a single Christian female; habits that are <u>doing you no favours</u> in the attraction department. It might be time to get out the laptop and do some serious social media curating.

A <u>**curator**</u> is someone who selects content or images with a real eye for detail, with a specific vision in mind, for a particular audience. (Like in a museum or art gallery.) And rather than just throwing up every random pic, tagging yourself willy-nilly all over the internet and posting mindless memes and quotes every two hours, you need to get yourself in hand and **become your own FB curator.**

Let me address three main issues I see cropping up regularly on the book.

1. **Ugly or forgettable profile pics.**

Your profile picture is the entrance to your portal. It's the doorway. The 'gateway', shall we say. **If it's not appealing, no-one is going to even bother crossing the threshold.** You must make sure that your profile pic combines the right ingredients of <u>authenticity, personality and beauty</u>.

A great profile pic is neither too sexy nor too plain. It's a happy medium of *attractive* and *mysterious*. I think an **ideal profile pic** shows you from the chest/torso up, is close-up enough to see the colour of your eyes, and presents you as happy, carefree, confident and kind. This is achieved through your facial expression, hairstyle, outfit, background, and lighting.

Now, it's not about being a model. **Just be you.** But you'd be crazy not to put in a little effort with hair, makeup and clothing, and get one of your many snap-happy friends to take a couple of decent pictures of you somewhere nice – in nature, with a sunset, or in front of a cool mural. Throw on a couple of filters, and you'll be all set.

If your current profile pic has any of the following features, **you need to change it!**

- can't see your face
- you're frowning
- it's a poor-quality photo
- there are too many people in the picture
- you look ugly (we all have those ugly pics)

- you look drunk/you're kissing your ex (not that you'd have those pics)
- you are eating or drinking (this rarely looks good)

2. **Too many posts and too many pictures.**

You've got to remember the golden rule of dating: <u>less is more</u>. This applies to EVERYTHING (except clothing). Your goal with social media is to 'drip-feed'. That means that you **occasionally** post an interesting article or funny meme, you **occasionally** post a status update (once or twice a week), and you **occasionally** update your profile pic or post photos of a recent event or holiday.

When posting photos, less is more. No one wants to scroll through 50 snaps of the same view, particularly if you're not in it. You just want to offer something to **tantalise the tastebuds**; an entrée, so to speak. Is your Facebook page a fancy French restaurant, or all-you-can-eat ribs and wings? After visiting a fancy French restaurant, a person might think, 'What a gastronomic delight that was. My appetite is piqued; seduced...I can't wait until next time'. Whereas two pounds of buffalo wings only leads to one response: 'Urgh, I feel disgusting...' Which response do you want your viewers to have?

You have to leave some stuff to discuss on an actual date, remember. A little mystery goes a long way.

3. **Too many personal and intimate details and pictures.**

One of the major problems with the social media generation is the complete **inability to maintain any sense of privacy** about our private lives. In which other civilization in history would 784 people scattered around the globe know what you have for breakfast, every day, and how you feel about it!? It's obscene. The casual way in which millennials proclaim the most **banal and intimate facts** about their lives is frightening. And when you're trying to <u>attract marriage material</u>, you need to be careful. **Decent, civilized, upwardly mobile men will not be drawn to you if your FB page is littered with angsty, sexy, ranty, boring and/or inappropriate material.**

It has been said that ***discretion is the better part of valour*** (by our old friend Shakespeare in the play *Henry IV*). This means that sometimes it's best not to take bold, rash action, but to hold off and use a measure of prudence – to make a wise choice about what steps should be taken. 'Discretion' is defined in the Oxford dictionary as '<u>The quality of behaving or speaking in such a way as to avoid causing offence or revealing confidential information</u>'.[2] These days, it's common for Facebook profiles to cause offence *and* to reveal confidential information. But if you're in the market for a man, I would strongly advise you to **avoid over-sharing on any topic** (including in pictures), and to be tasteful, discreet, and modest. (The Bible repeatedly encourages women to be discreet in all their dealings. There's just something feminine about it.)

Your FB page should be like the *foyer* of your house, not the bedroom. That is, it should offer a <u>promise</u> of what is to come; a little <u>taste</u> of the personality and culture of the inhabitant. NOT an open-slather ransacking of your personal life.

So go and **take down the photos** of you pre- and post-makeup before an event. Take down the photos of you lying on your messy bed (in a revealing top) with random personal items strewn around the room. Take down the photos of you lounging on the sofa cramming your face with Doritos during your last Netflix binge. **No guy wants to see this!** I repeat, even if you have great boobs/bum/legs, a serious Christian guy does NOT want to see the boobs/bum/legs of his future spouse plastered all over the internet. It's a huge turn-off.

In the dating world, which is a world you need to jump into with both feet (if you're serious about getting married), you need to **treat your social media like an assault rifle**. Powerful and effective in the right hands, but deadly if you don't know how to use it. <u>**A bad Facebook page can kill your future spouse's mojo in two seconds flat.**</u>

So, I would suggest you avoid posting anything that reveals:

- your cleavage
- your half-naked body
- your pimples
- your shaving cuts, broken nails and grey hairs
- your body issues
- your wild, drunken, parties (you wouldn't do that though, right?)
- your bedroom (would you let 563 casual acquaintances inside?)
- your depression and anxiety
- your recent failures or breakups
- your negative feelings towards other people
- your loneliness and isolation
- your strong political feelings
- your anime addiction
- your soft toy collection
- your cat
- you get the idea.

But **a big fat YES** to smiles, sunshine, friends, family, happiness, freedom, peace, faith, generosity, vision, achievement and fun. Is this always your reality? No. Do we all have bad days? Yes. Do we need to tell the whole world when we are ugly crying, binge-eating or menstruating? **NO.** *Discretion is feminine.*

And you know what? All of this advice applies to going on dates, too. When dating, you need to be discreet, feminine, and hold something back. It's not appropriate to spill your guts with someone you've known for two days (or two weeks). You really don't know how trustworthy a guy is, and you need to keep him interested. Stay cool!

So – go and have a good look at your Facebook right now. **Try to see it through the eyes of a man, particularly a man to whom you are a complete stranger.** Do some major culling of photos, statements, memes, posts and everything else (particularly bad photos). Set up a great profile and cover pic that communicates 'happy, free, kind, beautiful'. He is going to love exploring the possibility of you!

CHAPTER 26

Are blind dates safe?

If you're doing everything you can to meet men and to get married, then no doubt you are going on the occasional (or regular) blind date. It could be with someone you've been set up with through a friend or colleague, someone you met at a coffee shop or bar, or someone you've met online. Technically, on a blind date neither of you has ever seen the other person, but with social media and the internet, it's pretty unlikely that you haven't at least tracked down a pic. Either way, you **don't know the guy from a bar of soap**, and you're going out together for a date.

Unless you've been moving in the same friendship or work circles as him, it's highly possible that *any* man you go on a date with at this stage of your life is going to be **someone you don't know**. You've probably done the rounds of the men in your circle, and so your only option is to try dating guys you don't know at all. *That's ok.* If you're waiting for the type of guy who can be your friend or colleague for a few months (or years) so you can get to know him, and then ask you out – you're going to be waiting a long time. At this stage of the game, you don't have time to waste waiting for Mr Right to stumble upon you in your work cubicle – it's not going to happen. **Get out there and get dating!**

No one I know of really likes the idea of a blind date. It's awkward and potentially terrifying/horrible. But it's what you've got to do. And when you do, here are some tips to follow to make sure you don't become a victim of the various awful things that *can* (but probably won't!) happen when you go on a blind date. You might find this information a bit depressing, but you need to hear the truth from someone! (Me.) Read on.

First of all, remember this: **YOU DO NOT KNOW THIS PERSON.** Until you can trust that he is who he says he is, that he is a decent person, and has your best interests at heart, you simply can't give yourself over to him. It's not safe. Even if the date 'feels' good, and you've been chatting online for weeks and feel 'really connected', you really don't know if he's a psychopath or a wolf in sheep's clothing (or he's already married). Follow these guidelines to ensure you get home alive.

1. Meet him at a **pre-arranged, <u>public</u> location**, such as a restaurant or bar. Don't give him your home or work address or get him to pick you up. Even if the date is going well, don't tell him these details yet. Wait until you're a few dates in.

2. Tell a conscientious friend, family member or flatmate that you are going on a blind date, and **give them the details**: his name and some info about him, the name of the restaurant, the time you'll meet, and the time you'll check in with them afterwards. Ask them to call you or come and find you if you don't touch base at the pre-arranged time.

3. Get as much **info about the man** as possible prior to the date. He should give you at least his full name, phone number, and some other identifying detail such as where he works, what church he goes to, or where he lives. (If he won't give you that info, that's a red flag. And no, it doesn't go both ways. You are

not a danger to him and you are not obliged to give him so much identifying info. But he should.)

4. Try hard to **gather at least some insight** into whether the man is who he says he is, prior to the date. Look him up on Google and Facebook (don't add him!). Search up his work website. Find him in old university records or church newsletters. Sure, it feels like you're a double agent when you do this – but **you literally have no evidence that anything he is telling you is true**, until you do.

5. Ideally, you will be able to **track down a mutual acquaintance**. If you can, contact the person to ask if the guy is legit. You might find this awkward and embarrassing, but it's actually totally smart and what a normal, sensible girl would do.

6. On the date, **trust your gut instinct**. If something seems 'off' about the man, and you just don't feel good about it, give yourself permission to cut the date short and leave, or at least don't agree to a second date. **Here are some lines you could use:**

   - 'I'm sorry; I'm just not feeling well at the moment. I really appreciate you meeting me, but I'm going to have to go.' (Do not accept his offer to walk you to your car or take you home.)
   - 'Look, it's nice of you to come and meet me, but I don't feel comfortable about this. I'm going to go.'

   If you say something like this and he gets angry, controlling, manipulative or possessive, you need to stand up for yourself. **Don't negotiate,** just repeat your statement in a firm tone. 'I'm not comfortable, and I'm going to go.' Then stand up and leave.

   If you can sense that the guy is a legit psycho or feels dangerous, **you are allowed to do a runner.** Excuse yourself to the bathroom and make a quick exit. Or go up to the head waiter or manager and discreetly explain your situation and ask for help. If your date chases you out and gets angry or starts a sob story, just keep walking into a public area and approach someone for help if you need to. **You do NOT have to be polite to a dangerous man.**

You may feel bad about cutting a date short and costing a man money, even if you can tell the man is dangerous, so if you want you can always put a $20 note on the table to contribute.

7. Don't drink too much alcohol. You need to have your wits about you. For some of you, this may be one drink. For others, none. This is really important. This man is not necessarily safe. **You need to be alert.**

8. Make sure your **phone is charged** before the date, and keep it close to you. Definitely take it with you if you go to the bathroom. Prior to the date, think about who you will call if you need help, and give them a heads up beforehand. Try to have some cash on you that you can use if necessary. And always carry cash or card to use for a taxi, or to pay for your parking.

9. If the man really is a complete stranger (BTW chatting intimately online with someone still doesn't change that), when you finish the date, even if it went well, **don't let him walk you to your car.** Being near a car with a man is putting yourself in a vulnerable position, particularly if it's in a dark street or in an underground carpark. Men are stronger than women and he could push you into the car. It's best to just finish the date and wander into the crowd, or go into another shop for a browse or a drink, until he clears off. Alternatively, you could arrange to have friends actually in the vicinity, who you could meet after the date and help you get home safely.

10. If you can sense that the 'public' area where you met is starting to look deserted, and there's no one around, particularly at night

time, end the date quickly and **get out of there**. You need to have other people around!

11. Use your body language to communicate 'I'm a kind, respectful woman, and I value myself and won't put up with any funny business'. **Stand up straight, put your shoulders back, smile, and make direct eye contact.** Although you want to flirt a little bit, your main goal for this first date is to communicate to the man: 'I'm giving you a chance. Prove to me who you are. I'm not committing anything yet.' **Your first blind date is not to make him fall in love with you. It's to give him a chance to earn your trust.** He needs to do the work here!

12. **Don't kiss him on the mouth after one date.** I mean, this is up to you really, but…really? You don't know this guy from a bar of soap, remember? **You really don't have any proof at all that anything he has told you is true.** You must communicate to him that you have a high standard for yourself and expect to be treated with respect and dignity. Don't communicate to him, 'I don't care if your name really is Matthew – let's make out!'

13. Each ensuing date **should corroborate more and more** of what he has told you is true. It's not enough to just be wined and dined by someone. You must be able to learn if they are who they say they are. You need to see evidence. Here's some easy ways he can show you the truth:
    - take you to a work function and introduce you to some colleagues
    - show you his staff page on his work website (make sure it's a legit company!)
    - introduce you to his family members (particularly parents)
    - take you to his church and introduce you to his friends
    - show you his educational certificates, driver's licence, passport etc.

- show you photos of where he grew up, family, etc.

  Obviously you don't want to ask him outright on the first date, 'Show me your licence!' But you do need to be **watching and listening closely** to see if everything is adding up. I may sound cynical, but everything he actually *says* out of his mouth is literally worthless until it's corroborated with evidence. So don't get caught up in the romantic words and lovely sob stories – wait until you see the evidence.

14. I would recommend that you do not **make anything official** until you have properly met and spent quality time with his family and friends (or at least that you have discovered some mutual friends who are very trustworthy, and give him the thumbs up).

15. If he **seems overly keen**, particularly if he is much better looking than you, consider the possibilities. Is there a chance that he:

    - is just after a good time (easy sex/a nice meal with a total stranger or someone in a different city – for that matter, why is he dating girls outside of his own city…?)

    - is just after a green card (citizenship can be priceless, and worth anything to some people). If so, will he dump you after the wedding? Will you find yourself being swept off to another country to cook and clean for his 50 relatives? (Different cultures have different expectations of wives.)

    - is already married? Maybe he just likes dating on the side, to spice up his life. Maybe his wife is cold and distant and gives him no sex. Maybe his wife is sick or an invalid, and can't love him. Maybe he likes the excitement and risk of illicit relationships. Maybe he is looking for a genuine, long-term mistress.

    Here's a tip for the naïve: **men can lie.** So if you ask a man outright, 'You're not just wanting a green card, are you? Ha ha.'

He will say, 'Of course not, silly! You are just too beautiful not to date! Here, have some more wine.' Then he will go home and re-strategize, or won't ever contact you again.

16. Remember this: **a healthy relationship has nothing to hide.** If you start dating this man and get caught up in the emotions and romance, then you realise a few months in that you only ever hang out together, have never seen his workplace, have never met his friends or family, and only went to his church once (and sat up the back and left straight away) – you REALLY need to step waaaaay back and invite some wise counsel into the situation. Get your mum to lock you in your room for a week if necessary, and take away your phone. Don't get caught up with a deceiver.

A final word. I've done a lot of online dating, and been on a lot of blind dates. I followed all these rules, most of the time. When I didn't, I regretted it. These guidelines are not weird, silly or over the top. They are smart and sensible. There are a lot of men out there who are deceptive, weird, or quite evil – and you just can't trust a man based on some good online chats and a few nice dinners. **You must have your wits about you and go in with your eyes wide open.**

With that all said, please, **go on blind dates**. You will meet some nice guys in doing so – and one of them might be your future husband. Just be sensible, and trust your gut.

SECTION #6

A Few Big Questions

When it comes to topics like dating and marriage, there are always grey areas, once-offs, and exceptions to the rules. So with all the advice I've given, while you're hopefully more equipped to make some good decisions, it's still up to you to follow your own path and to do what you believe is right for you (and live with the consequences).

This section covers some of those grey areas and answers some of the difficult questions that can occur when you're not dating in a perfect world. And again, while I think I make some pretty strong arguments in these chapters, it's always *your* choice about how to respond. The only thing I would urge you to do is to *tread carefully*. Marriage is not a decision you want to mess up.

CHAPTER 27

Can I date a non-Christian?

I've heard of lot of older girls mulling over this dilemma – *should I or shouldn't I consider the possibility of dating and marrying a non-Christian?* It's a legitimate question, and a real issue. There just aren't that many Christian guys around to choose from, so what's a girl to do? You might even find yourself deeply attracted to a certain man who isn't a Christian – and he might be attracted to you too! Should you give it a go? Well, it's certainly not a decision to make lightly, and is a move that deserves a lot of **deep thought, prayer, and wise counsel**. Here are my thoughts on it.

If something happened to all the people of the earth and you alone were stuck on a **deserted island** with the only living male left on the planet, chances are that the two of you would 'get together' and assume some sort of partnership, most likely involving sex in order to provide each other with comfort and companionship, and to **keep the human race going** (or at least produce some more labourers to help you dig wells, build cabins and get coconuts off trees). What if the man was a non-Christian? Potentially, you'd be more concerned about the survival of humanity than about his doctrine. So there's that.

But that's pretty unlikely. However, as you well know, it seems like there aren't any single Christian guys over 30 left on the planet. So – should you expand your horizons? Here are some questions to ponder, and my own take on the answers.

How badly do you want to get married?

Remember, you can get married anytime until you die. Maybe you'll meet Mr Right at the age of 60. But probably, you want your own biological kids. So, **the clock is ticking**. Again, how badly do you want your own biological kids, and what cost are you willing to pay to get them?

And where kids are involved, there are **no guarantees**. You don't know when menopause will hit you – it could be tomorrow, or it could be at age 59. You could marry a non-Christian and then find out that you can't have kids, or he can't. Or you could have kids, and then he might leave you – and you end up as a single mum. Could you cope with that, and with the ensuing effects on the kids? You've got to think about what you want your **family life** to look like.

You may indeed get the kids you've always wanted, but you might be miserable for the next 50 years, because you're in an unequal marriage. And your kids might end up resenting you for giving them a spiritually divided and unhappy family, should that be the result. **You just don't know.** It's a huge gamble! (Marriage is a huge risk anyway, even if you do marry a Christian. But the more security you can get, the better.)

My opinion: Unless you live in North Korea and can't get out of the country, my preference would be to **keep on moving until you do find a Christian**. There are 7 billion people in the world, half of them men, and Christianity is arguably the biggest religion on the planet. So – your chances are good. Like I've said before, move churches, move cities, move countries – because there *are* Christian guys out there. Move to regional areas where there are more men than women. (It's a numbers game!)

That said, you do need to take into account the emotional toll that may occur if you moved to a vastly different place. **Maybe you would be better off** with a non-Christian if you could stay in your current community, near your own family, rather than marrying a Christian and living the rest of your life being lonely, out in the boondocks. It depends so much on what type of man he is, what type of faith you have, and your temperament, people group, history, resources, skills, etc.

Whose authority is he under?

This is a key question. If this guy doesn't follow Jesus, who does he follow? Everyone believes something, and everyone is on a spiritual journey. I mean, he might be a 'non-Christian', but what *is* he? **Every man is under an authority, and by marrying him, you will move under this authority as well.** There's a lot more categories to spirituality than just 'non-Christian'. Is he a practicing or non-practicing Muslim, Jew, agnostic, atheist, new-age dabbler, Buddhist, Hindu, astrologist…? What has he been in the past? What type of family does he come from? What is his cultural heritage? Has he had any spiritual experiences?

If he is a classic white westerner from a modern, non-religious family, chances are that he hasn't had much spiritual input, but places his trust in his own dad, a mentor, a favourite sportsperson, a political group, his close-knit group of peers, or his own intelligence and capacity to make money. Or maybe he went to a religious school and carries around some of the beliefs he learned there. In any case, you better do a decent analysis of that person, group or school. Because their beliefs will probably be his beliefs.

Why do beliefs matter anyway? Well, they impact everything. What a man believes about the big existential questions:

- **who am I?**
- **why am I here?**
- **what's wrong with the world?**

will impact every decision he makes. This includes: how he spends his money and time. How he relates to his boss and his work. How he treats you and the kids. What he thinks about infidelity, divorce, discipline, marital roles, civilian duties, recreation. And so on. You've got to remember that life is hard, and it gets more messy the older you get. So, how will this man respond to and lead your family through the following possible events?

- illness and disease
- infertility
- miscarriage
- in-law dramas
- problems with the kids (eg. disability, rebellion, drug use, teen pregnancy, school failure)
- loss of job
- loss of income
- bereavement
- infidelity
- change of government
- bad neighbours
- being betrayed or mistreated by boss, peers, etc.
- being invaded/war/conscription
- and so on.

As a woman and a wife, you will be under his leadership as these events unfold throughout the span of a lifetime. The kind of man he is will majorly impact the way you and your family get through these issues. **The value system by which he rules his life, will end up ruling yours.**

When a conflict of views arises, you may need to acquiesce to his opinion, in order to save the marriage relationship. This is fine when it's just choosing what to eat for dinner (fish or chicken?) but when it comes to something serious, having to 'give in' can have dire consequences.

My opinion: It's definitely best to marry someone who *at least* has been brought up with a **Judeo-Christian foundation**. So, someone from a conservative family in a Western country. Someone whose Grandma took them to Sunday School. Someone who at least has a Bible somewhere in the house.

If you haven't studied history, anthropology, sociology, or world politics, and haven't travelled much, you may not realise that there are whole massive chunks of the world that have **entirely opposing belief systems** to you. And I mean, totally different – particularly when it comes to politics, gender roles, family loyalty, raising kids, spending money, and all those big things.

So, *if* you experiment with dating a man with 'no' faith (although everyone has faith in something), or a man from a different religion, you better be **studying your butt off every night** researching the history of that belief system and how it plays out in marriage. You better be hanging out with lots of girls and couples in that belief system and watching how it works, and decide if you can submit to it and handle it. You better be spending lots of time with his family and learning about the family dynamics. Because sister – it's very unlikely that he'll be changing for you. You will be the one who has to adapt. Can you handle it?

What does the Bible say about marrying a non-Christian?

Well, there's two ways to look at this. On the one hand it doesn't say anything very explicit, probably because women in Bible times had very little say in who they married. Most of the marriages were arranged and generally stayed within local religious and cultural groups (this was before online dating and overseas travel, remember!)

But on the other hand, it says quite a lot. When the Bible doesn't seem to give specific advice, we can still glean from the general principles that are outlined. Here are some thoughts on the topic of marrying a non-Christian.

In 2 Corinthians 6:14 we read Paul warning the Corinthian church (which was still engaging in some secular practices): *Do not be yoked together with unbelievers. For what do righteousness and wickedness have in common? Or what fellowship can light have with darkness?*

Now, Paul makes a good point here. In using the 'yoke' symbolism, he's referring to the ancient agricultural practice of 'yoking' two oxen together with a big wooden bar, so that they could plow the fields in sync. If you put two oxen together that are of different shapes, sizes, strengths, or attitudes, you wouldn't have a very successful team. There are various interpretations of this scripture, with some commentators believing it applies to business partnerships[1], some to marriage[2], and some to a larger picture of the dangers of Christian culture becoming intermingled with pagan culture[3]. But the point is pretty clear – when worldviews clash, how can two parties (or a whole community) walk in agreement, and stay committed to one Lord and Master?

All throughout the Old Testament we see situations where the Israelites moved around the place and settled in or near foreign lands. And repeatedly, God told them not to intermarry with the other cultures. Why? Mainly, because the other cultures followed different gods, and He knew that as soon as marriages and kids started happening, at least some of the people would eventually turn away to the other gods.

This happened when King Solomon – the wisest man who ever lived – started marrying women from pagan cultures. (He ended up with 700 wives!) Eventually, his wives turned his heart away from the Lord. *As Solomon grew old, his wives turned his heart after other gods, and his heart was not fully devoted to the LORD his God, as the heart of David his father had been.* (1 Kings 11:4)

It's pretty obvious that if you align your life with someone who has vastly different beliefs to you, some of their philosophies and behaviours will rub off on you. Joshua had actually cautioned the Israelites about this, 500 years earlier. When he was about to die, he gathered them together and gave them this warning:

Therefore watch yourselves carefully, that you love the LORD your God. For if you turn away and cling to the rest of these nations that remain among you, and if you intermarry and associate with them, know for sure that the LORD your God will no longer drive out these nations before you. Instead, they will become for you a snare and a trap, a scourge for your sides and thorns in your eyes, until you perish from this good land that the LORD your God has given you... (Joshua 23:11-13). Joshua seems to be warning that intermingling with cultures, communities and in marriage alliances with those who have different idols is a pathway to cultural destruction. What type of culture do you want in your marriage and family? Are you a truly committed Christian with a mature, no-compromise faith? And if so, do you want your non-Christian husband and potentially secularised children to become 'a scourge for your sides and thorns in your eyes'? Do you want to be constantly pushing against the tide in your marriage and disagreeing with your husband on small and large matters? That sounds incredibly frustrating and painful.

My opinion: Being a wife has a lot of really tough responsibilities and can be agonising at times (even if you share your faith), particularly if you are used to being independent and doing whatever you want. Marriage requires a lot of self-sacrifice, humility, and patience, as well as learning how men 'tick' and working out how to communicate effectively. If you end up with a husband who doesn't 'get' your faith, isn't interested in God, doesn't go to church with you, and most importantly, isn't submitted to Christ's headship, don't you think your marriage could become unbearably difficult? Husbands are mandated to love their wives 'as Christ loved the church', and to 'lay down their lives' (and lifestyles!)

for their wives (Ephesians 5:25). But if a man hasn't accepted Christ's love, sacrifice, and leadership in his own life, and surrendered to his authority, how will he offer such love and leadership to you, and have the humility to make sacrifices for you?

You must realise that marriage is far more intimate and complex than simple friendship. It's not like having a non-Christian flatmate. As a wife, you will need to lay down your own pride, independence and personal goals (to some extent) in order to be receptive and vulnerable to, and supportive of your husband. That is the wife's job – to be a 'helpmeet' (Genesis 2:18). Now, no-one is forcing you to get married, remember. If you want to retain your self-sufficient, please-yourself lifestyle, you totally can! But if you choose to become someone's wife, and want to model your marriage on Christ's relationship with the church, you immediately take on a role of service – **so think about who you want to serve**. Do you want to serve a man who isn't going to lead you to Christ, love you like Christ, or use the wisdom and counsel of the Bible and the Holy Spirit in guiding your family and making family decisions? Yikes!

In every marriage, you really need lots of love to smooth over the difficulties and the cracks. Theoretically, a Christian man who is submitted to Christ and has found 'heart freedom' in Christ, will be able to tap into a larger reservoir of love, patience and grace, which can then flow out onto you. He may also be more open to the goal of being transformed through the Holy Spirit and growing in his practice of patience, love, forgiveness, grace, and so on. This is the ideal marriage situation!

So I caution you to think carefully about the importance of marrying someone who has a similar maturity in the faith to you. As the prophet Amos points out to the Israelites in Amos 3:3, 'Can two people walk together without agreeing on the direction?' (NLT) Marriage is a journey (a long one). If you want to have a nice, companionable journey with a like-minded traveller, I encourage you to prioritise marrying a man who is headed in the same direction as you. Anything else could turn into a painful battle.

For those of you who are currently dating or engaged to a non-Christian, or planning to, or who feel affronted by these thoughts so far…my heart does go out to you. It's a jungle out there, and at the end of the day you just want someone to care for you, be good to you, protect you and provide for you. I get it. There's no law in your country (I hope) against marrying a non-Christian. It's a decision you have to make for yourself. But you really have to weigh it up, because it will have a major impact on the rest of your life, and I do mean major.

Will marrying a non-Christian affect our future children's faith?

Absolutely. Let me boil down the psychology for you. 'Mum' is seen as the nurturer, the go-to for the early years, the one to set the foundational culture and atmosphere in the home while Dad brings home the bacon. But because 'Dad' is the one the kids typically see as 'out there in the big wide world', his behaviours and preferences are seen as more 'adult' than Mum's. So when kids start to grow up, they want to branch out and explore the world, and taste and see the kind of life that their Dad has. If Dad only attends church to keep Mum happy, or only goes during the kids' early years, they will develop the perception that church is just a children's activity – nice for when you're little, but not something you continue as you become a real adult. This particularly applies to boys, who are typically more adventurous than girls, and are keen to leave behind the trappings of childhood and seek out more masculine activities and 'men's only business'.

Statistically, this was indicated in a large Swiss study released in 2000.[4] Basically, the results overwhelmingly showed that Dads' church attendance had a major impact on the kids' decisions to continue attending church as they grew older, whereas it didn't matter so much whether or not Mum attended.

If you marry a man who isn't a Christian, don't expect him to be super keen to take the family to church every Sunday. Most men work very hard during the week and want to guard their weekends for family time and personal hobbies, as well as some much-needed down time. Usually, only men who are truly committed to the Lord and to the community of faith will sacrifice quarter of their weekend for church. So think realistically about how that might play out in the long term for your family.

(Here's a concerning thought – what if he is strongly committed to another faith, or becomes a disciple of another faith during your marriage? Are you okay with your husband going to and taking your children along to the Mosque, Synagogue or New Moon Yoga Meditations and Crystal Chakras? Eek!)

Now obviously, church attendance is not necessarily an indication of faith, nor is non-attendance an indication of faithlessness. But it's a helpful rule of thumb for the purpose of this question. The point is, your children receive their identity through their dad. That is the spiritual role and privilege of the father, and nothing you can do will change that. So even if you are the most super-Christian mum out there, your children will be looking to 'Dad' to see how to live their lives. Which leaves you with the question…how does this man live his life?

Well, how do I know if he's really a Christian?

This is such an important thing to ask, because lots of girls have been caught out and thought they were dating a Christian…and had a rude awakening! Some guys are quite keen on Christian or 'church' girls because they tend to be a bit more old-fashioned, are sometimes into cooking and cleaning and serving, and are more likely to be virgins. So a man might pursue you and try to convince you that he 'believes in

God' and 'love is the main thing' or something like that. But when it comes to the crunch, this is not the kind of guy who is going to put his life on the line for Christ.

Here are some strategies to **figure out where he's at with God**. No one can know the heart of man, sure, but 'from the heart the mouth speaks' – so, in a way you can.

- Pentecostal girls: use the phrase 'born-again' around him and see how he reacts. Can he also describe himself as a born-again Christian, or does this language freak him out?
- Ask him about his conversion experience. It should have detail. Ask him about how his life has changed since.
- Ask him: 'What does it mean to you to be surrendered to Christ?' (But maybe not on the first date!)
- Watch his behaviour. Is he kind, forgiving, self-controlled, humble? Does he give to the poor? Does he bitch about his boss? Does he backstab his neighbours?
- How does he talk about Jesus? As a friend, master, spiritual guru, good teacher, cool iconic figure…does he talk about Jesus at all?
- See if he is a regular church-goer and is known in his church community. If he doesn't seem to go anywhere or have a home church, that's a red flag. If he doesn't know the Pastor's name, that's a red flag. If he takes you to 'his' church, and doesn't know anyone there, that's a red flag.
- If he pushes you for sex before marriage, he's not committed enough. Get out of there!
- Does he have a relationship with Jesus, or is he just religious? A religious person trusts in their own good deeds to save them. A true Christian knows that he is a sinner in need of a Saviour (Jesus), and that only faith in Jesus can save. A true Christian

can bow their knee to Jesus and say that 'Jesus is Lord' (Romans 10:9).

- Does he have any knowledge of Christendom? Eg. famous preachers, churches, church history, recent Christian events, major Christian artists, and so on.
- What is the religious culture or background of his family? How do they treat each other? Do they pray before meals? How does his dad treat his mum?
- Can you talk about things like 'the Holy Spirit', 'the cross' and 'salvation' without him getting uncomfortable?
- Sneak a look at his Bible. Does he have a Bible? Is it worn, underlined, and readily at hand? Or is it a fresh, still-in-the-box, Old King James leather-bound version stuck on the top shelf? These are clues, girls, clues...
- Drop a couple of scriptures and see what he does with them. Or if he asks you what you've been reading, you could say, 'Oh, I'm really getting into Paul's epistles at the moment'...and see how he responds.
- If you're over 30, wear a WWJD band one night and see if he says anything.
- Trust your gut. Deep down, you know if he's legit. If you want to marry him, go right ahead. But you must *be honest with yourself.*

Won't he eventually convert, once he sees how amazing my faith in Jesus is?

Statistically and anecdotally, I would say no. You absolutely cannot bank on this. I would suggest that if a Christian man married a non-Christian woman, there would be more chance of a conversion taking place. Why? Because marriage is not an equal partnership. It's a system with a headship – that's the husband. And the head sets the course of the system. Just think, whenever a company wants to change the culture, it changes the CEO – because culture comes down from the top. It's the same in marriage. It's very unlikely that he'll change because of you. And if you have to give him an ultimatum – *convert or we're breaking up* – well, that wouldn't make it a very authentic decision, would it?

A lot of girls like the idea of 'missionary dating' or 'flirt to convert'. But you have to think of the power imbalance. A girl who evangelises a man takes on the role of mentor, counsellor, teacher, or parent. This is not attractive to a man! He may learn and grow under your tutelage, he may come to church with you, and he may even 'get saved' – but he probably won't marry you afterwards. Remember, the man is meant to save the damsel in the distress – not the other way around.

It's not to say it can't happen or doesn't happen – but it's highly unlikely that a man will convert because of you, *and then marry you*. And if he does – do you really want to be the more spiritually mature person in the marriage? Unless he has a radical conversion and grows spiritually in leaps and bounds, you may find yourself feeling like a Sunday School teacher instead of a wife. Are you okay with that?

What if I don't care anymore, and I just want someone to help carry the groceries, buy me flowers and give me children?

Well – good luck to you, sister. I get it. Life is tough and being an older single totally sucks. It is lonely and it is hard. If you find a lovely, kind, supportive and financially viable single man who wants to marry you, who isn't a Christian…who am I to stop you? But go in with your eyes wide open. It's a big risk. How important is your faith? If it's a massive part of your life and lifestyle, then marrying a non-Christian might put you in a pretty lonely marriage, with two people doing their own thing and living parallel lives. Be honest about your situation, and make the best choice you can with the resources and wisdom you have.

What if he's better than all the Christian guys?

Now, I know there are so many Christian guys out there who are absolute deadbeats, narcissists, or players. They have major unresolved issues and are lacking maturity in a whole variety of ways. These guys have a lot of growing to do. And by the same token, there are tons of non-Christian guys who are awesome, lovely, kind, great at their jobs, humble, generous, and great with kids.

A guy just being a 'Christian' certainly doesn't guarantee a happy marriage. So when it comes to this question – you're on your own. Only you can decide what you can live with. But be informed: marriage is a lot harder than you think it's going to be. Does this man have the character, grace, mercy, kindness and leadership that you need to feel safe and secure under his headship, for the rest of your life?

CHAPTER 28

What's wrong with living together before marriage?

Reading this book may be making you feel pretty exhausted with the whole relationship thing. I mean, if it's so complicated, why bother trying to get married? Why enter such an intense covenant agreement, which requires major lifetime commitment, to someone who could turn out to be sub-par? Maybe it would be less risky to just 'try before you buy', and live with a man prior to committing to a marriage for life. I mean, he might turn out to be a complete dud, right?

Well, unfortunately, if you want to be in a **truly intimate** relationship that is built on <u>trust, respect and commitment</u> (which are the building blocks for relationship!) – *marriage is it*. When I say 'intimate', I don't mean 'sexual'. (Sex can be a lot of things, including not very intimate at all. Don't mistake physical *intensity* for relational *intimacy*.) Intimacy can more accurately be explained as '**into-me-see**'. It means that two people actually see into each other's hearts, that they know each other, and trust one another with their true selves. And unlike sex, intimacy doesn't happen overnight.

Arguably, though, 'knowing' someone inside out is not even the crucial factor in the beginning of a marriage relationship – **it's actually**

the commitment itself that makes the relationship so powerful. Think about arranged marriages, including marriages in Bible times – most of those women wouldn't have known their future husbands at all, but the covenant of marriage entered into by the two families would have created a very firm foundation upon which both parties could rely on and draw upon in hard times. **The 'trust' component automatically offered by the gravity of the commitment itself actually provides a potential springboard to intimacy.** I mean, if a guy is willing to buy you an expensive ring, propose to you, bring you into the community of his friends and family, make vows to you at the altar, be faithful to you, re-order his life around marriage and family, and go to work for 60 years to provide for you – that's a pretty good sign that you can trust his love for you!

Remember, love is more than feelings. Love is work. It's a decision. It is a choice. Love is saying: 'I choose to trust you, and I want to let you into my life and earn your trust. I will work hard to win you over again and again as we do life together. I choose you over all others, to cherish you and to hold your heart with great care.'

This issue of trust is crucial when it comes to relationships. You can't ever achieve intimacy with someone you don't trust. It's impossible, because you will always hold part of yourself back from them. They will never see the *real* you. Now think about it: **marriage** is daunting enough in terms of trusting someone with your life, but **cohabitation** really takes it to another level! How can you trust someone who hasn't even defined what the relationship is or where it's going? Sure, you can date this person and give them a chance to make a plan. But to actually move in with them and give them your body sexually, without requiring any level of certainty about the future? (Plus sharing finances, chores and pets, with no definition of roles, responsibilities and goals?) That is super scary! It reminds me of the parable of the man who built his house on shifting sands[1] – very, very foolish.

Why is cohabiting different to marriage? They look the same, don't they? Well…they do look kind of the same, but they're not the same. It's kind of like you rocking up at a job every day in uniform, doing what the employer tells you to do, using the lunchroom and hanging out with the staff, parking in the staff carpark and going to Friday night drinks with everyone. *But*…you're not actually employed there. You're not on a contract. You're not getting paid. You have no rights (and technically, no responsibilities). And – you don't really belong there.

When you live together with a man, even if you are totally 'sold-out' to the home-making idea yourself and believe he will marry you, you have **zero** assurance that he is 'covenanting' with you on the same terms you are, and **zero** legal and familial kinship bonds that give you the reassurance of the relationship that you really want deep down. Talk about walking on thin ice. You just never really know when it's going to crack. And to throw sex in the mix, with all the extreme psychological elements, let alone biological outcomes…far out. That is just asking for trouble. People these days might think someone is crazy to get married, but I think – it's crazier to move in with someone without getting married!

I bet you know heaps of girls who are living with their boyfriends, or maybe you are living with your boyfriend at the moment. You may have reached the point where you now tentatively use the word 'partner' to describe him, instead of boyfriend. It's the way things are these days. Does that make it right or good? Nope. Without even discussing the moral pitfalls of this way of living, let's now take a quick look at the psychology behind cohabitation.

The bottom line: when a man is deeply in love with a woman, he will make a conscious decision to *depart from all other options* and choose her above all others. And vice-versa. 'Commitment is fundamentally about making a decision . . . making the choice to give up other choices,' says psychologist Scott Stanley of the University of Denver. 'It can't be a commitment if it's not a decision'.[2] This may sound harsh, but don't you think it's a million times better when you know that a man has *really* chosen you above all others? And no, deciding to move in together is *not* a true commitment. When's the end date? Unless it's specified, you have no idea whether the 'commitment' is for life, or will run out at the end of his rental lease. *Are you honestly ok with that?*

In fact, guys who are happy to live with you but not marry you are called '**renters**'. As comedian and dating coach Steve Harvey says, 'People who rent don't care anything about the property they're with – they let it get run down, beat up, don't care what it looks like. They use the space, and when they find something better, they decline the new lease and they move on out and on to the next rental...After all, boys shack. Men build homes.'[3] *Ouch.*

Now it is true that lots of people who live together do end up getting married. But you have to ask yourself why. The reality is that couples who live together often cohabitate just for the sake of convenience, and get married for the same reasons of inertia. This is known as '**sliding, not deciding**'. Psychologist Meg Jay points out: 'Couples who live together before marriage enjoy a companion and a teammate, but sometimes, couples stay in relationships longer than they should because once they live with someone, it can be harder to find the escape hatch...Once you buy dishes, share a lease, have a routine, and get a dog, it can be difficult to cut your losses and accept that the relationship isn't working.'[4] Double ouch. And sure, plenty of cohabiting couples do end up getting married...but it's not quite the same, is it.

Girls, is this what you want for your life? A guy who marries you because of *inertia*? I believe you are worth more than that. And if every girl knew her worth and didn't make it so easy for men to get easy sex – there would be a lot more men making the commitment to get married! You wonder why some men these days are slack, lazy, not chivalrous, not dynamic, not appealing? It's because they don't have to be. Women have made themselves (the prize) so cheap, that men barely have to lift a finger to win them. **But you are worth more.** And only *you* can communicate to men what your worth is.

I have to state the obvious – men are simple. They don't ask too many questions. If you give them a free pizza, they won't ask why; they will take it and eat it. If you're lucky, they'll say thanks. By moving in with a guy, **you are communicating to him** that *that is all you expect* – a roof over your head and some shared dinners. And maybe the title of 'partner'. The problem is – none of this has been laid out, no one has agreed to anything specific; no one really knows the terms of the relationship! Super awkward. Deep down, girls in this situation want their partner to cherish them, serve them, and make sacrifices for them, like a good husband would – but the man has zero obligation to do so! Why should he, when he already has the prize? (Your luscious body and sweet companionship!)

Girl - are you giving your man mixed messages? If so, then it's not all his fault, is it? **You have a personal responsibility to yourself and to him to communicate your requirements for the kind of relationship you want.** If you move in with him without requiring an engagement ring, a wedding date, a marriage – then that is exactly what you will (or won't) get. And if he's not willing to meet your requirements? Well, it's up to you to decide how much you're willing to compromise on your own life to have the attentions of this man, for an indefinite period of time. Don't say I didn't warn you.

I could be wrong, but it seems to me that 99.9% of girls want to get married. People have been getting married since the beginning of time, for some very basic reasons: physical protection, financial stability and growth, social status and safety, companionship, sex, and kids. As Ecclesiastes 4:9 points out, two are better than one! And while cohabitation offers a shadow of these things, it doesn't really give you the whole package, because it doesn't give you the *commitment*. So you might feel like you have all those things, but at the end of the day it can all come crashing down in a very sudden moment.

It's true that all marriages don't retain the commitment offered during the wedding vows, for various reasons, and they can come crashing down too. But because divorce is very expensive, legally difficult, time-consuming, heart-breaking and socially scarring, not to mention a logistical nightmare, it makes someone think twice before choosing to break off the relationship. It's a lot harder to get divorced than it is to just pack up your half of the kitchen appliances and break lease.

It's a rare lady who can *honestly* say, 'Yeah, we can live together and act like a couple, and maybe have some kids, and I don't care if we ever get married.' And yet girls move in with their boyfriends all the time, quietly hoping that they will notice how great it is to never run out of toilet paper and to eat three square meals a day, *and hoping that one day they will propose.* Actually, what their boyfriend is noticing is how great it is to have free sex and food and cleaning and friendship while still being able to keep their future options open. Who's the winner here, girls?

Sometimes, that girl keeps living there for 5, 10, 15 or 20 years, waiting and waiting for the wedding that will never come. And does she decide to have kids with him or not? What if he doesn't want to? Can you even have that conversation when there's no official obligation to each other? Having kids is a gigantic issue in the cohabitation debate. It's all fun and games living with your boyfriend, posting cute pics of the two of you at the Sunday morning farmers' markets, double dating with your friends, and choosing home-wares at Kmart together – until you wake up and you're 35. And then…that biological clock is ticking and you are wondering, waiting, if the conversation about kids is ever going to get off the ground. You have no guarantee that the conversation can ever really *take* place, let alone the action plan for building a family together.

Furthermore, bringing children into an unstable family situation is highly damaging for those kids. The number one thing kids need in life is the security of knowing that their mum and dad are committed to each other and to them, for life. Children are not accessories. They are real human beings with significant needs for secure attachment and a stable home life, and if you can't provide this for them, they will suffer. There is no question about it.

I know we don't live in an ideal world, and due to the brokenness of humanity, people make bad decisions and sometimes are negatively affected by others' bad decisions, or sometimes, life throws you a curve ball that changes everything, like illness, poverty, war or bereavement. Maybe you've experienced this, and you can see areas in your life where children (you as a child, your children or others') have been damaged because of difficult circumstances. In those cases, you just have to move forward and make the best of things. But if you do not yet have children, please be wise about how and when you plan to bring them into your life. *They are not accessories.* Cohabitation and a 'slide' into parenthood is not ideal for kids, nor for you.

The main thing is to stop any wishful thinking and to be honest with yourself. Life is not a movie. If you want to have a home and family one day, don't think it will be a natural step in the process of cohabitation. **Maybe it will, maybe it won't.** There are no guarantees.

Sometimes, after a few years in a cohabiting relationship, the guy packs up his gear and says, 'I think it's time we start seeing other people' and moves off into a new life, leaving the girl devastated and confused. But technically, no official commitment was made and he hasn't exactly gone back on his word – because he never gave his word. Their expectations of the relationship were vastly different. These kinds of unofficial agreements are really blurred, and people end up getting devastatingly hurt because of them. Is it hard to say no to this kind of living arrangement, when you really like the guy, and it would be far more economical to share the rent with someone? Of course it is. But it's harder to find yourself deeply committed to someone, having invested years of your love and time and money into a life with someone, and then to have it all pulled out from under you with **a casual break-up chat**.

You were designed to enjoy security of relationship with a guy who is serious about you, who knows beyond the shadow of a doubt that he wants to commit to you and *to take responsibility* **for being your protector, provider and pursuer.** Anything less in a relationship will lead to a life of anxiety and stress for you – which is not ideal, and in my opinion is not worth settling for. And in our culture, and cultures all over the world, a man's proper commitment to you is communicated to you personally and to your friends and family publicly through the legal and spiritual sacrament of marriage. There is no clearer way for a man to make his intentions known. And if he's serious about you, why wouldn't he?

Yes, it's hard to find the right one (and for him to find you). And sometimes it's hard to believe that someday someone will want you enough to marry you. Maybe I'm an idealist, but I didn't want to settle for something less. You have to be tough, sister. Tough enough to stay true to your convictions and to use as much common sense as you can muster up. It will be worth it in the long run. Don't waste your time on boys. A real man is someone who can and will take responsibility for a wife and kids – and they are out there! Remember, 'boys shack, men build homes' (Steve Harvey).

Marriage is awesome, sacred, special and strong. It is also a massive commitment and definitely not something to enter into lightly. The problem is, there's not really another viable option if you want a truly intimate relationship, and if you want the stability and security that every woman naturally desires in a relationship. I guess that's what it all comes down to. (Do you really believe God is capable of miracles? I do.) And don't be fooled by the secularism of our times. Not everyone is cohabiting, or sleeping around, or 'never' getting married. People are getting married all the time. It is still possible!

CHAPTER 29

Can I stay friends with my ex?

I'm sure that some of you have one or more ex-boyfriends hanging around in the background of your life, just waiting for another chance, or generally being a nuisance. It's a topic I want to address, because it can affect your future prospects. I have had girls ask my advice on whether or not they should stay friends with their ex, so let me give you some thoughts.

Firstly, I would ask *why* you want to stay friends. As Greg Behrendt, Liz Tuccillo and Lauren Monchik point out in their great 2004 book *He's Just Not That Into You*[1], **it's called a break-up because it's broken**.

What was it that caused you (or your ex) to end the relationship? Did he have some glaring character flaw? Were you incompatible? Was it long-distance and just too hard to maintain? Did you both lack the necessary relationship skills to get deeper with each other? ***Or was he just not that into you?***

Whatever the reason, if there's a man hanging around your life who shouldn't really be there, something's gotta give. Let's break this down into some various scenarios and solutions.

1. **He broke up with you but you're still keen.**

Ok. I get it. I've been there. This is the situation where you write letters to him, you apologise, you promise to change, you go hot and cold and hot to try and mess with his head, you drive past his house to see if he's home, you check to see if he's texted you in the last five minutes, you date around with deadbeat guys who are just time-killers to try and make him jealous, you write songs about him, you journal about him, and you know *but you know* but you KNOW that God has brought THIS man to you and IT IS GOING TO WORK OUT. Sound familiar?

Well. I hate to break it to you, but **if he wanted to be with you, he'd be with you.** Once I dated a guy for a month or two who I thought was so 'perfect' for me I could have screamed. He ticked (nearly) all the boxes! But then, in a **horror twist**, he tells me he's been planning a year-long overseas trip and can't back out of it. Of course, I say I can wait a year. I can wait five years! But no, he says that would not be fair to me. So, heartbroken, I watched him (metaphorically) ride off into the sunset, never to be seen again. Back to square one.

Anyway, I have asked my husband about these kinds of situations, and he assures me that if a guy is into a girl, he will make it work, somehow. No matter what the reason is, **if he's not with you, he doesn't want to be with you.** And there's a 99% chance he's not going to change his mind in a few months or years.

Could you be the 1%? Maybe, although you may have to wait a really long time. This is a legitimate question for older Christian girls, who think they've nabbed Mr Perfect but then he breaks it off or just keeps stringing you along on the side…and we all know you're never going to find anyone else quite so perfect…or are you? **What's more perfect: a 'perfect' guy who doesn't really love you and won't commit, or an imperfect guy who is totally into you and totally committed to you?**

Argh, it's a tough one, I know. My advice is to <u>lay low</u>, keep your options open, and move on as much as you can. *Do not pursue him. Do not give him girlfriend privileges.* If he wants you, he'll come back. I really love the strategy of the leading lady in the 1961 version of *The Parent Trap*[2]. She was classy. She was cool. She knew that to get her man back, she needed to give less of herself, not more, trusting that he would realise what he was missing! (Spoiler alert: it totally worked.)

The other alternative is to give him an ultimatum – 'Do you want me, or not? If not, I'm out of here.' Yes, the ultimatum is a risk. But if you don't do it, you could be waiting forever! The problem is, **a man becomes *more* of a catch as he ages** and gets richer (and more mature). You, on the other hand, have a biological clock ticking away, signalling impending doom as everything starts heading south. Yikes! Only you can decide how long you want to wait.

Also – remember Bradley Cooper's character in *He's Just Not That Into You* (the 2009 movie)?[3] He ended up marrying the girl he'd dated for ages, because if he didn't, and I quote, 'he'd look like a dick'. **And do you remember what happened to that marriage?** Let's just say… it did not end well.

A tip for young players: the only way, and I mean **the *only* way, to get back a guy who has dumped you**, and there are no guarantees, is to go totally underground and be unreachable. Remember, *guys want what they can't have.* If he has dumped you, getting *more* of you is certainly not going to make him interested again. He needs *less* of you, so that he can miss you, so that he can meet other girls and realise that you're way better, and so that he can wonder what you're up to these days and if you're still single. If he decides he wants you again, don't worry, he will come and find you.

2.   **You broke up with him but you miss what he did for you.**

Ooh. Read that again. If your boyfriend was one of those guys that is just great to have around – he pumps up your car tyres, offers you his jacket on a cold night, makes sure you lock your car doors, buys you treats, cooks the odd dinner for you, drives you to the airport, helps you build your IKEA desk, sorts out your finances…well, who wouldn't miss a guy like that? But let's get this straight. He had feelings for you (which is why he did that stuff) – then he made a move on you and asked you out – you said yes – you had a relationship – you realised you weren't into him like that – you dumped him – he's heartbroken – and you want him to stick around and mow your lawn? Girrrl…that's cold.

Here's the thing. A romantic relationship is **transactional** (we can argue about that another time). Have you heard the old saying, men give love to get sex? And girls give sex to get love? Well, in a crass way, it's kind of true. There's nothing new about this. It's been happening for millennia. To put it more kindly, men and women complement each other in certain ways, and when they are both humble, selfless and giving, they give to the other what the other needs, and the other gives to them what they need.

It's like humans and plants. Humans breathe out CO_2, plants breathe it in and breathe out oxygen, which humans need. It's the circle of life. So, in our context, men give money, treats, security, care, protection, fidelity, attention, and public honour to their woman, and women give respect, kindness, encouragement, appreciation, admiration, fidelity, and within marriage, sex.

So I'm sorry, but **you can't have your cake and eat it too**. It's not fair to stay 'friends' with him and keep stringing him along just so that you can enlist him to help you move house next month. That's manipulative, selfish and disrespectful. Don't do it.

(Non-Christians may call this type of relationship **'friends with benefits'**. So if you're ok with giving sex or physical intimacy to a guy you don't love that much, just so he comes over and moves your fridge… well…I feel sad for you. It's not going anywhere, and it's going to cause havoc when a spouse comes along for either one of you. Think long-term and have a bit more self-respect…and find yourself a loving father figure to provide the care you need!)

3. **It was a mutual break-up, but you still enjoy his company more than anyone else's because** *he knows you like no-one else does.*

For some reason, I'm picturing a lone cowboy out in the paddock, staring back at the one girl who's ever taken the chance to know him. (Or is that the cover of a Nicholas Sparks book?) Where do I even start…

Firstly, **is there really such a thing** as a mutual breakup? Genuine question here. I mean, it's got to be pretty rare that both parties in a relationship realise, at the same time, that they'd be better off alone. So first of all, make sure you're not in category 1 or 2, rather than this one.

Secondly, of course you have history. **The longer you've dated, the more history you have.** All those private jokes, romantic moments, mundane routine days, shared experiences, shared possessions, shared family connections…sure, it's not ideal to close off that part of your history and pretend it didn't exist. That's why I **don't think** God really designed men and women to date around. Because trust me, it hurts like hell, it's exhausting, demoralizing, and makes marriage harder than it should be. It's storing up history with another person who you're not going to be married to. Less than ideal.

But what are you going to do? Keep building *more* history with this guy? Oh, your future husband is really going to appreciate that. I can just imagine, he starts dating you and soon realises that old 'Pete' is hanging back in the wings, just there ready to offer a little piece of personal knowledge about you whenever it's needed. **Yeah, thanks a lot Pete!** (Think *Win a Date with Tad Hamilton!*[ɪ] from 2004 – one of the greatest movies of all time.)

Let's talk about sex. In the Old Testament, sex was often subtly referred to as 'knowledge'. As in, *carnal* knowledge. As in, *Adam **knew** his wife Eve, and she gave birth to son.* Here's the thing: knowledge is intimacy. The more you know someone, the more intimate you become. Imagine that *metaphorically* you and your boyfriend were having **tons of sex**, then you broke up. But you keep having sex, because you *used* to have sex. You *knew* each other, so you keep getting drawn back to each other, to keep *knowing* each other more and more. Doesn't this sound dysfunctional? (Actually this happens in movies all the time, doesn't it. It never works out.)

My point is, it's not logical to keep developing a deeper and deeper relationship just because you were already pretty deep. That's like digging a deep hole that you can't get out of (but realise you don't want to be in), and **instead of stopping and waiting** for the rescue team, you just keep digging anyway, like, *what the heck?* In fact, let me get all Freud on you – *you keep digging because you don't believe that a rescue team will ever come for you.*

Girl – don't give up. You've got to keep waiting and hoping for someone that you really do want to marry. You've got to keep trying and improving yourself and moving around and meeting people and doing what you've got to do to attract a worthy man. *Don't give up.*

Here's the other thing about staying friends with an ex. In a relationship, you develop **soul ties** with a person. All the stuff I've been mentioning, the shared experiences, both good and bad, the protection of each other – this develops soul ties. You are literally tied to this person in your soul (or heart or whatever word works for you). If you are still so tied to someone, how is someone new ever going to get in? How is a new guy ever going to build up enough 'credits' with you to compete with 'Pete'?

If you are sure you can't marry Pete, and you do want to get married one day, then **Pete has to go.** You need to take a huge risk and make the painful and necessary decision to cut him off. You need to de-tangle your soul ties (maybe by journaling, grieving, a letter for closure, in therapy, moving cities or whatever works for you), and open up your heart so that someone new can throw you a line.

If **no one is asking you out, ever**, you should check yourself for old soul-ties. Men can vibe these kinds of things. Maybe they can vibe that you're still tied up elsewhere.

4. **You're not that into him but you want to keep him around in case you never meet anyone else.**

Go back and read number 2.

5. **You broke up with him but he's hanging around like a lost puppy.**

Ok, this is just sad. But common. You are not into him, you don't really want to hang out with him, but he's one of those 'hangers-on'. He accepts the scraps from your table, if you will. Well, there's two ways this can go. **Either you keep him around as a useful minion, or you respectfully and firmly put an end to it.**

If you want to pick the first option, go back and read number 2. If you want to take the second approach, here's how you do it.

- Privately, clearly explain to him that the relationship is over. Assure him that there will be no future.

- Give back anything that he owns. Don't receive any gifts or favours from him. And don't ask for favours!
- Respectfully request that he no longer try to sit next to you at church, follow you to your car, or text and call you.
- Delete him from your social media (this is key).
- Preferably, get a new boyfriend asap.

On a serious note – in rare cases, you may find yourself in what could be called a **domestic violence** situation. Some guys, due to their own insecurities and ego problems, **cannot handle being dumped** and then ignored. Sometimes, these guys get very controlling, manipulative, and violent. (You would have experienced signs of this during the relationship. Trust your gut feeling.) If you have a boyfriend like this, tread carefully. Usually the violence *increases* after the break-up. Talk to a trusted professional counsellor, social worker or law enforcement officer about how to break up with this person. Or Google local DV support services in your area, for advice.

6. **You want to stay friends because you're afraid of being alone - but you're also afraid of intimacy, and of anything deeper than friendship.**

Hmmm. Look, ideally, a girl will grow up in a secure family unit with a kind, protective father, then will marry out of that family into marriage with a kind, protective man. No baggage, no in-between, no fuss. But these days, this is a rare scenario. A lot of girls these days don't have that kind of family, or don't have that kind of dad, or have moved away from their family, or are so independent they don't want to sit under that covering anymore. These kinds of girls usually have good male friends, who help to fill some of the gaps. Totally understandable.

What's also understandable is developing a romantic attachment to one of these friends, and perhaps starting an on-again, off-again kind of relationship that never seems to get to marriage (like Ross and Rachel from *Friends*[5]). I would suggest that this kind of girl probably has some **daddy issues.** She's felt uncovered for so long, she's scared of being vulnerable. **So she wants to be covered, but she's scared of the vulnerability required of marriage.** It's a tough situation.

The best way to avoid these on-again, off-again, non-marriage scenarios is to **come back under the covering of a father** or father-figure, and get some of those old needs met. You need to get a 'top-up' of fatherly love, protection and provision, and stop treating this guy as your surrogate daddy. (That's probably why you don't want to marry him, by the way.) Then you'll be freed up to start a relationship with someone new.

7. **You really like this guy and he still likes you - but you know he's not right for you.**

Ooh, this is heart-rending, isn't it. To have a guy in your life who is just super lovely, and is into you – but for whatever reason, he's not the right fit. Maybe he's not a Christian, he lives far away and can't move to you, he's waaay too old (or too young) for you, he's incarcerated (so many questions to ask here!), your cultural differences are immense, or one of your families forbids the relationship. It's a sad, sad scenario. What to do?

Well, it's up to you. Do you think the differences can be overcome? Or are they real deal-breakers? This would be a good occasion to bring in some wise counsel. You need to get perspective on this one.

The thing is, marriage is not just about finding someone who is in love with you, who you can love and respect in return. It's got to work on a practical level, too. It's just not logistically viable to try to have a relationship with someone in another country, for example, unless one of you is fully committed to moving overseas for life. That's a huge commitment! You're better off falling in love with someone from your own country – your own city, if possible!

And if one of your families forbids the marriage - whether you think they have legitimate grounds for their feelings or not – well, it's going to be a rough road for you two. When you're dating, you are in a little love bubble, and nothing seems to be a problem. But once you're engaged… the poop hits the fan! All of sudden, the layers of history and culture and values and family dynamics start to surface. They cannot be avoided and will have a major impact on your entire future as a family. So act with caution!

Wisdom is key in this situation. Don't just pray about it and place trust in your feelings or what you think God is saying to you. Don't just throw caution to the wind and hope that it will all turn out in the end. You need to search the scriptures and trust God's principles, and you need to get wise counsel from older Christians and marriage experts who have experienced more of life than you have. Then weigh it all up. Remember – marriage goes for a *really* long time.

And finally, you and your man need to be on the same page for this one. If you think the obstacles can be overcome and he doesn't, then it's not going to work. Either you're both all in, or the relationship is doomed from the beginning.

8. **A note on social media and communication in regards to ex-boyfriends.**

Your Insta or FB profile is like a window to your life. Like, literally, the front window of your house. **Who do you want looking inside?** When you break up with someone, I personally think it's wise to disconnect from them on social media. It's not that you can't have *males* on your social media (although even then I'm particular) – but it's not wise to have your *exes* on social media. Do you know how many affairs have started from people reconnecting over Facebook? Tons! It's probably not going to happen in your first year of dating or marriage…but a few years in, when things get boring, or hard, **it's not that difficult to start fanning the old flames** via a 'harmless' little comment or text on the old FB.

Here's a verse you should inscribe somewhere: **'It's the little foxes that ruin the vines'** (Song of Solomon 2:15). It's the tiny things, over time, that can bring down kingdoms (and marriages). Relationships are incredibly fragile. The devil is out to ruin marriages, you know. **Expect to hit the battlefield as soon as you say 'I do.'** So you need to clear the margins, or for the fine country folk reading this, do a bit of 'back-burning'. That's when you purposely burn up some of the bush near important things (like your house) to create a wider firebreak, in case of bushfire. It's preparation for the onslaught that you expect to come.

Thus - if you're not connected to a man on social media, **you can't exactly 'stumble' into an illicit connection.** And the same goes for calls and texts. A married man should not be ringing you or texting you about personal things. (And if they're professional things, be careful. Remember how many men have affairs with their secretaries? And this includes pastors!) And **you shouldn't be ringing or texting a married man**, or the boyfriend of another girl, about personal matters – unless he's your brother. And you certainly shouldn't be **spending time one-on-one** with a man who is 'taken', nor should a man spend time one-on-one with you if you are in a relationship with someone else. I know this sounds a bit archaic and prudish, but **why do you think** hundreds of cultures around the world have been using these kinds of rules for thousands of years? *Because they know what happens.*

You've got to understand **how strong the power of sex is**. Men and women are born with an instinct and a desire to connect, emotionally and sexually. It's a biological drive that has to be kept very disciplined and channelled into the right pathways. Anything that can cause the river to divert, so to speak, must be given immediate attention. **Guard your heart. Dam your rivers. Back-burn the bush!**

CHAPTER 30

Should I date or marry a divorcee?

Ok, first up let me point out that I am in NO way an expert on this topic…I have very few divorcees in my circle, nor have I ever had a divorcee boyfriend (nor been divorced). So feel free to question the validity of my advice (you should be questioning everything, anyway – that's what smart people do!) But based on my reading, observation and common sense, I can outline a few pros and cons of dating a divorcee.

If you have experienced divorce in your own life, may I extend my sympathies to you. No one enters a marriage thinking that they'll end up divorced, and from where I stand, it looks like a horrific experience. I'm so sorry that this has been part of your story. So there is no judgement from me for those who have gone through it. But for those entering the dating scene who may be naïve to the realities of divorce, I think it's important to consider the following points.

Firstly, please understand that divorce is a massive deal. It's not like a high-school dumping. It's a major relationship break-down, emotional pounding, and social identity crisis. When kids are involved, it causes family disintegration and can lead to financial ruin or at the very least, indentured servitude (usually of the father). Logistically, it's a nightmare.

It's never pretty and it hurts everyone involved, a lot. I've read that a divorce is as painful as a death (possibly more, because you still have to deal with the ongoing tensions forever!) Because divorce is so common in our culture these days, people often talk about it in a casual way, like it's just par for the course. But it isn't. It's brutal, expensive, and heartbreaking, particularly for the children affected.

There are a few references in the Bible to divorce – primarily by Moses and Jesus (see Deuteronomy 22 and 24, Mark 10 and Matthew 19). They essentially point out that divorce was never God's intention for human relationships (and if you've been through one, you'll know why). Their general consensus seems to be that divorce should only be an option if one or both parties have such hard hearts that they cannot humble themselves to act correctly in the marriage partnership, causing major division and pain.

I'm not going to go into whether divorce is right or wrong – it's an incredibly complex issue that is beyond my paygrade (although no doubt there are many illuminating Christian resources out there you could look into). But I think it's imperative to try and wrap your head around what a heavy weight divorce can be on a family. It's huge. I've also read that many people post-divorce wish they had never gone through with it, because of the incredible ongoing emotional and financial toll it takes. (It sounds like maybe the grass is not always greener on the other side.)

So when it comes to dating a divorcee, you can't really say, 'Oh yeah, he was married before, but that was in the past.' That would be like saying, 'Oh, yes, he did serve in the armed forces in the Middle East conflict for a couple of years; that was pretty intense; but he's back now so it's all good.' You have to realise that these kinds of events are often very traumatic for the people involved. Undoubtedly, there will be major baggage. So tread carefully.

Let's talk about the pros and cons for awhile, and then we'll look at whether or not it's 'worth it' to date a divorcee. Again, these are just my ideas and certainly aren't exhaustive. Nor are they prescriptive or an attempt to stop you marrying a divorcee. (You might be in a certain situation where you just have to make it work within the divorcee context. Or you might meet a super lovely, emotionally healthy divorcee who is majorly into you!) And you may have more insight than me – so use it.

I would suggest that there are a few **positive elements** to dating and then marrying a man who has been married before. Firstly, unlike the guy who's still single at 45, Mr Divorcee (let's call him Mr Div) has at least had some solid relationship experience. It may not have been the best experience, but at least he's had some! He has had a taste of what it's like to live with a woman, how to communicate with a woman, the responsibilities of leading a wife and/or family, how to manage in-laws, and how to clean the toilet (hopefully).

Secondly, if he's pursuing a committed relationship with you, he's obviously someone who likes the idea of marriage and family life. He's smart about the fact that he needs a good woman, and wants to share his life with a companion. That's positive.

Thirdly, if he already has kids and you are ambivalent about having kids, it gives you the nice option of being a pseudo-mum without actually having to do the main bulk of the child-raising (not to mention pregnancy and labour!). This is also a great bonus for women who are past child-bearing age but really want to shower love and care on some kids.

Fourth, if you are also a divorcee, he will possibly have a similar state of maturity or at least life experience as you when it comes to the realities of marriage and family. I can imagine that marrying a total innocent when you yourself have been through marriage, childbearing, child-raising, and divorce, could become a bit annoying after awhile!

Fifth, and this is the kicker – he's available.

Now let's move onto the **negative elements** of marrying a Mr Div. There are a lot more of these, so I'll do a numbered list.

1. **Baggage.** This guy has a past. All the big things in life – work, money, a wedding, sex, in-laws, kids, health, lifestyle, housing – he's already gone through with someone else. He has history with another woman, possibly the woman he considered 'the One' and hoped to grow old with. And there's nothing you can do to erase that history.

2. **Grief.** Depending on who initiated the divorce (and in 70% of cases, it's the woman[1]), he may still be drowning in a swamp of shock, devastation, guilt, regret, fear, sadness, and probably a lot of anger. A divorce can shatter a man's existence, forcing him to move into a tiny flat and pay most of his wage towards supporting the children, losing relationship with them along the way, all while having to re-establish his confidence and social status. It is usually a massive blow for a man, and can take years to come to terms with. He may never be able to fully move on.

3. **Awkward social adjustments.** Just because Mr Div is now with you, it doesn't mean that the whole network of relationships he built while he was married instantly disappear. He will have to work through the very sticky situation of figuring out how to relate to the various friends, family members, colleagues, and church acquaintances that were connected to he and his wife. You will need major patience to stand by and watch while this is all unfolding.

4. **Dramas with the ex-wife.** If Mr Div has kids, you will never be separated from dealing with his ex-wife. Most of this is due to logistics. Who's the one picking up the kids for their weekend

with dad? Probably – you. Who's the one reminding each kid to take their school excursion form back to mum to sign? You. Who's going to get in trouble from the ex-wife for feeding her children non-approved foods? You. It's just the reality of dealing with kids. There's a lot to manage, and when you are sharing children across two or more homes, it's a logistical nightmare.

Then there's the emotional component. No doubt you will be hearing the occasional tirade from Mr Div about his ex-wife, and you'll have to field the children's questions from time to time about you, Mr Div, their mum, what's happening, and so on. Messy. And what if you run into Mr Div's ex at the shops? Awkward, to say the least. What if she tries to run you down on social media, stalk you and ruin your life online? It's possible. Many people today are living this existence, and I applaud them for their patience, resolve and commitment to making things work out the best they can for the sanity of everyone involved. But I can tell you this for sure – it's not fun and it's not easy.

5. **Difficulty in disciplining (his) children.**

Depending on how Mr Div sets the culture as you enter his home, his children will probably find it very hard to want to respect and obey you. Even if they can't help liking you as a person, or they are relieved to see their dad happy again, in most cases they will try to resist developing positive feelings for you and will resist submitting to the new family system. Mainly this is because they feel a deep loyalty towards their biological mother, and feel that submitting to and being nice to you is like giving her a slap in the face. I would suggest this is also the case if the mother has died, and your new husband is a widower.

It's very hard for children of divorce, because they have lots of very deep, mixed feelings, and aren't sure what to do with them. They need to have some relationship with you, in order to survive, but they are resentful that this is the case. Potentially, they will make your life difficult, or act in a passive-aggressive manner towards you until you want to scream.

My advice would be to play it cool for the first months (or years), depending on the age of the children. Don't come on too strong, and leave the majority of the discipline up to their dad. Try to stick to basic household instructions only. Let them get to know you at their own pace, and be ready to accept their 'bids' for positive engagement, whenever they may be offered to you. Perhaps at the start you could consider operating in the style of a nanny, governess, teacher, or aunty (depending on their ages). This may be more acceptable for the children, initially. Don't expect a warm welcome if you rush through the door yelling, 'Your new mummy is here!'

The key is for their dad to teach them to accept you, and then to respect you. This will take time. If he's not great at this, a few quiet conversations or even some marriage counselling may be needed.

6. **Financial restrictions.** Particularly if there are kids involved, chances are that Mr Div will have to put part of his pay-check towards child support every week (as he should). The tricky thing is that he's also having to pay another rent or mortgage to provide somewhere for himself to live. There's the extra fuel involved in driving to pick up and drop off the kids for their various custody timeframes. Airfares for flying the kids back to mum, or to their maternal grandparents. Extra costs for schooling and extra-curricular, that Mr Div may not have chosen if he was back in control of the family. Money for fun presents and outings that Mr Div feels obligated to offer his kids when they do visit, just to keep them happy (because he no

longer has a great backyard or pool, now that he's living in a tiny flat or back with his parents.) Everything is doubled.

On top of that are the massive legal costs for finalising the divorce, and dealing with custody issues. Have these been paid in full? On credit? Are they ongoing? Divorce is a huge sinkhole for cash. (As the old saying goes, 'divorce is a luxury for the rich.') And then if you and he have kids, he basically has to pay to run two separate families. That's a huge financial pressure for a man.

7. **No more kids may be desired.** A divorcee with his own kids may not want to enter into 'kid-land' again. The sleepless nights, nappies, discipline, and most of all the financial commitment required, might just be too much for him to handle. He's possibly already weighed down with the financial burden of his first family, and probably has dollar signs flashing in front of his eyes when he thinks of the things they'll need as they get older. He may not have the will or even the financial capacity to be able to consider more children. And that's his prerogative. If he says: 'I don't want any more children' when you're dating – believe him.

8. **He may have a culture of divorce.** If Mr Div initiated the divorce, it's possible that he maintains an ideology that it's ok to call it quits if things get tough. And if he did it once, he may do it again. In fact, research shows that second marriages break down more frequently than first marriages.[2]

9. **What went wrong the first time?** You really have to wonder. People don't get divorced for no reason. Who initiated the divorce, and why? Maybe he's a secret alcoholic. Or has anger issues. Or can't hold down a job. Or is consistently critical and mean. Take some time to understand what caused the divorce in the first place, and take even more time to assess whether this

man has dealt with the character flaws that contributed to his first marriage breakdown.

Hopefully by now you are starting to get a feel for the complexities of dating and marrying Mr Div. But the question still remains – is it worth it? Well, only you can answer that. This is where self-knowledge is imperative. **What kind of person are you?**

Do you desperately want children, or could you live without them? Would it drive you insane knowing there was 'another woman' in the past, or could you deal with that? Are you ok with managing some kids who aren't yours, for the next ten or fifteen years, or would that be a deal-breaker for you? Do you have the kind of patience and grace required to enter into a marriage with a man who may be burnt-out and grieving, and must devote some percentage of his time to managing the logistics and emotional issues that are part and parcel of divorce?

If I were you, I wouldn't actively go out seeking a divorcee to date and marry. But if a divorcee approached you and was really keen, perhaps you are at an age and stage where you think it's sensible to give it a go. If so, may I recommend you consider the following:

- Don't be the rebound girl. Some men will latch onto a new 'option' just to escape from an unhappy marriage. They might see you as all sunshine and rainbows; the complete opposite of their ex. Be warned: the shine comes off everyone eventually, even you! If he is not seeing your negative aspects, which we all have, he's not seeing the real you. Don't marry him while he's in the infatuation stage. He has to realise that you are just a normal person and not someone 'way better' than his ex. (And besides, maybe she only became so 'awful' as a result of being married to him!)

- Ensure he loves you for you. Is he committed to helping you flourish, or is it all about him? Don't just be his support person or personal cheerleader. If you want this to last long-term, he has to be willing to get involved in your life, too. If he doesn't have space for your joy and your pain, then he doesn't have space for you in his life. Check out Dr Jordan Peterson's lecture clip on YouTube: 'How to Know Your True Friends'[3] – because friendship is the one of the best foundations for a solid marriage.
- Use strong boundaries from the beginning. Show that you have self-respect. Don't let him use you as a weapon or a shield against his ex. His business with his ex-wife has nothing to do with you, and you should not be involved. He has to figure that out on his own. And don't just become a free babysitter for his kids. You have a life, too. Remember, you're not his personal maid – you should be his princess.
- Be very respectful and discreet around his kids, if he has them. Launching on them straight away with hugs, kisses, presents and pet names is going to backfire. They have been through the worst experience of their lives, and will possibly hate you. (It's not personal.) Possibly, for many years they will wish that you two would break up, so that their dad will go back to their mum. Treat them pleasantly but keep your distance for awhile. Let them decide how they want you to fit into their lives. And take the lead from Mr Div – he may have certain ways he thinks you should interact with them.
- Encourage Mr Div to get some personal counselling, if he hasn't already. Divorce causes major grief, and major grief usually needs major support. It's important that he process his feelings, work through his baggage, and come up 'cleaner and lighter',

ready for a new relationship. (This will benefit you!) But be careful not to become his counsellor. That is *not* your role.

- Be wary of dating a man who is separated but not yet divorced. Apart from the messy ethics of it, there's no way he has fully processed the break-up and moved on. If he's dating you while he's separated, I'd say you might be the rebound girl. If he really loves you, he can wait. It will encourage him to speed up proceedings. But to be honest, this is not something to rush. It will take him time to work through his emotions, as well as the logistical and financial changes. Let him sort all that out before he dumps it on you!

None of this is exhaustive or prescriptive, nor will it apply to every situation. But I think it's valid. As I've said, divorce is horribly messy for everyone involved, and is majorly traumatic for children. I would tread very carefully when dating a divorcee. That said, there are many blended families who have overcome the hurdles and manage to maintain healthy relationships and fruitful family lives. It is possible. But you will need a great deal of grace, patience, understanding, time and extra support to get there. **It's not the right path for everyone.**

If you are 'fortunate' enough to be dating a divorcee without kids, the relationship will probably be a lot smoother for you. But I would be wondering why the first marriage broke down. It takes two to tango, remember, and marriage is not something to be entered into lightly. Why did they divorce? Check carefully for character flaws that may have led to the dissolution of the marriage.

Again – marrying a divorcee is not for wimps. Maybe you have what it takes, maybe you don't. I would suggest that this course of action is only for women with real maturity, a realistic perspective of life, lots of patience and grace, and great communication skills. Godspeed!

CHAPTER 31

How do I know if he's really in love with me?

Let's get one thing straight. Men are simple. If they like you, you'll know about it. If they are in love with you, it will be obvious. There will be no doubt in everyone's mind that his intentions are to win you over, date you and marry you. So what are the signs?

If a guy is into you, he will do three things: PURSUE, PROTECT & PROVIDE. What does this look like?

PURSUE:

He will text you. Call you. Initiate dates. Come to your house. Pick you up from work. Email you. Tag you in posts. Buy you flowers. Stop by your desk. Like your posts. Compliment you. Tell you what he's been up to. Invite you to things. Go to the things you're going to. He will not leave you alone! As marriage expert Dr John Gottman teaches, he will make 'bids for connection' to keep engaging you.[1]

PROTECT:

He will defend your honour. Stick up for you. Give you his jacket on a cold night. Walk you to your car. Walk you to your door. Walk you to the bus stop. Call you when you get home to see if you're ok. Pick you up when your car breaks down. Check that you've locked your doors at night. Kill spiders for you. He will make you feel like a cherished princess.

PROVIDE:

He will pay for you. Buy you lunch. Buy you dinner. Buy you presents. Refuel your car. Leave treats on your desk. Go out to get bread and milk for you. Bring everything required for a picnic. Save you a seat. Get you a drink. He will look after all your needs.

None of this is new. It's the same cross-culturally, and across time. But unfortunately, thanks to radical feminism and the breakdown of the family, it's more complicated now. Men have grown up without solid fathers or father figures to show them how to be men. And women have grown up without solid fathers to protect and provide for them. As a result, women have become so tough and independent that men are scared to be chivalrous. **They don't feel needed.** These days, a lot of men are scared and feeble, and women are demanding and critical. This leaves you in a difficult position. Because of the veritable switch in gender roles, combined with rampant promiscuity, men aren't very motivated these days to really step up to the plate and treat women like princesses – and women are so entitled and self-centred that very few men are 'good' enough for them. What will you do with this conundrum?

My advice is this. Firstly, act like a woman. Chivalry is *not* dead and **if you invite it, you will experience it**. A man will step up if you <u>inspire</u> him to do so, not with your demands, but with your appreciation and vulnerability. Secondly, get over yourself and give the decent guys a chance. You're not going to marry the next Billy Graham or George Clooney, so lower your expectations and when a man comes along who is really into you, thank the good Lord and give it a go.

All you need to ask is, does he *pursue, protect,* and *provide* for you? If so, he's into you.

Now, I can't finish this chapter without emphasising a very important point. If a man is not clearly pursuing you, <u>even if you believe</u> 'the Lord told me he's The One' – *he is not into you*. Let me repeat that. I don't care if you've had angels from heaven descend into your kitchen and sing 'The Wedding March' as you pack the dishwasher, or if you've had 'prophetic dreams' of your white-picket-fence homestead and this man striding through the door in his suit and tie...***if he is not pursuing you, he is not interested.*** I know that you don't believe me and that you will ignore this advice. But you will not succeed in marrying this man. **The only way to know if a man likes you is if he likes you.** (Makes sense, doesn't it.) Please, I beg you, sit back and look for signals <u>from the man</u> (not from God) that he is interested. Anything else will lead to heartbreak.

CHAPTER 32

How do I know if I'm really in love with him?

What does it mean, to you, to be 'in love' with someone? Think about it. Does it mean you can't stop thinking about them, you're obsessed with them, you feel butterflies in your tummy, you can't eat, and you doodle their surname in your notebook all day long? If this is how you describe it, you're right, in part. This is what the first stage of love can be like. It's all chemistry and hormones at this point. But as marriage guru Dr John Gottman points out, there are actually three stages of love, as follows: **lust, trust and loyalty.**[1]

Anyone can be 'in love'. People 'fall' in and out of love all the time. That's one reason why people have affairs – they often still love their spouse, but they just 'couldn't help' falling in love with another person. So if you're only looking to be 'in love', I would posit that your goal falls short of what's required for a successful marriage.

May I suggest that while chemistry is important (don't marry someone you find boring or repulsive!), what's more important for a woman is <u>trust</u>. The number one thing women need to feel happy in a relationship is **security**, particularly as they get older and more vulnerable in some respects. There are many ways a man can offer security to you, and depending on your values and your background, each woman may experience security in a different way.

It could be all about the money, for you. You want a man who can offer a stable, high-paying wage to sustain the household. Or it could be about Christian values and a strong character – a man who you know is firmly committed to his beliefs and will lead the family towards the Lord. Or it might be about social status and community engagement – you want someone who is entrenched in the local 'tribe' and is highly esteemed by your social group. Or it might be about intellectual capacity – you feel a bit lost when it comes to 'knowing things', so you feel secure with a man who is really smart. Or it could be about physical strength and size – you feel confident when partnered by someone who could beat up the baddies in your life. None of these is right or wrong – it depends on what you need.

So let's rephrase the initial question. Rather than asking, *How do I know if I'm really in love with him?* I'd suggest asking, *Am I certain that this man can and will give me the security I need?*

This sounds a bit clinical, but it's a crucial point when you're an older woman. You can't afford to throw your life away on some unknown bad boy who swoops in on his Harley Davidson and gets your engines going in 5 seconds flat. You need to be a bit more circumspect about who gets to hold your heart. Why do you think much of the world has relied heavily on the practice of arranged marriages? It's because getting married based on first impressions, lust and feelings of being 'in love' is rarely enough to sustain a life-long, life-giving marriage.

I do think it's crucial for a man to be 'in love' with a woman, before she marries him. A man really needs to be 'into' a woman in order to be motivated to serve and lead her. But it's a bit different for women – in our case it's crucial to feel security, trust and respect for the man, above all else.

Let me draw your attention to Ephesians 5:33, which literally says that men need to **love** their wives, and wives need to **respect** their husbands. Do you see the difference? If you respect a man, and he's in love with you, your love for him will easily follow. But if you love him and don't respect him...you will end up mothering him, resenting him, or leaving him. The key is respect and trust. That's why so many girls prefer marrying older men – or have affairs with their bosses! Because nothing turns a girl on more than a man she respects.

So in conclusion, the question is flawed from the outset. These questions are more pertinent: Do you feel safe with this man? Do you seek his opinions and help? Would you feel content to be with him forever, and not be looking around for a better offer? Does he pursue, protect and provide? Are you clearly #1 in his life? Do you have shared values and goals? Can you trust him in the areas of life that are most important to you? If so...I'd say you're onto a good thing.

CHAPTER 33

Does it matter if we are from different cultures?

In this day and age, multiculturalism is normal and most of us are used to mixing with people of all different races and nationalities. You may have one or more friends who are from a different country and speak a different language to you. You may be from a mixed-race family yourself, or be living as an immigrant far from your original birthplace.

It's great to gain a more well-rounded view of the world in getting to know others who are different to you. However, when it comes to marriage, you must really think through the challenges that will occur in marrying someone from a different culture. Even if they have lived in your country for a long time, there will be certain cultural values ingrained into them because of their parents and grandparents, and their education. You might think some of these values are really 'cool', but can you live with them?

For example, it's invigorating to observe the openness in family relationships of people from Middle Eastern, Mediterranean and Latin American cultures – everyone shouting and laughing, hugging and kissing, and spending hours chatting (and arguing) over every meal. These are 'hot-blooded' people. Who wouldn't want that, right? Well, living with it could become a bit much if you are someone who is used to plenty of personal space, freedom to make your own choices, and an organised calendar.

Pacific Islanders, Indians, many Asian cultures and most tribal communities around the world have a much more tactile commitment to their aging relatives than Westerners. You could be expected to embrace multi-generational living, having grandparents, cousins and extended family moving in and out whenever necessary, or at the very least dropping into the house all the time. You will be expected to help care for these people, cook, clean, make space, and so on. Are you ok with that?

English people are very reserved, not overly emotional, and quite private. They might not reveal their deepest feelings, and will find it unnatural or rude to engage in conflict and connection in an overly emotional way. Will that bug you?

(Obviously I'm using generalisations and stereotypes here that won't apply to everyone. But it's worth considering!)

Apart from these superficial (but extremely relevant) aspects of culture, it is vital that you assess the deeper values and belief system of a man's cultural background. Western nations such as Australia, the USA, and the UK (among others) were founded on a Judeo-Christian worldview. Although many of these countries are now operating as secular and non-religious, the basis for their constitutions, laws, education and economic framework was originally the Bible. This affects everything, including health care, women's rights, protection of children, and employment freedoms, for example.

Areas of the world such as the Middle East, Africa, India, and South-East Asia were founded on different principles, therefore the psyche of the population is entirely different. Even if a man has lived in your country for a while, *he will still have his country's values ingrained in him*. A man who has truly given his life to Christ will be committed to learning new values that are Biblical, such as protecting women and children and treating all people with dignity and respect. Thus, he can overcome cultural values that are in opposition to Christian living. However, *this will not happen overnight*. Be wise, be careful, and take the rose-coloured glasses off.

If you are dating someone from a different culture, take time to understand what that means, and what his expectations will be of you and of himself if you get married. Meet his family and community and spend *lots* of time there (not just the weekend!), travel to his home-town, and observe him in various contexts. Be aware that the dating norms and typical marriage timeline of his people group may be different to yours. Watch how wives are treated in his community, and how he and his friends speak about women. Ask him his plans for the future.

Where will you live? Will you live there forever? How will you live? How will you spend your time? Who will earn money? Will you have any power in financial decisions? Who will care for the children? Will you use contraception? What are his sexual expectations? What are his views on fidelity? Will you access Western medicine? What kind of house will you have? Who will live in your house? Will you be free to visit your family and friends? Will you be permitted/expected to work after having children? Will you be number one in his life, or will his parents and family still have the final say? Where will you seek support if necessary? What will happen to you if you disrespect him or do not follow his wishes? Who will get legal custody of children if anything goes wrong? Are you fluent in each other's language? (Communication in marriage is already hard enough, without having to deal with language differences!)

Realise that your assumptions and his assumptions about these things will probably be quite different. You need to know what you are getting yourself into! Research, observe, ask questions, talk to other mixed-race couples, get couples counselling – do what you need to do to feel comfortable with your choice.

It's also important to assess how comfortable *he* is with dating someone of your culture. Does he take an interest in it? Does he want to learn about the history of your country, your customs, your language and your cultural norms? Does he show that he is willing and able to adapt to some of your preferences? Two people of different cultures getting married means that both of you will have a lot of adapting to do. It will take extra work and you will probably be surprised at how ingrained their (and your) values and customs are. So this option is not for the faint-hearted. Prepare to work hard and to change, a lot!

CHAPTER 34

What dating to marriage timeline should I expect?

This is a very pragmatic question, but an important one. Even though every relationship is different, a healthy one will follow a fairly routine path, with marriage at the end of it. You may not have had much relationship experience, or grown up around many healthy marriages – so you may not really know what it should look like. While I must include a disclaimer that no-one can really say what a romantic timeline should look like, and that every situation *is* different, I feel confident about offering you a basic breakdown of events. Furthermore, it strongly depends on your (and his) age. I'm assuming that many of you reading this are over 30, so let's look at the common timeline of a Christian couple in their 30's.

Phase 1: Early dating. 1-3 months duration.

In this phase, you are flirting, texting, going on dates, getting to know each other, and storing up fun and romantic memories. You have the chat where the relationship is defined. (Eg. 'Will you be my girlfriend?') A note on this: a man should define the relationship. If he's not making it clear, after 2-3 months you can ask him, 'Where do you see this going?' If he says, 'Oh, we are just playing it cool, getting to know each other', that's when you need to *pull back*. (Remember, guys always want what they can't have.) It is *not* your role to define the relationship or to ask a man to be your boyfriend.

However, there is an argument for a mature single woman to sweetly approach a mature single man she knows and to ask if he would like to go out for coffee (or similar) to get to know each other more. ONCE. This might kick start him a little bit, or at least let him know that you're interested (maybe you've been friends for years, but he didn't think he had a chance, or hasn't clicked that you'd be a great match). Then it is up to him.

Phase 2: Getting a little more serious. 1-8 months duration.

In this phase, you are meeting each other's families and friends. You're taking time and making plans to travel to meet distant relatives (rather than just coincidental hang-outs with family). You're meeting each other's colleagues and going to each other's churches, and becoming known publicly as a couple. If he's active on social media, he should have changed his 'relationship status' by now (again, that's his role, not yours!) – if he hasn't, don't say anything, but just play it cool and pull back a little. As Jane Bennett says in *Pride & Prejudice*[1], **let his behaviour be your guide.** You should probably be chatting now about the future – marriage, family values, where you'd like to live, and so on. If he's keen on you, he will be talking to you about this by now.

Phase 3: Engagement. 1-8 months duration.

If you're both over 30, he should pop the question within about a year of officially dating. If he doesn't, pull back a little bit. Go on a long holiday, without him. Answer his calls less, and don't agree to every date.

Suggest that you're thinking of dating other guys, if he's not serious yet. (That should freak him out, if he's into you.)

A true engagement should include a real ring (not one from a cereal box), and a public announcement. If he offers you some sort of weak semi-engagement, that *does not count*. He might not be that into you! Pull back! After the engagement, there's the wedding planning and deciding on where to live, etc. (Mainly this will be a time of saving money, asking for money, dealing with two sets of families, trying not to have sex, and experiencing major stress all round!)

Phase 4: Marriage.

So essentially, from first date to wedding day, if you're over 30 and both Christians, I would expect that the timeline would be anywhere from 3 to 19 months. If it's much longer than this, I would be wondering why. Unless there's an obvious reason, like wanting to save up a certain amount of money, issues with relocation for work, or wanting to finish a course of study before getting married (although sometimes these are just excuses), it would be pertinent to ask a few savvy friends and mentors about their thoughts on him 'dragging the chain'. It's possible that he's just not that into you – maybe he's just killing time with you while waiting for 'the one' to appear. In that case, sweetly and graciously step back – if he comes running for you, you'll know he's keen. (Under NO circumstances should you show him this book and say, 'Look, it's been 20 months; you're behind schedule!')

Remember – when a man realises he is about to lose something, it immediately forces him to evaluate its worth and value. For example, he may question himself: 'Is this just a convenience? A titillation? Or the woman I don't want to lose?' You have the power in the relationship because you are the (future) provider of all good things (i.e. sex). So don't be initiating the deep chats, defining the relationship, pressuring him into getting married, or nagging him about it. If he's taking too long and is being a bit flippant with you, just pull back and go underground for a bit, and see what he does. **If he wants you, he will come to you.**

Finally, as I said before, every timeline is different, every situation is different, and only you can decide what you want to do. I know girls who have written urgent letters to recalcitrant boyfriends (some then got married, and some got dumped), girls who have given ultimatums (and got married, or dumped), and girls who have proposed (and gotten married, and then divorced – NEVER, EVER PROPOSE). So it's up to you.

CHAPTER 35

It all sounds so hard – is it even worth it?

You know what? Relationships are really hard. Marriage is ugly as well as beautiful. **Knowing and being known is excruciating at times.** Losing your freedom and independence in many ways is frustrating. And don't get me started on having kids. That is really, really hard (as well as great). So you do have to wonder, is it worth it?

Well, here's the difficult truth of the matter. The creation account in Genesis 2 makes it pretty clear that women were designed to be help-meets to men, because it's not good for man to be alone. The thing is, **men need women.** Research shows that men are better off when they're married.[1] And if a man's wife leaves him or dies, it's very common for him to find a new woman pretty quickly. Men need women!

Think about it. Men without women are often 'lost'. Without a female influence or training, sometimes they can be uncivilized, unsociable, and clueless about domesticity and child-raising. They often prefer to take the easiest routes in life, and have very little motivation to improve themselves. They get sicker and die quicker. But with good women, men are both softened and strengthened, and can become wealthier, healthier and happier all round. **Women inspire men.** They help men. They give men a reason to be better. They provide children to the men so that their hard labour in the world is for something useful – maintaining a family. A woman gives a man purpose. And experts consistently point out that the best thing for the stability of a society is for men to be married, working, and raising families.[2]

But I suppose this leaves us with the question – **do women need men?** (Cue the cries of the feminists.) Well, yes and no. Also, it depends.

It depends on where you live. If you live in a first-world country where there are rights, welfare and education for women and children, and women are allowed to pursue a decent job and to keep their earnings and to own land, and there is proper health-care and childcare and a government pension, so that you are healthy enough and supported enough to actually have a job and pay your own way and live comfortably all the way to the end by yourself, then – not really. You can survive without a man.

It depends on where you see yourself in God's design for humanity. If you are a conservative Christian believer with a comfortable acceptance of the Biblical outline for female life, you may fully accept your role as being a man's helpmeet, and may be happy to live for that purpose. If you take issue with the purpose for which women seem to have been designed, you may prefer the modern, feminist approach and feel that marriage and family is inconsequential (or at least, that you shouldn't have to serve a man to follow God's plan). You may be so economically independent and enjoying your freedoms that you couldn't really be bothered surrendering to marriage.

It depends on how you define the purpose of marriage. In *The Book of Common Prayer*[3], widely used by the Church of England since the 16th century, marriage is proposed to meet the human needs and desires for sex, procreation of children, and companionship. So perhaps you only want marriage to fulfil one of these desires, or maybe all of them. There are other ways to get these needs met (some good and some not so good), so perhaps you don't want to go through the hassle of marriage to fulfil them.

It depends on whether you are under decent protection *from* men. If you're not, you are at risk of being a target for unhealthy men to mistreat, misuse or abuse you. You have to remember that whether or not you *want* a man around, there are men around. And unless they are all having their various needs met in appropriate ways, or they are as pure and kind as Jesus himself (which no man is), then you are at risk. So perhaps having a man's protection, from other men, could be useful for you.

And it depends on what makes your soul truly satisfied. And this is the kicker. The vast majority of women, across culture and across time, strongly desire to be attached to an appropriate male counterpart. Neither men nor women were designed to be alone. And although some women hate the idea of having to find companionship in marriage, the reality is that it's the most efficient, productive, natural, long-term solution to the deep disease of loneliness.

I'm reminded of the character of Jo March in Louisa May Alcott's magnificent book *Little Women* (1868)[4]. Jo is full of angst as her sisters are marrying off and 'leaving her', because she wants to maintain the familial joys of childhood forever. But alas, we all grow up. She struggles deeply with the cultural norms of her day, which leave women few options for adult life and survival beyond marriage or wealth. In a fit of anguish she cries: 'Women have minds and souls as well as hearts; ambition and talent as well as beauty, and I'm so sick of being told that love is all a woman is fit for. But…I am so lonely!'

Can you relate to Jo? I know I did. And it's true that women have minds, souls, ambitions and talents, and that they can use them for good purposes in the world. And if that satisfies you – go for it! But I wonder if there is still a longing deep inside you, for a husband. Perhaps you wish there wasn't!

Let me **shed some light** on this dilemma. According to the Genesis creation account, it's true that the woman was created for the man, to be his helpmeet and to help the man not be lonely anymore. That's not in question. We know that women operating in their Godly role are great for men, and that men need us. But why do *we* have such a strong urge to have husbands of our own?

I think I would need five PHDs to answer that question properly. There are so many reasons that are all caught up in our biology, anthropology, economics and socialisation. But apart from the big hole of loneliness inside that we all feel from time to time, I think one of the major drives for women to have their own man is that most women can't avoid feeling a deep, inner compulsion to apply their maternal instincts to the noble, challenging and life-lasting mission of mothering *their own children*. And to do this, we need men.

A husband provides not only the 'seed' to create a child, but within that, half of the genetic code for that child – a massive contributing factor to the very identity of your offspring. He provides physical and financial protection for you and the child, particularly in the vulnerable stages of pregnancy, breastfeeding and early childhood. And he provides friendship and companionship in his own masculine way – typically, not being as emotionally 'needy' as you, and therefore able to offer his strength and stability to you as you go through the emotional rollercoaster of marriage, motherhood and child-rearing.

This is how marriages have been playing out for millennia, and when it 'works', it works really well. Men and women have a complementary design as well as complementary spiritual roles and positions – so they really do just 'fit' together. Marriage and family life is about building something together – something timeless, meaningful and wonderful.

Part of the reason I'm writing this book, though, is because in the modern western world, these age-old understandings have been completely dismantled, and modern women are really confused. I don't know about you, but over the years I've received tons of mixed messages from educational institutions, books, the church, relatives, politics, society, and particularly the media, about what it means to be a 'woman'.

For example, the Disney kids' movie *Frozen* (2013)[5] was one of the first pop-culture stories that normalised the idea of women making their own way in the world, toying with romance, and *not getting married* (or coupled) *at the end*. This is an increasingly pervasive ideology, which without a doubt will affect future generations' perspective of marriage and family.

Think about how much things have changed in the last 100 years. It's now 'normal' for women to have children 'on their own' using anonymous sperm donors, for women to be 'self-partnered', or to live in lesbian relationships – which are all manifestations of **a rebellion against a woman's need to be vulnerable to a man.** We have completely done away with our 'need' for men. (It must feel weird to be a man these days.)

Sure, marriage is hard. In some ways, life *is* easier without a man. But we weren't designed to live alone, and we sure weren't designed to have children alone (just talk to the single mums you know – I can't think of a much harder job in life).

Although it's hard to hear, the reality is that there are no short-cuts or ways to 'beat the system'. If you're a Christian committed to Biblical values, and you want to have kids, you need to get married. If you want to have sex, you need to get married. If you want a man to protect and provide for you – get married.

Now, if you just couldn't be bothered, you realise you're too selfish, and don't think the sacrifice it is worth it, that's fine. **You are not mandated to marry.** You can serve God as you are, definitely. You can serve the world and change the course of society through your work and service. Or if you want, you can just live it up and enjoy a self-centred life! Not being married *does not make you a lesser being*. It does mean that as a Christian, you will be giving up certain privileges, like sex and biological children. And that is a heavy choice to make. But many women take this path. You wouldn't be alone.

Being unmarried is not wrong. In fact, it can give you more time to enjoy the presence and work of God. (Being married with kids takes up a lot of time and energy.) Think of nuns. Across time and culture, nuns are women who have given up the goals and privileges of sex, children and in many cases, private property and riches, to come under the covering of a church and to serve God and the community in selfless ways. (I think the 'covering' is key. The covering is what protects these special ladies from the evils and persecutions of the world.) And hey – just like Maria in *The Sound of Music* (1965)[6], maybe you'll commit to the path of singleness, and then fall in love with an amazing man way down the track, in the most unexpected way. That would be awesome!

I guess it comes down to how you want to use your **time, energy, and skills.** Do you (primarily) want to serve a husband and family, or do you want to serve the Church, or do you want to serve the world? (And no, they are not mutually exclusive!) Or – do you want to serve yourself?

Married women who happen to be reading this may be thinking – *Girls, marriage is not that great! I wish I was still free and single!* And again, here's the dilemma. There is no perfect life. There is no perfect situation. As soon as you grow up and start adulting properly, you will find that no matter which path you take, it's going to be hard. It's going to require personal sacrifice and a shouldering of responsibilities. You're going to see some of the shine come off of things, and realise that everyone is just doing the best they can with what they have, to struggle through the difficulties, boredom and the hard slog of life. But it's not something you can avoid forever. (Welcome to adulthood, yay!)

Which path will you choose? What realities are you ready to face? How will you meet your needs for companionship? It's up to you.

CHAPTER 36

Am I too broken to get married?

wonder if some of you are just too tired of it all to even bother trying anymore. Perhaps you have given your best to others for so long that you have nothing left. Maybe you are **worn out** by your job or your family dysfunction, or crushed by constant dating disappointment. You may have become too intimate with various boyfriends and feel that your love is all used up. Maybe you've been humiliated, betrayed or forgotten. If this is you, let me gently encourage you – your life is not yet over. Life is a long time. You can come through this wilderness and find meaning just over the horizon. I believe that **God has a bright future for you**. Please don't give up! Let me share some of my story with you again.

Just before meeting my now husband, I had gone through yet another relationship break-up with a man who just wasn't emotionally ready for marriage, and with whom I wasn't really compatible. I was 33 and was so disillusioned and exhausted. I was tired of dating, tired of trying, tired of the fear and the work and yawning dark chasm that seemed to be my future. And I basically had a meltdown. **For three days I prayed and cried to God** to give me a future, to show me the way and to give me a husband. I reminded God of his promise in Psalm 68:6, that he 'puts the lonely in families'. I called on his mercy and pleaded with him to remember me and to look after me. And I repented of my brokenness, promiscuous attitudes, social dysfunction and worldly thinking.

And you know what? **He heard me and he came through for me.** I don't know what battles were being waged on high on my behalf, but I am so relieved and grateful that the Lord saw me and heard my cry. I'm now happily married and am slowly recognising and taking hold of a new lease on life (although it's still hard to believe, sometimes!)

But here's the thing. I have all those **years of baggage** to contend with. Although I always tried to follow God and was fully committed to my faith, walking through the quagmire of modern womanhood with very little protection or helpful guidance from a local community of elders, has taken a huge toll on me.

Unless you live cloistered at home under the protection of your parents, use extreme self-discipline and/or don't take too many risks, it's a rare girl in her 30's (or older) who can still present a fresh face to the world. Western culture today, in the workplace, church, educational systems and the media, encourages women to strive, to take risks, to push themselves and to suck all the juice out of life. While there is a lot of excitement in this kind of living, I think it's hard to do this well long-term as a single woman, without pushing yourself over the edge.

Personally, and some of you might relate to this, I feel pretty **knocked around** from having had this lifestyle. I have quite a few regrets, a lot of sadness, emotional exhaustion, and some lingering anger about a lot of situations in my past. Mainly, I'm mad at myself. I feel foolish that I didn't have better boundaries, and ended up burning out in ministry. I wonder if I never should have moved away from my hometown and family. And I'm disappointed that I wasn't able to bring my best self to my husband. I even said to him on our second date, 'You don't want a girl like me. I'm tired, burnt-out, depressed and used up.' Thank the Lord, he saw through the muck and could still see the glimmer of light (my true self) poking out from the inside.

So, I've had some continuing work to do on myself. I'm still working through forgiveness for myself and others. Two things are helping me to do this:

1. **The forgiveness of God.**

   No one is too broken for God to redeem. No one has gone so far that there is no return. He is the ultimate long-suffering Father, who is waiting and ready to receive you back into his house, with great celebration.

   I'm reminded of the story of **the prodigal son**, told by Jesus in Luke 15:11-32. There are two sons – one is the perfect do-gooder, and the other is rebellious and runs off into the world. He wastes his dad's money, makes a fool of himself, and ends up in the mud with the pigs. He realises he has nowhere to turn, so he goes back home, with his tail between his legs, not sure what type of reception he'll receive. But his dad is absolutely overjoyed to see him. He doesn't worry about the mud on his son's clothing, or hassle him about where he's been and what he's done. He puts a celebratory robe on his back, gives him a special ring, and throws a party! 'For this son of mine was dead and is alive again; he was lost and now is found' (v. 24). What a picture!

   Did you realise that God feels that way about you? **If you're lost, or if you are 'dead' in sin – he will be ecstatic to welcome you back into the family, no matter what state you're in.** His love is big enough to cover your sin. When you repent, he doesn't even see your sin anymore!

   Here's a beautiful verse on which to meditate: 'Forget the former things; do not dwell on the past. See, I am doing a new thing! Now it springs up; do you not perceive it? I am making a way in the wilderness, and streams in the wasteland.' (Isaiah 43:18-19) This could be a scripture for you. The Lord wants to bring you through your wilderness, and to see you flourish. Believe it!

2. **The love of my husband.**

Like the Lord, my husband is long-suffering and patient with me. He uses heavenly eyes of wisdom to see through the 'mud' to the feminine spark that remains within me. Regardless of my dysfunctional patterns (we all have them), occasional anxieties and lingering moments of depression, he brings out the best in me by being a loving listener, strong visionary, and forgiving friend. He's not perfect and I also have space for *his* pain (very important in any partnership), but it has taken his soft heart and kindness to woo me back into a burgeoning self-acceptance and inner freedom.

None of this has been easy. **I don't want to sugar-coat it.** If you've been alone in the world for many years, by circumstances or your own choosing, it's possible that you also have some hardness, some failures and some regrets. But *it's not over for you.* God still loves you and sees you as **his beautiful daughter**. He still has good works for you to do. He still has things in store for you to enjoy and celebrate. (And I believe He has a good man ready to pursue you at the right time!)

May I share another lovely scripture with you from 2 Timothy 2. In this chapter, young Timothy is being exhorted by his mentor, the Apostle Paul, about how to be a good worker for the Lord. I think it relates to all of us.

'In a large house some dishes are made of gold or silver, while others are made of wood or clay. Some of these are special, and others are not. That's also how it is with people. **The ones who stop doing evil and make themselves pure will become special.** Their lives will be holy and pleasing to their Master, and they will be able to do all kinds of good deeds. **Run from temptations that capture young people.** Always do the right thing. Be faithful, loving, and easy to get along with. Worship with people whose hearts are pure. Stay away from stupid and senseless arguments. These only lead to trouble, and God's servants must not be troublemakers. They must be kind to everyone, and they must be good teachers and very patient.' (2 Timothy 2:20-24, CEV)

You see, the Bible gives us a clear way out of our problems. If we will run from temptation, seek to be pure, and repent of our sin, we can please God and be used for a special purpose. It does involve some action on our part – the action of **repentance**, which means turning around 180° and changing our behaviour. If we would only stop doing evil, everything would eventually sort itself out. **The tricky bit is figuring out what *is* evil.**

In our current culture, even the church is muddying the waters of what's right and wrong, and because we now have a very politically correct society, it's pretty hard to get any decent guidance – it's more popular to be told, 'You just need to figure out what is right for you.' Well, in some cases that's not helpful at all! On top of that, many of you reading this come from broken families in which you were not shown how to live in harmony with a spouse; families that may have been characterised by fighting and stress rather than belonging and acceptance. So it can be really confusing trying to figure out how to live in relationship, and you may doubt if you've got what it takes to overcome the disadvantages of your past.

But there is a way. We are not such great and mighty creatures that we can come up with our own moral compass or relationship methodologies (just look at the state of the world – that approach is clearly not working!) What we must do as Christians is to be constantly seeking to do God's will. **We must study the Bible; really study it, to know what his 'ways' are.**

I urge you to make a time in your week to meditate on Psalm 119, which is simply a gorgeous piece of poetry proclaiming the richness of knowing and following God's word. I particularly love verse 32: **'I run in the path of your commands, for you have set my heart free'**. (WEB) God's commands are so safe, so clear, and so life-giving that we can simply run along the path he has set out, knowing that it will lead us to freedom! Take time to learn his ways and commit to them.

(I remember a moment from my high-school teaching days when an 11th grade student who was always in detention burst into the room, declaring to his friends, 'Boys, I've figured it out! If you just follow the rules, you don't get in trouble!' He was truly amazed at this profound piece of wisdom he had finally discovered. But it makes sense – when you stick to doing things right, things will go well for you.)

May I exhort you with a final image. God made you. He loves you. He has not forgotten you. If you have strayed from the path, or collapsed on the path, He is there, ready to set you back on your feet and guide you in the right direction. Don't give up. Like the character of 'Christian' in the seminal Christian allegory *The Pilgrim's Progress* by John Bunyan (1678)[1], you can put the past behind you and move forward with the protection of the Word of God.

Christian may have entered the Valley of Humiliation overconfident and puffed up with false pride, but he departs with humble reliance on the Word of God and prayerful gratitude to the Lord of the Highway who has come to his aid and saved him from the Destroyer. He goes forward with his sword drawn. He has learned his lesson and now relies consciously on God's Word for protection.

It's not over for you yet, sister!

CHAPTER 37

What is the role of a Godly wife?

These days, while girls are great at being social workers, fashion designers and engineers, a lot of girls have literally no idea how to be a Godly wife. They have not grown up in traditional homes and observed traditional marriages and gender roles. And even if they have, culture has made this type of lifestyle seem so strange and different that no-one is really sure what's 'right' anymore.

This section assumes that as a committed Christian, you want to go into marriage prioritising the marriage relationship itself, and the strengthening of the interdependent relationships within the home and family. I believe this approach encompasses the Biblical understanding of a woman who takes on the commitment of being a wife.

Let me start by pointing out that being a 'wife' is very different to being a friend, flatmate, colleague, friend-with-benefits, girlfriend, or partner (even a co-habiting partner). **Being a wife is next level.** It's a legally, spiritually, financially, emotionally, sexually, socially binding role which carries a lot of weight. Being a wife is not for weaklings.

I warn you in advance – this topic could fill many books and there's no way I'm able to thoroughly cover the theological, sociological, anthropological, political, economic, cultural etc. aspects of this theme – and they are all open to interpretation! But I will share some of my thoughts with you in this long chapter, in the hopes that they will help to crystallise your own. I'm going to use a few sub-headings to help us stay on track.

1. **Your attitude as a wife**

What do you picture when you think of yourself as a wife? Cooking sumptuous meals in a cute little apron? Being escorted by your dashing husband to fabulous social events? Decorating your home just the way you like it, and not having to deal with annoying siblings or flatmates anymore? Being able to tick the 'husband' box and then get back to your corporate career? Take a moment to think about it.

For some girls, it can be tempting to see marriage as simply a means to an end – leaving the single life and finally getting 'off the shelf' – but becoming a wife is a complete vocation in itself. One definition for the word 'vocation' is: 'A person's employment or main occupation, especially regarded as worthy and requiring dedication.'[1] I love the use of the word 'dedication'. In my opinion, to at least have a chance at a successful marriage (because it takes two) and to be a good, Godly wife, you do need to dedicate yourself to the 'occupation' of wifehood. It doesn't just come naturally, and the older you are, the harder it can be, because you are so used to being independent and not having to consider a husband.

So, how does one go about preparing for this noble, Godly task?

Firstly, I must point out that wives in today's modern, western world are in a category of their own. To be honest, when I look at the way the wifely role is portrayed in most TV shows and movies these days, I'm not surprised that women are confused, and that many marriages are failing. The modern woman is often portrayed as a domestically lazy, professionally overworked, cynical, over-sexed, binge-drinking, manipulative, independent, ball-busting whiner who only cares about getting what she wants. You don't often see a character who is selfless, forgiving, modest, kind and respectful, and *available* to her family.

I love watching old classic movies like *The Swiss Family Robinson* (1960 version)[2] and *Seven Brides for Seven Brothers* (1954)[3]. And I've noticed that the way women and wives act in those old movies is very different to how women act today. The way those old-school women operated is incredible! They worked hard, like women today, but their work was generally focused on their home lives. (Sounds like Proverbs 31, especially verse 7.) They remained submitted to older couples and women who would show them the ropes. They were **strategic** in how they ran their marriages and families. They were thoughtful, purposeful and respectful in the way they communicated with their husbands. They realised that men and women were different, and that men needed to be treated with delicacy and tact, in order to get the best results for everyone. *They realised that the marriage and family would not manage themselves.*

These (fictional) women presented their best selves while remaining true to themselves and being mentally tough. They arranged their lives in such a way and took time for themselves so that they could be rested, properly dressed, and calm. They enforced appropriate personal boundaries without being shrewish and demanding. They were emotionally resilient, and they were verbally **gracious**. (Otherwise known as 'manners'.) They were committed to their situation and made the best of it. <u>They knew they were fortunate to have a committed man to run the family.</u> And they really knew how to play the long game!

I find it helpful to observe visual representations like these, along with real-life 'role models' (who are yours?) to help me understand how to behave as a wife, not just to figure out what's 'right', but to figure out what *works*. There's no point getting married if you're going to make a huge mess of it. That's just painful for everyone.

And underpinning all this, of course, is what the Bible says about being a wife – there's quite a lot! When I look at women in the Old Testament, which was in many ways a very primitive and brutal time, I learn about how to 'survive' as a woman in tough circumstances (like we discussed in Chapter 19). But the actual advice about what a Godly wife should look like is located more often in Proverbs and the New Testament. Let's have a look at a couple of the key passages. The obvious place to start is in Proverbs 31.

> **Proverbs 31:10-31:**
> *¹⁰A wife of noble character who can find?*
> *She is worth far more than rubies.*
> *¹¹ Her husband has full confidence in her*
> *and lacks nothing of value.*
> *¹² She brings him good, not harm,*
> *all the days of her life.*
> *¹³ She selects wool and flax*
> *and works with eager hands.*
> *¹⁴ She is like the merchant ships,*
> *bringing her food from afar.*
> *¹⁵ She gets up while it is still night;*
> *she provides food for her family*
> *and portions for her female servants.*
> *¹⁶ She considers a field and buys it;*
> *out of her earnings she plants a vineyard.*
> *¹⁷ She sets about her work vigorously;*
> *her arms are strong for her tasks.*
> *¹⁸ She sees that her trading is profitable,*
> *and her lamp does not go out at night.*

19 In her hand she holds the distaff
and grasps the spindle with her fingers.
20 She opens her arms to the poor
and extends her hands to the needy.
21 When it snows, she has no fear for her household;
for all of them are clothed in scarlet.
22 She makes coverings for her bed;
she is clothed in fine linen and purple.
23 Her husband is respected at the city gate,
where he takes his seat among the elders of the land.
24 She makes linen garments and sells them,
and supplies the merchants with sashes.
25 She is clothed with strength and dignity;
she can laugh at the days to come.
26 She speaks with wisdom,
and faithful instruction is on her tongue.
27 She watches over the affairs of her household
and does not eat the bread of idleness.
28 Her children arise and call her blessed;
her husband also, and he praises her:
29 "Many women do noble things,
but you surpass them all."
30 Charm is deceptive, and beauty is fleeting;
but a woman who fears the Lord is to be praised.
31 Honour her for all that her hands have done,
and let her works bring her praise at the city gate.

This scripture really packs a punch, doesn't it! I know a lot of women who struggle with Proverbs 31. This woman just seems too perfect! But you know what? She didn't necessarily do all of these things at the same time, or achieve all of these states of being and good attitudes all at the same time. If you look at this passage as describing the lifetime journey of a woman as a wife and mother, it becomes a bit easier to understand. And – with the help of the Holy Spirit, some good strategies, and some relational savvy, it is possible to be like this woman. I know a number of older ladies who could be described as 'Proverbs 31' women…so it can be done!

I encourage you to take a pen and jot down some notes next to each portion of the scripture above. Have a think about what the various skills and attitudes might look like in our day and age, and take note of which areas you already excel in, and other areas in which you could improve.

Here's another great scripture to give us some advice on how to be a Godly wife:

> **Titus 2:3-5:**
> [3] *Likewise, teach the older women to be reverent in the way they live, not to be slanderers or addicted to much wine, but to teach what is good.*
> [4] ***Then they can urge the younger women to love their husbands and children,***
> [5] ***to be self-controlled and pure, to be busy at home, to be kind, and to be subject to their husbands, so that no one will malign the word of God.***

The key characteristics I want to point out in this passage are purity of spirit, self-control and submission. You see, a married, Godly woman *submits herself* not just to the role of 'wife', but to the <u>actual man</u> she is married to. It is a laying down, a surrendering, a dying to self – an opening up and a humbling towards her man. A Godly wife allows herself to be led by her Godly husband (even though he's not perfect). Just think about this for a minute. Modern women are celebrated for being wild and free, boundary-less, self-centred, outspoken and even obnoxious. But this is not how the Bible teaches women to be. Sure, I realise that extreme feminism is a knee-jerk reaction to the poor state of masculinity in our society – but it's still not the right approach, and it doesn't get the right results (pop quiz: are the feminists happy?)

By the way, did you know that this is all just a result of the Fall of man in the Garden of Eden? In the second part of Genesis 3:16, when God is doling out the consequences for Adam & Eve eating the fruit, Eve is told: 'Your desire shall be for your husband, and he shall rule over you.' Some commentators interpret this to mean that there will always be the potential for conflict within the marriage relationship, because Eve will <u>want</u> Adam to lead her, but will *resent* him leading her – and as a result, Adam will become either too domineering (to force her to follow), or will give up and become passive, letting Eve lead (which deep down she actually doesn't want to do).[4]

Do you see this happening in marriages all over the place? I do! So many women are always complaining – either their man is too overbearing, inflexible, or even abusive (hence many wives understandably leave their marriages), or he is too passive, weak, or uninspiring (leading to many wives being eternally frustrated and trying to manage the family on their own). So you see, because of sin, it's pretty hard to find the right balance as a wife. We have this internal struggle; we want to lead *and* we want to follow, and we just can't be satisfied. Men aren't perfect and they don't always lead us exactly where we want to go, in the way we want to be led…but we still want them to try. (It must be tough being a guy these days.) All that to say - being a 'satisfied wife' is an incredible life goal – put it on your bucket list!

Finding the right balance obviously depends a great deal on the quality of husband you have, and whether he has accepted and grown into his proper masculine role, *but* it also depends a lot on how you strategically relate to your husband, in order to help him become his best self (which will benefit you as well). This is why it is key to study the scriptures, to educate yourself about gender differences (yes, they are real), and to learn some relationship skills, so that you are best prepared for marriage.

It's also super helpful to develop an 'attitude of gratitude'. No, you're not going to have the ideal husband. No, you're not going to get everything you want in life. But can you choose to be grateful for what you do have, and what you do get? Life is full of major suffering, for many people around the world. Having a husband who doesn't necessarily get everything right all the time is a small issue in the grand scheme of things. So have a think about your current attitude towards men and marriage, and consider whether or not you need a perspective shift.

2. **Your influence as a wife**

I think being a <u>Godly</u> wife is about two things: **service and support**. In Genesis 2:18, the woman created for Adam is described as his 'ezer kenegdo' – his strong helper, a companion who complements him perfectly, who is the right fit – like a key in a lock. So the wife is essentially in a service position; a complementary role to the man's directive leadership. The man provides the **headship** role for the family, as described in 1 Corinthians 11:3: 'But I want you to realize that the head of every man is Christ, and <u>the head of the woman is man</u>, and the head of Christ is God.'

Words like 'headship' and 'leadership' can be pretty loaded, so you might feel more comfortable with the word 'covering' instead. The husband covers the wife, spiritually and physically. He is responsible for her and will one day answer to God about how well he stewarded her. The wife comes 'under' the husband. A good husband will cherish his wife and make her life more comfortable, more fulfilling, and more fun.

I think a lot of women throughout history and today are terrified of being a 'submissive wife' type. They have conflated the idea of 'submission' with women they've seen or heard about who live in terribly oppressive domestic scenarios. And it's true that a percentage of women do end up in difficult situations, depending on their choice of husband, or perhaps their cultural context. However, this is not because the 'Biblical wife' approach is flawed. **It's because humans are flawed.** Obviously, the type of man you choose to marry is going to have a major impact on your experience as a wife.

The concept of submission goes both ways, and being a wife is not about losing all your freedoms or ability to have your own will and your own mind. In fact, the Apostle Paul encouraged Christians to 'submit to one another out of reverence for Christ' (Ephesians 5:21). It's not just about the wife submitting to the husband, but about two Christ-followers humbling themselves before the Lord and putting the other person first, out of love, in a kind of symbiotic and mutually beneficial partnership.

As soon as you become a wife, your life is no longer about you. You start to take on some responsibility for the health and happiness of your husband – and he starts to take on some responsibility for yours. It's what's called an 'interdependent' relationship (which is what makes it different to a flatmate relationship). It's (ideally) a collaborative, back-and-forth, influencing-each-other type of symbiotic dance.

In marriage, **you are essentially a 'mirror' for the other person**. You can reflect back to them their good and bad parts, and what you choose to reflect back to them actually helps to shape them further as a person, and grow you together as a couple. (Or kill the relationship.) For example, if you are always criticizing your husband, and focusing on what's wrong or lacking (in your opinion), the marriage will start to shut down. He will no longer want to show you the good parts of himself, because he will lose any motivation to do so (seeing as they are not 'good enough' for you). And he won't be too keen to point out and celebrate *your* good parts, either. So the negativity cycle will spiral from there.

Marriage expert Dr John Gottman teaches that for a relationship to be healthy, there needs to be a certain ratio of positive to negative interactions across the day.[5] He believes that the 'magic ratio' is 5:1 – meaning that for every one negative interaction you have, you need to have five positive ones. His studies have indicated that marriages with higher negativity ratios than this often end in divorce. So being positive towards your husband is key. (Seems obvious. This would be a good time to go and read 'The Five Love Languages' by Gary Chapman.[6])

Interestingly though, using the mirror analogy, if you only reflect the good parts, the marriage will become flat and superficial. Gottman goes on to explain that too much positivity (described by some psychologists as 'toxic positivity'[7]) can also lead to the failure of the marriage – because the marriage is too shallow, and is based on denial of what's really going on emotionally for either or both parties. True relationship involves truth. Without revealing your own negative feelings, your desire for certain things to be different, or your constructive criticisms containing ideas for improvement, you're not bringing your whole self to the marriage, nor are you giving the marriage the 'oxygen' it needs to give it some movement and life. The marriage simply can't grow, so it remains stunted and unfulfilling.

You may be in a dating relationship or have a history of relationships in which **everything looks good on the surface**, but as soon as conflict arises, the relationship hits a stalemate. But all good relationships need to include healthy conflict in order to grow – so make sure you are learning how to do conflict well, and that you choose a husband who is mature enough to engage in conflict with you! (Go back and re-read Peck's 'stages of community' in Chapter 2.)

As a wife, you are in the unique position of **strategically reflecting back** to your husband good and bad parts of himself (and yourself) that can literally make or break the marriage. And therein lies your power as a wife. **Being a wife is not a powerless position** – in fact, it's one of the most powerful roles that anyone can have. You can tell when a man has an awful wife – he becomes a shell of himself. And likewise, when a man has a great wife, he becomes confident, successful, and happy.

You see, power is influence. As a wife, you have a huge influence not only on how your husband lives and on who he becomes, but on your children, too. Have you ever heard the saying, 'The hand that rocks the cradle rules the world'? Being in a position of influence within the domestic sphere, while it may at times seem mundane and unappreciated by the world at large, is actually one of the most powerful positions any person can have in this life.

This is where **'the art of being a woman'** comes into play. (This is an art which has largely been lost in our generation.) A smart and wise woman, led by the Holy Spirit, self-aware, prepared and attentive, **will influence her husband towards behaviour and decisions that are for the benefit of the whole family.** She will not do this in a harsh manner, like a steam-roller, nor will she demand her rights and belittle her husband until she has worn him down. She will not do it through playing a victim or martyr role, by guilt-tripping him, giving him the silent treatment, or making emotional ultimatums. She will be strategic, reasonable, compassionate, kind, tough and patient. And with practice, prayer and preparation, she will be able to have a very significant voice in the family unit.

3. Your responsibilities as a wife

When you take on a position of employment with an organisation, you don't just get a name badge that says 'employee' and then get to stay home and watch TV in your pyjamas. No, you actually have to go to work, and work! You have certain obligations to fulfil. Marriage is the same. When you take on the role of 'wife', it comes with its own (gigantic) set of responsibilities. Eek!

Before you break out in a cold sweat, I think it might help to remember that the marriage relationship is, on some levels, **transactional**. Both people should benefit from the marriage situation (otherwise, why do it?)

Think about the vows made at a wedding – one person says, 'I promise to do ABC' and the other person says, 'I promise to do XYZ'. No woman in her right mind would go into a marriage where the husband vows: 'I promise to be a lazy slob, to never talk to you, to mistreat you, to pay no attention to the kids, and to cheat on you whenever I want.' And no man in his right mind would go into a marriage where the wife vows: 'I promise to let myself go, to never put any effort into my appearance, to constantly nag and criticise you, to cook terrible food, to put all my time and energy into my job and my friends and not into the family, and to constantly compare you to the better men I see on a regular basis.' Do you see what I'm getting at? Both parties enter a marriage with the hope and desire not just to bring their best selves to the relationship, but also to receive a huge level of love, support, appreciation, attention and fidelity.

So being a wife is a huge responsibility. **It's foolish to think you can just secure a man and then go off and do your own thing, while living together.** The whole point of marriage is to go on the adventure of life together – not two separate adventures! This is where feminism has made things a bit tricky. Many modern girls have their own dreams and goals <u>that they believe should supersede those of the husband</u>. And many modern men have given up and accepted this, too, and end up taking a passive role in the marriage. News flash: this approach doesn't work long term. Women eventually despise passive men, and men are turned off by masculine women.

If you want to attract a real man, you have to realise that you need to be a real woman. A woman who is wife material is someone who is ready to serve and support a man in his grand adventure. I know that this is hard to swallow, but that's just because feminism has so indoctrinated our education and church institutions that we can't imagine a life where we have 'no identity' of our own. Well, here's something to chew on – being a wife (and mother) is a huge, valid, and important identity. As I've pointed out, women have incredible power over <u>the direction of culture</u>, from right within the home!

Can you be a wife and still be a teacher, an accountant, or a chef, and find meaning in outside work? Sure. Can you still have your own friends and do things that you like to do? Sure. **But when you get married, your number one priority needs to be the marriage.** If it isn't, there will be consequences. I'm not trying to freak you out; I'm sharing these thoughts so that you can start to tweak your ideas of marriage, and get emotionally prepared for what it's really about.

The way I see it, the husband is like the **CEO**, providing vision, direction, and resources to direct the energies of the company (the family). He also holds the final responsibility for whether it succeeds, and has to answer to God (who is like the **board of investors**) for his stewardship of the people under his care. The wife is like the **general manager**, organising, allocating, scheduling, delegating, and looking after the people below her (the kids). She gets her general direction from the CEO, but has freedom to arrange how it all works. She appeals to the CEO when anything is too tough, and he helps resource her or redirect when necessary. This is how the family unit is supposed to work.

The reason why this is different to a **cohabiting partner relationship** is that two people living together (who aren't married) are more like **colleagues**. They have a general consensus on how things should be done, have things in common, and work towards shared goals. It's likely that one of them will take on a bit more of a leadership role in the relationship (sometimes the woman!), but it does look very different to a real marriage. (And what happens when they have kids?)

I think a successful marriage works because the husband is under the authority of Christ, and the woman, being under the headship of the husband, is thereby **protected and led** in a responsible Christian manner. A Christian woman can pray and petition the Lord to intervene on her behalf when there are difficult situations – *and He will*. She has an 'upline' beyond her husband, and there is great security in that.

In a healthy marriage, when kids come along, they can see and understand **the proper line of authority** in the home. And trust me, kids actually love the boundaries and safety provided by having a strong leadership structure in their parents. Having a dad and mum who work as a team, with dad as the boss, makes kids feel really safe.

There are tons of responsibilities for wives – mainly, looking after your husband, kids and home. **Any woman who neglects these duties is not pulling her weight.** In the next chapter we'll look at some of the practical tasks you'll need to do on a regular basis, and how to prepare for these.

Let me conclude with a final caveat: you don't *have* to get married. As long as you have a decent job, somewhere to live and someone to help protect you in tough times, you can potentially live a very enjoyable and fruitful life as a single woman (or a serial dater, although I don't recommend that!). Marriage is a lot of hard work. Are you up for it?

CHAPTER 38

How do I succeed at home-making?

L et's turn now to some of the more **practical ways you can prepare** for wifehood. To be honest, along with everything we've already discussed, I really think that **attentiveness, humility and fidelity** are the key elements to set you up for success. If you have those, this other stuff doesn't matter too much. But it will certainly make both of your lives a lot easier if you have some practical skills in the following areas. And of course, I must point out that every culture and every family has a different way of organising the family structure and household roles. You and your husband should discuss these responsibilities and come up with a realistic 'plan of attack'. Because these jobs do have to get accomplished!

1. **Cooking.**

Although the modern woman may feel that her competence in the boardroom sets her apart from the kitchen, she couldn't be more wrong (unless she's really rich). **Everyone has to eat**, and someone has to cook. In most homes around the world, that someone is YOU – the wife. Just because you work (if you work), it doesn't mean you get a free pass from doing anything at home. You will have to cook, so you may as well learn how to do it, and learn to like it. It is **your responsibility** to ensure that your family is fed. Whether you like it or not, it's a major part of your role and cannot be ignored. Have you heard the old saying – *the way to a man's heart is through his stomach*? Well, it's partially true. Men love food, and they love good food. So get good at cooking!

Think about it – say you get married at age 30 and live until you are 90. That's up to 60 years of cooking (or about 22,000 dinners)! And that's not including breakfast, lunch, snacks, and hosting parties and events!

If you need help in this area, watching the fancy cooking shows on TV, while they are interesting, is probably not going to teach you the basics. No one can afford to eat like that every night (and the washing up would send you mad). **You don't need to be a *chef*, but a *cook*.** A chef is for fine dining; a cook is for serving up regular hot meals to average people, using everyday ingredients and sticking to a budget. If you're just starting out in your cooking journey, the best thing to do would be to get a simple cookbook and start practicing some of the basic meals that most people like – pasta dishes, curries, meat and vegetables, and so on. There may be certain recipes that are staples in your culture, so focus on those ones.

Grocery shopping can be an enjoyable activity, and I suggest you create a loose menu plan for the week, write up the list of necessary ingredients, and then go shopping just for what you need. It's a much more efficient and cost-effective way to stock up on food. Try various supermarkets and local markets to see what your options are in terms of value for money. If you're really pressed for time, you can always place a regular online order and get your groceries delivered to your house, for a small fee.

The only way to get out of being the regular household cook is to arrange a cooking roster with your husband, order in pre-packaged meals, eat takeout every night, or get a personal chef. In some homes, the husband will do all the cooking and you will do some other type of work around the house. The point is: you do have to eat somehow! (And I think men like it when their wives cook for them. There's just something nurturing and homely about it, isn't there?)

2. **Cleaning.**

Again, unless you can afford a regular cleaner, guess who will be cleaning the family home? You! If you never had to do regular chores when you were growing up, you may have never cleaned a toilet in your life. Maybe it just magically got cleaned every week and you never gave it a second thought. But guess what? The cleaning fairy is not going to live at your house. So you will have to do it yourself.

The main things you (or someone) will need to do **regularly** (besides grocery shopping) are:

o   Clean the toilet and the bathroom sink.
o   Scrub the shower/bath.
o   Vacuum and mop the floors.
o   Wash and hang out the clothes, sheets, towels etc.
o   Fold the clothes, sheets, towels etc.
o   Iron the clothes.
o   Wash the dishes and clean the kitchen (EVERY NIGHT).
o   Empty the bins.
o   Tidy up.

Other jobs you'll need to do less regularly include:

o   Cleaning the windows.
o   Getting cobwebs off the ceiling.
o   Dusting.

o   Sweeping the entrance/outdoor areas.

o   Cleaning out and rearranging drawers.

o   Beating the rugs.

o   And depending on where and how you live: gardening, mowing, shoveling snow, repairing fences, etc. Hopefully your husband will do this!

o   Etc.

Ideally, you will be able to allocate some jobs to your husband to do. **Men prefer projects with a clear goal**, rather than ongoing small tasks. For example, if a man knows he has to wash the dishes every night, he is prepared and he can see a clear start and finish to the job. Whereas 'cleaning out and rearranging drawers' is a bit vague and probably totally un-motivating to a man. So **ask him** what he would like to do to help you. (If he does it differently to you, or slower, **be smart** and say nothing except 'thank you' at the end. Otherwise you'll end up doing everything yourself!) And if you've never done some of these jobs, <u>learn how to do them</u>. You're tough, you're smart, and you're tenacious (you got a degree, didn't you?) You can learn how to clean a toilet.

Cooking and cleaning are the two biggies, and don't be naïve - they *do* take up a lot of time each week. You have to factor them into your life. They don't always show you those things on the rom-coms – but they are a huge part of marriage. Many ongoing household arguments are based on the logistical difficulties of getting the cooking and cleaning done (and who should be doing it), so it's best to discuss this prior to marriage and to work out some realistic systems.

Apart from cooking and cleaning, here are some **various skills** that are useful to have up your sleeve when you get married (particularly once you have kids):

- **<u>Listening</u>, making conversation, laughing, caring and hugging (these are vital!)**
- Sewing on a button. (Men love this. It's equivalent to how you feel about him changing a car tyre. Swoon.)
- Filling out forms and paying bills.
- Budgeting.
- Selecting and signing up for various insurances.
- Organising maintenance people to come and fix broken appliances in the home.
- Hosting and entertaining in a gracious and generous manner.
- Tastefully decorating the home.
- Giving and receiving gifts, planning birthday parties, and organising events.
- Researching and organising holidays.
- Caring for pets.
- Maintaining and cultivating a calendar of tasks and social events (this becomes a massive job once you have school-aged children).
- Organising appointments of all kinds for yourself, husband and children.
- Knowing how to dress for various occasions.
- Plus of course the gigantic responsibility of raising children!

Does this sound like a **1950's domestic science class**? Probably, and modern women might frown at these lists. But you know what? Even the feminists who are married (or cohabiting) end up doing this stuff in the home. Someone has to do it! And if you want to bring honour to your husband and be an asset to him (from which you will also benefit), then get some of these skills up your sleeve before you get married. He'll be so blessed!

If you are feeling a bit uptight about what you're reading, and thinking that it seems **oppressive to women**, please remember that *you don't have to get married.* Or, you could get married and have a 'modern family'. But I wonder, will you be fully outworking the wifely role that God has gifted to you? Will you be helping your husband become all that he can be? Will you have a happy home? (This includes the happiness of the husband and kids, not just yours!)

Or will you be living **mainly for your own pleasures** and advancing yourself, at your husband's (and children's) expense? *It's not all about you!*

All I suggest is that you study the Bible to understand the great mystery of the marriage relationship. I absolutely concur that it is the man's role to be primarily responsible for the family and to lay down his life (and lifestyle) if necessary, like Christ did for his bride, the Church. And I also acknowledge that unfortunately, no man on earth is quite like Christ! (You can always be a nun, remember.) **But if you choose to marry, and you want your marriage to be glorious, it makes sense to follow Biblical wisdom…which gives you the best chance of success!**

Surround yourself with older married couples you respect. Be in their homes. Watch how they communicate, how they fight, how they repair hurts, how they forgive. Glean from the older wives and ask them for their best advice. Learn about their household management and weekly routines, and what they have found works best. Seek to understand the nuances of marital conflict, marital fidelity, and friendship in marriage. Read every Christian marriage book you can get your hands on. (There are heaps listed in the back of this book.) **Learn, learn, learn!**

Even though it takes decades to master being a 'wife' (and I'm not sure you can ever reach 'success'), it is something that can be learned. Imagine you were about to climb Mt Everest. Would you just wait until the day of the hike, without planning or preparing in any way? Of course not! Knowing how intense and serious the task would be, you would be doing as much research, training, practice and knowledge-building as you could. Marriage is the same. Don't think to yourself, 'Ah, I'll just wing it. We love each other, and that's the main thing, right?' Um – wrong! (Marriage is actually really hard!)

Don't rely on your future husband to clean up your messes and drag you into a suitable starting position. And remember, he will have his own issues to bring into the marriage. You better toughen up and get ready to face them. **Present yourself as a trained, equipped, prepared lady of dignity and strength, ready to embark on the great adventure of marriage.** A Godly man looking for a Godly wife will see this and appreciate it.

And for the modern career woman, here are three more things you can do now that will help you a lot when you get married:

1. **Save money.** If you are an older single, by the time you get married you might want to start having kids straight away. This means that you'll potentially be switching to one income for a time – and it's not easy to live a middle-class lifestyle in the western world on one income. Save money while you are single, so that you can afford to pay for a wedding or a house deposit (or both) as soon as you get engaged. That said, I wouldn't bring it up on a first date! You don't want a man who is only marrying you for your money – that would be weird.

2. **Build your tribe.** Every woman needs a good circle of friends, and when you're married you will lean on these friendships for shared laughter, tears and advice. Men are different to women and marriage won't be the same as living in your fun girls' share-house. You will need to continue your friendships, in order to survive! Women need community – so build it now.

3. **Enjoy your time building intimacy with Christ, and learning about who you are as a daughter of God.** As a single woman,

I spent many years doing intensive Bible study (including Bible college), daily devotions, running Bible study groups, attending myriad church events, conferences and worship nights, going to spiritual retreats, and basically just having plenty of time to journal and to pray whenever I wanted to. I also read a lot of Christian books about relationships and being a Godly woman. All of this learning and growing and *time* soaking in God's presence and teachings has helped me so much as I have entered marriage and family life. I don't have nearly as much time or energy to focus on Bible reading and prayer as I used to – and I'm so grateful that I 'schooled' myself while I had time, and built a real depth of relationship in my faith walk that I've been able to lean on during these busy seasons. So enjoy your time with the Lord. It's like a honeymoon period, or like those few years at college where you have time to ponder the big questions of life (before starting the 9-5 grind!)

CHAPTER 39

What about sex?

There's sex in marriage, and there's sex outside of marriage. That pretty much covers it. But within that, there may be some nuanced questions that plague you from time to time, such as:

- How far is too far?
- What counts as 'sex'?
- How do I fulfil my sexual desires if I'm not married?
- What if I'm dying for physical touch?
- How do I recover from a broken sexual relationship?
- Should I disclose my sexual past to a new boyfriend?
- How do I come to terms with having had an abortion?
- Will not being a virgin ruin my chances of a Christian marriage?
- Won't it be awkward to get married and go on a honeymoon with no sexual experience?
- Will my health issues interfere with my sex life in the future?
- If I know I can't have children, do I have to tell my boyfriend?
- How do I cope with people's opinions about my virginity or lack of?
- Will I die a virgin?

These questions are huge. Sex is a massive, complex, polarizing topic, so I recommend you do some serious Bible study on the subject as well as get your hands on some of the great resources I'll list below. In this chapter, I'm just going to give a cursory answer to each of the above questions. (Please note that I'm only one person with one set of knowledge and experience. Take responsibility for seeking the correct Biblical approach yourself, and of course seek counsel from a GP, gynaecologist, sex therapist or psychologist as needed.) And beyond that, just use your common sense.

Modern culture has let sex out of the box, and we are reaping the consequences. Look down your street, turn on the TV, or read a magazine to see how screwed up we are now that sex has been commercialized, cheapened, exposed and exploited. It's a disaster out there. Don't become a statistic!

Question 1: how far is too far?

Although you think you will marry the guy you are currently dating, it's quite possible that you won't. And if you don't, would you feel awkward or ashamed describing your current physical intimacies with your future husband, when you do get married? If so – it's too far. There's a broad spectrum when it comes to Christians' views on what you're 'allowed' to do sexually before marriage. Deep conservatives would suggest that anything beyond holding hands is too much for dating couples. Some of these couples even save their first kiss for marriage. More liberal Christians might be comfortable with heavy kissing and 'petting'.

As a broad rule of thumb, I would suggest that anything involving fondling of private parts (even on top of clothing) is definitely too far. And let's just say it's best to leave a margin before you are going to fall off the cliff! Keep your wits about you and set up some practical rules to stop you going too far. My favourites are: don't be in a bedroom together with the door closed, don't be home alone together, have a 10pm curfew (nothing good happens after 10pm), and don't do unchaperoned sleepovers (and definitely not in the same room or bed!).

The further you go sexually with a man, the further you will probably go with your next boyfriend…and your next…and your next. Will there be any of you left to give to your future husband? Each time you 'bond' with someone and then are ripped apart, your ability to bond becomes weaker and weaker (like an over-used piece of sticky tape). If you want to have a close relationship with your husband, you need to 'save your sticky'.

Question 2: what counts as 'sex'?

This is really subjective. But if it involves the removal of clothes, activities that would make your Sunday School teacher faint if she walked in on you, or anything that makes you scared of getting pregnant – you're in sex territory!

Question 3: how do I fulfil my sexual desires if I'm not married?

This is another subjective one, which can be controversial. The thing is, until your libido is awakened, try to leave it dormant! (Song of Solomon 8:4) Don't go stirring it up or getting yourself all hot and bothered for nothing. This includes not going down the path of provocative movies, books, images, clothing, social media pages, and so on. It will take some discipline. Also, you could use physical activity to burn off all your energy in healthy ways, like team sports, high-impact training, or endurance challenges. Keep yourself busy and tired.

Some girls do masturbate to keep sexual tension at bay. This is not talked about much, but it is common among women as well as men. My take on it is that there's nothing in the Bible to explicitly condemn masturbation, although some would argue it counts as 'fornication' or 'sexual immorality', which is mentioned a lot in Scripture. As in all things, you need to follow your own conscience. With this in mind, acknowledge that your vagina is a very special and sensitive part of the body, and needs to be treated with dignity and care. Don't compromise your physical (or spiritual) health.

There is nothing wrong or evil about your body or your sexual desires. You don't need to live with shame and guilt for feeling sexually aroused or unfulfilled – we are sexual beings, after all. Our bodies are ready for sex from our late teens onwards. So getting married and becoming sexually active at, say, 35, means you've been putting sex on hold for 20 years! I'm not sure this was God's original plan for the body – it seems unnatural. The current late age of marriage is not too helpful for Christians! But if you've waited – well done.

The best way to deal with sexual frustration is to get married. As the Apostle Paul says, 'It's better to marry than to burn with passion.' (1 Corinthians 7:9) So don't delay!

Question 4: what if I'm dying for physical touch?

All of us are designed for human connection. We were not designed to live alone, to be alone, to not get regular hugs, and to not have a family around us to soften the harshness of life. And if you're someone who really loves physical touch, being single may be really hard for you. (If you have been alone for awhile, you probably either crave touch because you have a deficit, leading to promiscuous behaviour; or you have hardened yourself against the pain and don't feel anything when someone touches you.)

Here's what I recommend: live with other people. Develop a 'sisterhood'. Be open to people offering you a kind touch or hug. Be huggable – smell nice and brush your teeth! Get yourself a cuddly pet like a cat or dog. Volunteer to help hold the babies in the mother's room at church. Get regular massages. Visit your family often and get hugs from your parents and siblings. If you're desperate, pull out your old teddy bear. And if you feel sucked into a bad relationship just for the touch aspect – high-tail it out of there and go stay with a huggy friend or relative for a month!

Question 5: how do I recover from a broken sexual relationship?

The same way you recover from anything – time, attention to the wound, a change of pace and routine, care and support, and a recalibration of activities. You may need to spend a decent amount of time in prayer and reflection to let the Holy Spirit wash you clean of any shame and guilt you feel. You may need to see a counsellor to work through the grief of the break-up, or your anger at your ex. You may need to get checked by your doctor to make sure you don't have any lingering physical damage (sexually transmitted infections are prolific in our promiscuous culture). You may need to do some journaling or letter-writing to process the relationship and find closure. You may need to take a break from dating to give your heart time to heal. What you must *not* do is ignore the pain, brush it off, and jump into another sexual relationship just to feel better. That's a long road to a very painful existence.

And a word on sexual abuse: if you have been the victim of sexual assault, abuse or rape in your past, it is highly probable that this will have a deep and complex impact on your future sex life. Sex is a profound physiological act, and when this is combined with feelings of being violated, powerless, and unprotected, it usually leads to deep trauma. The body 'holds' onto trauma at a cellular level[1], so it's possible that even if you think you're 'over it', your body will balk when it comes to sex with your new husband. I recommend seeing a counsellor to work through the subconscious and conscious trauma of these tragic events in your past, prior to getting married.

Question 6: should I disclose my sexual past to a new boyfriend?

Not straight away. It's not about disclosing the exact details, but in showing him your values. After a few dates you might say something like, 'I'm a committed Christian but I have made a few mistakes in the sex department. I'm not happy about it, but I have worked through it and am now in a healthier headspace. I've decided to make some changes in the way I do relationships.' (Or whatever your story is.) At the very least, a guy deserves to know whether or not you're a virgin before you get married. (And it works both ways.) It's not that this changes your value, but it will create another layer of complexity to your sexual relationship. It's best to be prepared for the emotional complications.

Question 7: how do I come to terms with having had an abortion?

Many girls and women have abortions for a wide variety of reasons. Many women suffer terribly their whole lives from the guilt, shame, grief and loss of aborting one or more of their children. If this is you – I have compassion for you. If you are seeking forgiveness, it is available through the Lord Jesus. But the emotional scars (and sometimes physical complications) may be ever present. I urge you to seek professional counselling and medical care, to help you process and work through the various emotions you feel, particularly if you have not told anyone and feel like you are carrying a dark secret. This can plague you for life, if you let it.

The best way to get rid of the darkness is to shed light on it – and that means, bringing it out into the open with a **safe** person who will hold your confidences with great care and discretion. And like any emotional pain – the only way to get through it is to get through it. You will have to do the 'grief work' to find healing, with kind and supportive people who will join and journey with you. It will be worth it. And I believe this is definitely something you would need to disclose to your future husband before marriage (potentially during the engagement period, or just before).

Question 8: will not being a virgin ruin my chances of a Christian marriage?

Probably not. There are a lot of single Christian guys walking around out there who aren't virgins. It would be pretty hypocritical of them to not accept you just because you're the same! And for the Christian guys who are virgins – I think they're a mix of both views. Some of them may not be comfortable marrying someone who's already given herself to another man (or men). And that's their prerogative. You don't have to get nasty about it; just bow out and wish them all the best. And then there are other Christian guys who are virgins, who will be able to overlook your non-virgin state.

Question 9: won't it be awkward to get married and go on a honeymoon with no sexual experience?

Probably. It's pretty weird to go through all the lead-up and stress of engagement and the wedding and then have to be on your A-game on the wedding night, with all systems firing. It's super weird to have been pummelled with the 'no sex before marriage!' warning for decades, then all of a sudden be let loose and expected to jump into the marriage bed in a flurry of lingerie and champagne. A lot of couples don't even have sex on the first night (or in the first week!), because they're absolutely exhausted from the wedding. That's fine.

Here's the thing – *marriage* is awkward. Take two individuals from different backgrounds and bind them in a covenant relationship together, expecting them to strip off their 'armour' and reveal all their vulnerabilities at once – wow, it's hard! So some awkwardness in all areas of married life is par for the course. The key is to work through it together, have a laugh, and figure it out. The more you talk together about sex, the healthier your sex life will be. And if you and your future hubby do have sex together before marriage – well, there will be emotional, spiritual (and maybe physical) consequences from that too. Tread carefully.

Question 10: will my health issues interfere with my sex life in the future?

Very possibly. Again, this is a topic that isn't discussed much, but is very relevant. I'm astounded by the number of girls who are silently suffering with a wide variety of health issues that relate to the pelvis and reproductive area, as well as other health problems that impact on relationships, such as chronic fatigue or gut issues. There are some specific things that can really cause problems on the honeymoon, most notably a condition called 'vaginismus', which is an involuntary muscle contraction that makes penetration impossible[2] (if you can't wear tampons, maybe this relates to you).

If you do suffer from any of these types of conditions, or think you do, I'd recommend you see a doctor who specialises in women's health, and a women's health physiotherapist. Let them give you a once-over and you can start the healing journey. At the very least, you can learn about your issues and be prepared for what might ensue once you begin a sexual relationship. Check out the great 2019 book *Pain and Prejudice*[3] for more information on women's reproductive health issues.

Question 11: if I know I can't have children, do I have to tell my boyfriend?

Of course. This is potentially a deal-breaker for a lot of men. Most men (not all) will desire to have a family, and most of those men (not all) will prefer to have their own biological children. So if you have health issues that will definitely prevent this, it's crucial that your future husband is made aware of this, and is given the option to discontinue the relationship. Anything else is basically lying. And he needs to know this before he proposes to you. If you leave it pretty late, and tell him the day before he proposes, for example, expect the news to have a major impact on the relationship. He may recover from the blow and still choose to go ahead with proposing to you, because he does love you. But more likely, he will need some serious time and space to reconsider everything. And you know what? That's his prerogative. Be respectful and be sensible about it – he needs to know.

Question 12: how do I cope with people's opinions about my virginity or lack of?

No matter what your life situation is, certain people will love to comment on it. And the more public you make it, the more comments you'll get. It's ok to be private about this kind of thing. You don't have to keep everyone up to date on your sexual status. But here are some quick responses you can whip out at weddings or awkward family Christmases.

If you're a virgin: 'I could go to a nightclub any night of the week and lose my virginity. But I'm protecting my heart and my body for my future husband.'

If you're not: 'None of us is perfect. I've received forgiveness for my sexual sins and I've moved on. I wish you would too!'

Question 13: will I die a virgin?

Virginity is not a disease, you know. If you're a virgin, that means you've never had to deal with an unexpected pregnancy or a sexually transmitted disease, your heart is a little more intact, and you haven't built a bad reputation for yourself. That's something pretty special! You should be proud of that. Besides, you could lose your virginity to a random dude whenever you want – but would you want to? I recommend you save it up for your husband, as a gift to him, to yourself and your health, and to your children, no matter how old you are when you marry. (And until you die, there is still a chance of marriage!) May I point out: sex, like nothing else, has the capacity to radically impact the orientation of your life. It's not something to be toyed with. This verse comes to mind again: 'Can a [woman] scoop fire into her lap without being burned?' (Proverbs 6:27) – sister girl, the answer is no! So keep your V plates on and bide your time. Mr Right will be so honoured that you waited.

Here are some more helpful resources to expand your knowledge:
The Best Sex for Life[4] by Dr Patricia Weerakoon
A Celebration of Sex[5] by D. E. Rosenau
Sheet Music[6] by Dr Kevin Leman.

CHAPTER 40

What if I'm called to singleness?

I used to tremble with fear sometimes, wondering if God had given me the gift of celibacy and wanted me to stay single for life. Because I really didn't want to! It's an interesting concept, the idea of being 'called to singleness'. Is it even a thing, for women? I don't know. I don't know of any woman in the Bible who was specifically destined by God to stay single. More often, God would use women in marriage and child-bearing to make big impacts on the world at the time (think about Esther, Ruth, Sarah, Mary, etc.)

The Apostle Paul was single (by choice?) and he said that in his opinion, it is better to be single so that you can focus more fully on the work of the Lord. **'An unmarried woman or virgin is concerned about the Lord's affairs: Her aim is to be devoted to the Lord in both body and spirit. But a married woman is concerned about the affairs of this world—how she can please her husband.' (1 Corinthians 7:32-35).** Well, we can't really argue with that. All of you girls who've been busy serving in church know how true this is. I used to have loads of time to do various church and charity work. Now that I'm married with kids, most of my thoughts are centred on how to best look after my husband and children.

I think it helps to acknowledge your heart's desires. There are some women who really do want to give their all to the work of the Lord, perhaps becoming a missionary or nun, or devoting themselves to a field of service that requires their full attention. These women don't necessarily desire marriage, because they have different dreams. But then there are other women (the majority, I would assume), who are desperately keen to have their own husband and family – and that is totally okay. It's a normal desire and there's nothing wrong with that. And think about it – **by having children, you are bringing more of the image of God into the world!** Talk about evangelism.

If you are getting older and you're still single, *and you really want to be married,* I would suggest that your singleness is circumstantial. You just haven't met the right guy at the right time! I'm no expert on these matters, but I think that if you are truly called to a celibate life, you'll know in your heart.

So if you're reading this book, and you really want to be taken 'off the shelf', I doubt that you are called to singleness. Why don't you pray about it? And listen to what God says. If you have placed marriage as an idol in your heart, and would give up anything to have it, then maybe God is waiting for you to return him to first place in your affections. How do you do that? You pray and you believe and you behave: 'God, I really want to get married. But I do put you first and I do commit to my faith above all. I choose to obey you, whatever you ask me to do, even if it's hard. Please show me that you understand the desires of my heart and care about my future. Let's face this together.' I believe God will come through for you.

CONCLUSION

You might have mixed feelings after reading this book. There's a ton of information here and most of it is really hard to do. And not one of us is going to nail this in every area – including me! If you are feeling overwhelmed, I get it. It's a really tough dating climate out there for Christian girls, and it can often feel like your life is stretching ahead of you with no signs of romance on the horizon, with many hurdles to overcome. But you must have hope! You are stronger than you think. Life is not over till it's over, and God can do miracles, even if you feel like a lost cause.

This book contains loads of ideas and advice that I've gathered from my own experience, psychological research, university lectures, Bible study, and heaps of anecdotes and observations from other girls within the Christian community. It might seem like an overpowering amount of information, but if you **just take one thing at a time,** and change even a minor aspect of your approach to dating, you could change the trajectory of your future.

I believe there is hope for you. I also believe the enemy is out to seek, kill and destroy all forms of healthy relationship, marriage and family. We are in a battle, so you need to gird your loins for the fight, and realise that yes, you are swimming against the tide. But Jesus has won the victory for us, and we can hope in his redemptive power to give us peace in hard times, and to intercede for us with the Father to hear our cries and to answer our prayers. Don't give up!

You are beautiful, loved and designed for relationship. If you want it – go out and get it! It might take months, or it might take years. But I believe that the search will refine you and shape you in such a way that you will reach a new place of maturity within yourself, open your eyes to new experiences and peoples, and hopefully…get married!

God bless you, sister. I'm praying for you!

REFERENCE LIST

Here's a list of the various books and articles I've referenced in this book. And I really recommend wider reading across the psychology of relationships – so check out some of the resources I've added at the end, from right across the Christian spectrum. As always, read with a discerning mind – check everything against the Bible, use your common sense, and discard anything that is not a 'fit' for you and your situation.

All Bible references are from the NIV version, unless otherwise stated.

Notes:

Chapter 2
1   Peck, M. S. (1998). *The Different Drum: Community Making and Peace.* New York: Touchstone
2   Silk, D. (2015). *Keep your Love On: Connection, Communication and Boundaries.* Redding: Loving on Purpose.

Chapter 3
1   Gray, J. (2012). *Why Mars and Venus Collide: Improve Your Relationships by Understanding How Men and Women Cope Differently with Stress.* New York: Harper Element.

Chapter 6

1 Aron, E. A. (1997). *The Highly Sensitive Person*. New York: Broadway Books.

2 Wolfson, R. (2005). *A Time to Mourn, a Time to Comfort: A Guide to Jewish Bereavement*. Vermont: Jewish Lights Publishing.

Chapter 7

1 Kubler-Ross, E. (2011). *On Death and Dying: What the Dying Have to Teach Doctors, Nurses, Clergy and Their Own Families*. New York: Scribner.

Chapter 9

1 Gray, J. (2012). *Why Mars and Venus Collide: Improve Your Relationships by Understanding How Men and Women Cope Differently with Stress*. New York: Harper Element.

2 Meyer, J. (2008). *Approval Addiction: Overcoming Your Need to Please Everyone*. Nashville: Faithwords.

3 Beattie, M. (1986). *Codependent No More: How to Stop Controlling Others and Start Caring for Yourself*. Minnesota: Hazelden Publishing.

4 Hemfelt, Minirth & Meier. (2003). *Love is a Choice: The Definitive Book on Letting Go of Unhealthy Relationships*. Nashville: Thomas Nelson.

5 Silk, D. (2015). *Keep your Love On: Connection, Communication and Boundaries*. Redding: Loving on Purpose.

Chapter 13

1 Peterson, J. (2018). *12 Rules for Life: An Antidote to Chaos*. Canada: Random House.

2 Packer, W. (Producer), & Story, T. (Director). (2012). *Think Like a Man*. [Motion picture]. United States: Rainforest Films.

3   Peterson, J. (2017, September 6). *Women's Desire for Real Men* [Video file]. Retrieved from https://www.youtube.com/watch?v=br8KtroS-40

Chapter 14
1   Guzik, D. (2018). *Isaiah 3: The Sins of Judah* [Commentary]. Retrieved from https://enduringword.com/bible-commentary/isaiah-3/

Chapter 15
1   Janetzki, P. (2009.) Smartrelationshipseducation.com

Chapter 16
1   Knight, M. & Janetzki, P. (2011). *Being a Bloke*. Brisbane: Peer Power & Peter Janetzki.
2   Krane, D., Kaufmann, M. & Bright, K. et. al. (Producers). (1994). *Friends* [Television series]. California: Warner Bros. Studios.
3   Stiller, B. (Producer/Director) & Conrad, S. (Writer). (2013). *The Secret Life of Walter Mitty*. [Motion picture]. United States: Red Hour Productions.

Chapter 17
1   Smith, E. E. (2014). *Masters of Love* [Article]. Retrieved from https://www.theatlantic.com/health/archive/2014/06/happily-ever-after/372573/
2   Harvey, S. (2009). *Act Like a Lady, Think Like a Man*. United States: HarperLuxe.

Chapter 18
1   Peterson, J. (2020). *Perspective: Personality Assessment for Individuals* [Online test]. Retrieved from www.understandmyself.com

2   Peterson, J. (2017, March 24). *Jordan Peterson on Relationship Compatibility and Personality Traits* [Video file]. Retrieved from https://www.youtube.com/watch?v=X3Ou4-PyPIA

Chapter 20
1   Fein, E. & Schneider, S. (1994). *The Rules: Time-tested Secrets for Capturing the Heart of Mr Right.* United States: Grand Central Publishing.

Chapter 21
1   Fein, E. & Schneider, S. (1994). *The Rules: Time-tested Secrets for Capturing the Heart of Mr Right.* United States: Grand Central Publishing.
2   Fein, E. & Schneider, S. (2013). *The New Rules: The Dating Do's and Don'ts for the Digital Generation.* United States: Piatkus.

Chapter 22
1   Fein, E. & Schneider, S. (1994). *The Rules: Time-tested Secrets for Capturing the Heart of Mr Right.* United States: Grand Central Publishing.

Chapter 23
1   Carnegie, D. & Associates. (2011). *How to Win Friends and Influence People in the Digital Age.* UK: Simon & Schuster.

Chapter 24, part 2
1   Ludden, D. (2017). *The Psychology of First Impressions* [Article]. Retrieved from https://www.psychologytoday.com/au/blog/talking-apes/201708/the-psychology-first-impressions

2   Schlessinger, L. (2010, November 24). *Dating Roles Haven't Changed* [Video file]. Retrieved from https://www.youtube.com/watch?v=VTtYiyzwN-k

Chapter 25

1   Clement, J. (2020). *Distribution of Facebook Users Worldwide as of April 2020, by Age and Gender* [Graph]. Retrieved from https://www.statista.com/statistics/376128/facebook-global-user-age-distribution/
2   Discretion. (2020). In *Lexico (Oxford)*. Retrieved from https://www.lexico.com/definition/discretion

Chapter 27

1   White, J. (2011). *Working with Nonbelievers (2 Corinthians 6:14–18)* [Commentary]. Retrieved from https://www.theologyofwork.org/new-testament/2-corinthians/working-with-nonbelievers-2-corinthians-614-18
2   Ortberg, N. (2005). *Is it a Sin to Marry a Non-Christian?* [Article]. Retrieved from https://www.christianitytoday.com/biblestudies/bible-answers/marriage/unequallyyoked.html
3   Bratcher, D. (2018). *Unequally Yoked: A Study in Context (2 Corinthians 6:14)* [Article]. Retrieved from http://www.crivoice.org/yoked.html
4   Craven, S. M. (2011). *Fathers: Key to Their Children's Faith* [Article]. Retrieved from https://www.christianpost.com/news/fathers-key-to-their-childrens-faith.html

Chapter 28

1   Matthew 7:24-27
2   Rhoades, G.K., Stanley, S.M., & Markman, H.J. (2009). The pre-engagement cohabitation effect: A replication and extension of previous findings. *Journal of Family Psychology, 23, 107*-111.

Retrieved from https://www.ncbi.nlm.nih.gov/pmc/articles/PMC 5956907/

3   Harvey, S. (2009). *Act Like a Lady, Think Like a Man*. United States: HarperLuxe.

4   Owen, J., Rhoades, G.K., & Stanley, S.M. (2013). Sliding versus Deciding in Relationships: Associations with Relationship Quality, Commitment, and Infidelity. *Journal of Couple & Relationship Therapy: Innovations in Clinical and Educational Interventions, 12(2), 135*-149. Retrieved from https://www.ncbi.nlm.nih.gov/pmc/articles/PMC3656416/

5   Jay, M. (2013). *The Defining Decade: Why Your Twenties Matter, and How to Make the Most of Them*. United States: Twelve.

Chapter 29

1   Behrendt, G., Tucillo, L. & Monchik, L. (2006). *He's Just Not That Into You*. United States: Simon Spotlight Entertainment.

2   Disney, W. & Golitzen, G. (Producers) & Swift, D. (Director). (1961). *The Parent Trap*. [Motion picture]. United States: Walt Disney Productions.

3   Juvoven, N. (Producer) & Kwapis, K. (Director). (2009). *He's Just Not That Into You*. [Motion picture]. United States: Warner Bros.

4   Fisher, L. & Wick, D. (Producers) & Luketic, R. (Director). (2004). *Win a Date with Tad Hamilton!* [Motion picture]. United States: Dreamworks Pictures.

5   Krane, D., Kaufmann, M. & Bright, K. et. al. (Producers). (1994). *Friends* [Television series]. California: Warner Bros. Studios.

Chapter 30

1   American Sociological Association. (2015). *Women More Likely Than Men To Initiate Divorces, But Not Non-Marital Breakups* [Article].

Retrieved from https://www.asanet.org/press-center/press-releases/women-more-likely-men-initiate-divorces-not-non-marital-breakups

2 Banschick, M. (2012). *The High Failure Rate of Second and Third Marriages* [Article]. Retrieved from https://www.psychologytoday.com/au/blog/the-intelligent-divorce/201202/the-high-failure-rate-second-and-third-marriages

3 Peterson, J. (2017, December 16). *How to Know Your True Friends* [Video file]. Retrieved from https://www.youtube.com/watch?v=k5ukKf4vi6g

Chapter 31

1 Brittle, Z. (2015). *Turn Towards Instead of Away* [Article]. Retrieved from https://www.gottman.com/blog/turn-toward-instead-of-away/

Chapter 32

1 Gottman, J. (2014). *The Three Phases of Love* [Article]. Retrieved from https://www.gottman.com/blog/the-3-phases-of-love/

Chapter 34

1 Austen, J. (1992). *Pride and Prejudice.* Ware: Wordsworth Classics.

Chapter 35

1 Harvard Medical School. (2019). *Marriage and Men's Health* [Article]. Retrieved from https://www.health.harvard.edu/mens-health/marriage-and-mens-health

2 Callan, S. (2014). *Building a Strong Society Requires Effective Family Policy* [Article]. Retrieved from https://pdfs.semanticscholar.org/3531/c17d8e26a4f58bfd6d71e6d93ad26e221454.pdf

3 Church Publishing. (1789). *The Book of Common Prayer and Administration of the Sacraments and other Rites and Ceremonies of the Church.* Church Publishing INC.

4   Alcott, L. M. (2004). *Little Women (6th Edition)*. New York: Signet Classic.

5   Del Vecho, P. (Producer) & Buck C., & Lee, J. (Directors). (2013.) *Frozen*. [Motion picture]. United States: Walt Disney Pictures.

6   Wise, R. (Producer & Director). (1965). *The Sound of Music*. [Motion picture]. United States: 20th Century Fox.

Chapter 36

1   Bunyan, J. (2003). *The Pilgrim's Progress*. Oxford: University Press.

Chapter 37

1   Vocation. (2020). In *Lexico (Oxford)*. Retrieved from https://www.lexico.com/definition/vocation

2   Anderson, B., Keyes, B. & Disney, W. (Producers) & McKimson, J. & Annakin, K. (Directors). (1960). *Swiss Family Robinson*. [Motion picture]. United States: Walt Disney Productions.

3   Cummings, J. (Producer) & Donen, S. (Director). (1954). *Seven Brides for Seven Brothers*. [Motion picture]. United States: Metro-Goldwyn-Mayer.

4   Golden, S. (2012). *Is Male Headship a 'Curse'?* [Article]. Retrieved from https://answersingenesis.org/family/gender/is-male-headship-a-curse/

5   Gottman, J. (2015). *The Seven Principles for Making Marriage Work*. New York: Harmony Books.

6   Chapman, G. (1992). *The Five Love Languages*. Chicago: Northfield Publishers.

7   Answers, A. (2019, March 20). *Toxic Positivity: The Harmful Habit to Stop Immediately* [Video file]. Retrieved from https://www.youtube.com/watch?v=t2kAkbdS2S4

Chapter 39
1   Rothschild, B. (2000). *The Body Remembers: The Psychophysiology of Trauma and Trauma Treatment.* New York: W. W. Norton & Company.
2   Harish, T., Muliyala, A., & Murthy, P. (2011). Successful Management of Vaginismus: An Eclectic Approach. *Indian Journal of Psychiatry, 53(2), 154*-155. Retrieved from https://www.ncbi.nlm.nih.gov/pmc/articles/PMC3136020/
3   Jackson, G. (2019). *Pain and Prejudice: A Call to Arms for Women and Their Bodies.* Brisbane: Allen & Unwin.
4   Weerakoon, P. (2016). *The Best Sex for Life.* Sydney: Growing Faith.
5   Rosenau, D. E. (1996). *A Celebration of Sex: A Guide to Enjoying God's Gift of Sexual Intimacy.* Nashville: Thomas Nelson.
6   Leman, K. (2011). *Sheet Music: Uncovering the Secrets of Sexual Intimacy in Marriage.* Chicago: Tyndale House Publishers.

Additional recommended resources:

A Step Up for Stepfamilies: A Guide to Becoming an Intentional, Thriving Family by Marcia Watts (2018, Independent Ink)

Approval Addiction: Overcoming Your Need to Please Everyone by Joyce Meyer (2008, Faithwords)

Boundaries in Dating: How Healthy Choices Grow Healthy Relationships by Cloud & Townsend (2009, Zondervan)

Created to Be His Helpmeet by Debi Pearl (2014, Carpenters Son Publishing)

For Women Only: What You Need to Know About the Inner Lives of Men by Shaunti Feldhahn (2006, Multnomah)

His Needs, Her Needs: Building an Affair-Proof Marriage by Willard F. Harley, Jr (2011, Monarch Books)

Love for a Lifetime: Building a Marriage That Will Go the Distance by James Dobson (2004, Multnomah)

Love Must be Tough: New Hope for Marriages in Crisis by James Dobson (2007, Tyndale Momentum)

Men are from Mars, Women are from Venus: A Practical Guide for Improving Communication and Getting What You Want in Your Relationships by John Gray (2003, HarperCollins)

Real Marriage: The Truth About Sex, Friendship and Life Together by Mark & Grace Driscoll (2013, Thomas Nelson)

Safe People: How to Find Relationships That are Good for You, and Avoid Those That Aren't by Cloud & Townsend (2016, HarperCollins)

The Man Book by Brian Andrew (2018, Live Happy Together)

The Meaning of Marriage: Facing the Complexities of Marriage with the Wisdom of God by Tim Keller (2013, Hodder & Stoughton)

The Proper Care and Feeding of Husbands by Dr Laura Schlessinger (2005, HarperCollins)

The Road Less Travelled by M. Scott Peck (2008, Penguin)

What Wives Wish their Husbands Knew About Women by James Dobson (1981, Tyndale Momentum)

Why Men Love Bitches - From Doormat to Dreamgirl by Sherry Argov (2002, Adams Media)

Wobbly: One Woman's Journey Onward and Upward by Vikki Roubin (2010, Vikki Roubin)

Womenomics: Work Less, Achieve More, Live Better by Shipman & Kay (2010, HarperCollins)

You Can't Play the Game if You Don't Know the Rules: How Relationships Work by Irene Alexander (2006, Lion Hudson Limited)

ACKNOWLEDGEMENTS

This book has been on my heart for a few years, and I've written countless drafts and blog entries on this topic. It's wonderful to finally compile the most salient points and to hopefully inform and inspire many Christian women in their relationship journeys. So may I first acknowledge all the beautiful ladies out there who are faithfully following God's principles for their lives, and fervently praying and hoping for 'Mr Right' to come along. Girls – you are amazing! Stay strong and find your inner courage to keep moving forward. You are not forgotten!

There are a number of friends who have helped me with ideas for this book and for the cover design, along with some marketing tips and tricks. Thank you to Roshni, Katie, Theresa, Beth, Hannah and Mikaela, among many others. You've got my back!

To all the women and girls who have unwittingly helped me so much on my journey of singleness, dating and marriage – I couldn't be here without you. Andrea, Ang, Anushka, Arezou, Bek, Brenda, Bronwyn, Claire B., Claire D., Di, Dimity, Emily, Emma, Esther, Heather, Helen, Insool, Jane, Jeanne, Jenny, Justine, Kara, Kate, Katie, Krista, Kylie, Laura, Lauren, Libby, Lil, Linda, Marcia, Marion, Martine, Moira, Monica, Ngaire, Ruthy, Sarah, Talitha, and all of the amazing friends, colleagues and flatmates who've stood by me over the years, along with the faithful prayer warriors who've been in the background of my life all along.

To my long-suffering parents, who have made many sacrifices to position me in the place I am today – educated, churched, married and happy. Thank you.

To my wonderful, God-given husband Nathan – thank you for bearing with me through the years of emotional ups and downs, failures and successes. I'm so glad you are a man who gives me wise counsel and Godly leadership. (And don't let me get too crazy.) You and my sons make it all worthwhile, giving me security for my present and hope for my future!

And finally I give thanks to God, my Lord and Father, the Author and Finisher of my faith, my Saviour and best friend, who for the joy set before him endured the suffering he faced, for hope of relationship with us! (Hebrews 12:2) How amazing is that. Thanks for holding onto me, Lord, keeping me on the straight and narrow, and bringing me out into a lush, green pasture. You're the best!

CPSIA information can be obtained
at www.ICGtesting.com
Printed in the USA
BVHW080525070421
604344BV00010B/646